The Letters of Vincent van Gogh
to His Brother and Others

1872–1890

The Letters of Vincent van Gogh
to His Brother and Others

1872–1890

(Abridged by Elfreda Powell)

With a memoir by his sister-in-law
Johanna van Gogh-Bonger

CONSTABLE · LONDON

Constable & Robinson Ltd
3 The Lanchesters
162 Fulham Palace Road
London W6 9ER
www.constablerobinson.com

Letters selected from the following books,
first published in the UK by Constable & Co:
The Letters of Vincent van Gogh to his Brother 1872–1886 Vols I & II (1927)
Further Letters of Vincent van Gogh to his Brother 1886–1889 (1929)
Letters to an Artist 1881–1885 (1936)

A copy of the British Library Cataloguing in
Publication Data is available from the British Library

ISBN 978-1-84901-465-6

Printed and bound in the EU

THIS BOOK
IS DEDICATED
TO
THE MEMORY OF

VINCENT AND THEO

'And in their death they were not divided.'
Samuel II. I, 23

Contents

❊❊

List of Illustrations

❦❦

Preface

❦

This abridgment of Vincent van Gogh's letters to his brother Theo, his mother, and artist friends Anton van Rappard and Paul Gauguin is based on *The Letters of Vincent van Gogh to His Brother* Volumes 1 and 2 (1927), *Further Letters of Vincent van Gogh to His Brother* (1929) and *Letters to an Artist: from Vincent van Gogh to Anton Ridder van Rappard* (1936), all originally published by Constable & Co. Ltd.

In this version, just a fifth of the original length, I have tried to reflect Vincent's life-long passion for art, for nature, for peasant life, for walking (and for all things English), and his long and painful search to find true self-expression and loving relationships. For his development as a painter was hampered by too much poverty, his love of women too zealous, his relations with family and friends too turbulent, and his final descent into mental illness horribly ironic, happening just when he had at last found his own unique style. For the sake of brevity, then, some, though by no means all, of his discussions about fellow artists and Theo's work as an art-dealer, as well as a host of thank you letters to Theo for money received have had to be omitted.

Without the steadfast financial and emotional support of Theo, 'my best friend, my brother' – to whom most of these letters are addressed – Vincent would never have been able to evolve as an artist. Sadly Theo outlived Vincent by only six months. After their deaths, these letters were lovingly collected, assembled and numbered by Theo's wife Johanna, whose Memoir formed the introduction to their original publication and is now included in full in this book.

Because not all of Vincent's letters were dated, where possible an estimation of the approximate date has been given in square brackets.

The numbering of the letters represents Johanna's original numbering system. Letters with a number followed by the letter R are taken from *Letters to an Artist: from Vincent van Gogh to Anton Ridder van Rappard.*

E.P.
February 2003

Memoir of Vincent van Gogh
By His Sister-in-law

❦

The family name, van Gogh, is probably derived from the small town Gogh on the German frontier, but in the 16th century the van Goghs were already established in Holland. According to the 'Annales Généalogiques' of Arnold Buchelius, there lived at that time a Jacob van Gogh at Utrecht 'In the Owl behind the Town Hall,' and Jan Jacob's son, who lived 'In the Bible under the flax market', selling wine and books, was Captain of the Civil Guard.

Their coat-of-arms was a bar with three roses, which is still the family crest of the van Goghs.

In the 17th century we find many van Goghs occupying high offices of state in Holland. Johannes van Gogh, magistrate of Zutphen, is appointed High Treasurer of the Union in 1628; Michel van Gogh, at first Consul General in Brazil, afterwards treasurer of Zeeland, belongs to the Embassy that welcomes King Charles II of England on his ascent to the throne in 1660. In about the same period, Cornelius van Gogh is a Remonstrant clergyman at Boskoop, and his son Matthias, at first a physician at Gouda, is afterwards clergyman at Moordrecht.

In the beginning of the 18th century the social standing of the family is somewhat lowered. A David van Gogh, who settled at the Hague, is a gold-wire drawer, like his eldest son Jan, who married Maria Stalvius, both belonging to the Walloon Church.

David's second son, Vincent (1729–1802), was a sculptor by profession, and is said to have been in Paris in his youth; in 1749 he was one of the Cent Suisses. [A Swiss infantry corps formerly attached to the personal guard of the King of France.] With him the practice of art seems to have come into the family, together with fortune; he died single and left some money to his nephew Johannes (1763–1840), the son of his elder brother Jan van Gogh.

This Johannes was at first a gold-wire drawer like his father, but he afterwards became a Bible teacher, and clerk in the Cloister Church at the Hague. He was married to Johanna van der Vin of Malines, and their son Vincent (1789–1874) was enabled, by the legacy of his great uncle Vincent, to study theology at the University of Leiden. This Vincent, the grandfather of our painter, was a man of great intellect and extaordinarily strong sense of duty. At the Latin school he distinguished himself and won all prizes and testimonials; 'the diligent and studious youth, Vincent van Gogh, fully deserves to be set up as an example to his fellow students for his good behaviour as well as for his persistent zeal,' declares the rector of the school, Mr de Booy, in 1805. At the University of Leiden he finishes his studies successfully, and graduates in 1811 at the age of twenty-two. He makes friends; his 'album amicorum' preserves their memory in many Latin and Greek verses; a little silk embroidered wreath of violets and forget-me-nots, signed, E. H. Vrydag 1810, is wrought by the hand of the girl who became his wife as soon as he got the living of Benschop. They lived long and happily together, first at the parsonage of Benschop, then at Ochten, and from 1822 at Breda, where his wife died in 1857, and where he remained until his death, a deeply respected and honoured man.

Twelve children were born to them, of which one died in infancy; there was a warm cordial family feeling between them, and however far the children might drift apart in the world, they remained deeply attached and took part in each other's weal and woe. Two of the daughters married high placed officers, the Generals Pompe and Graeuwen; three remained single.

The six sons all occupied honourable positions in the world. Johannes went to sea and reached the highest rank in the navy, that of Vice-Admiral; at the time that he was commandant of the Navy Yard at Amsterdam in 1877, his nephew Vincent lived at his house for a time. Three sons became art dealers; the eldest Hendrik Vincent, 'Uncle Hein' as he was called in the letters, had his business at first at Rotterdam and afterwards settled at Brussels. Cornelius Marinus became the head of the firm C. M. van Gogh, so well known in Amsterdam. (His nephews often called him by his initials C. M.) The third, who had the greatest influence on the lives of his nephews Vincent and Theo, was Vincent, whose health in his youth had been too weak to enable him to go to college, to the deep regret of his father, who based the greatest expectations on him. He opened a little shop at the Hague, where he sold colours and drawing materials, and which he enlarged in a few years to an art gallery of European renown. He was an extraordinarily gifted, witty and intelligent man, who had great influence in the world of art at that time; Goupil in Paris offered him the partnership in his firm, which only after van Gogh joined it reached its highest renown. He settled in Paris and Mr Tersteeg became the head of the firm in the Hague in his place. It was here that Vincent and Theo got their first training in business; Goupil was 'the house' that played such a large part in their lives, where Theo remained and made a successful career, where Vincent worked for six years, and to which his heart clung in spite of all, because in his youth it had been to him 'the best, the grandest, the most beautiful in the world' [letter Autumn 1883].

Only one of parson van Gogh's six sons chose the profession of his father. Theodorus (8 February 1822–26 March 1885) studied theology at Utrecht, graduated, and in 1849 got the living of Groot-Zundert, a little village in Brabant on the Belgian frontier, where he was confirmed by his father. Theodorus van Gogh was a man of prepossessing appearance ('the handsome dominie' he was called by some), of a loving nature and fine spiritual qualities, but he was not a gifted preacher, and for twenty years he lived forgotten in the small village of Zundert ere he was called to other places, and even then only to small villages like Etten, Helvoirt and Nuenen. But in his small circle he was warmly loved and respected, and his children idolized him.

In May 1851 he married Anna Cornelia Carbentus, who was born in 1819 at the Hague, where her father Willem Carbentus was a flourishing bookbinder. He had bound the first Constitution of Holland and thereby earned the title of 'bookbinder to the King'. His youngest daughter Cornelia was already married to Vincent van Gogh, the art dealer; his eldest daughter was the wife of the well-known clergyman Stricker at Amsterdam. The marriage of Theodorus van Gogh and Anna Carbentus was a very happy one. He found in his wife a helpmate, who shared with all her heart in his work; notwithstanding her own large family that gave her so much work, she visited his parishioners with him, and her cheerful and lively spirit was never quenched by the monotony of the quiet village life. She was a remarkable, lovable woman, who in her old age (she reached her 87th year), when she had lost her husband and three grown-up sons, still retained her energy and spirit and bore her sorrow with rare courage.

One of her qualities, next to her deep love of nature, was the great facility with which she could express her thoughts on paper; her busy hands, that were always working for others, grasped so eagerly not only needle and knitting needle, but also the pen. 'I just send you a little word' was one of her favourite expressions, and how many of these 'little words' came always just in time to bring comfort and strength to those to whom they were addressed. For almost twenty years they have been to myself a never failing source of hope and courage, and in this book, that is a monument to her sons, a word of grateful remembrance is due to their mother.

On the 30th of March 1852 a dead son was born at the vicarage of Zundert, but a year after on the same date Anna van Gogh gave birth to a healthy boy who was called Vincent Willem after his two grand-fathers, and who in qualities and character, as well as in appearance, took after his mother more than after his father. The energy and unbroken strength of will which Vincent showed in his life were, in principle, traits of his mother's character; from her also he took the sharp inquisitive glance of the eye from under the protruding eyebrows. The blonde complexion of both the parents turned in Vincent to a reddish hue; he was of medium height, rather broad shouldered, and his appearance made a strong, sturdy impression. This is also confirmed by the words of his mother, that none of the children *except* Vincent was very strong. A weaker constitution than his would certainly have broken down much sooner under the heavy strain Vincent put upon it. As a child he was of difficult temper, often troublesome and self-willed, and his bringing up was not fitted to counterbalance these faults, as the parents were very tender-hearted especially for their eldest. Once grandmother van Gogh, who had come from Breda to visit her children at Zundert, witnessed one of the naughty fits of little Vincent; she who had been taught by experience with her own twelve babies, took the little culprit by the arm and with a sound box on the ears put him out of the room. The tender-hearted mother was so indignant at this that she did not speak to her mother-in-law for a whole day, and only the sweet-tempered character of the young father succeeded in bringing about a reconciliation. In the evening he had a little carriage brought around, and drove the two women to the heath, where under the influence of a beautiful sunset they forgave each other.

Little Vincent had a great love for animals and flowers, and made all kinds of collections; of any extraordinary gift for drawing there was as yet no sign; it is only noted that at the age of eight he once modelled a little elephant of clay, that drew his parents' attention, but he destroyed it at once when according to his notion such a fuss was made about it. The same fate befell a very curious drawing of a cat, which his mother always remembered. For a short time he attended the village school, but his parents found that the intercourse with the peasant boys made him too rough, so a governess was sought for the children of the vicarage, whose number had meanwhile increased to six. Two years after Vincent a little daughter had been born and again two years later on the 1st of May 1857, came a son who was called after his father. After him came two sisters and a little brother. (The younger sister Willemien, who always lived with her mother, was the only one to whom Vincent wrote on rare occasions.) Theo was more tender and kind than his brother, who was four years older; he was more delicately built and finer featured, but of the same reddish fair complexion and he had the same light blue eyes, that sometimes darkened to a greenish blue.

In letter 338 [of 1883] Vincent himself describes the similarity and the difference in their looks, and in 1889 Theo wrote to me the following about Vincent's appearance, referring to Rodin's marble sculpture, the head of John the Baptist. 'The sculptor has conceived an image of the precursor of Christ that exactly resembles Vincent. Yet he never saw him. That expression of sorrow, that forehead distorted by deep furrows, which denotes high thinking and iron self discipline, is Vincent's, though his is somewhat more sloping; the form of nose and structure of the head are the same.' When I afterwards saw the marble I found in it a perfect resemblance to Theo.

The two brothers were strongly attached to each other from childhood; whereas the eldest sister, recalling youthful memories, speaks of Vincent's teasing ways. Theo only remembers that Vincent could invent such delightful games, that once they made him a present of the most beautiful rose bush in their garden, to show their gratitude. Their childhood was full of the poetry of Brabant country life; they grew up among the cornfields, the heath and the pine forests, in that peculiar sphere of a village parsonage, the charm of which remained with them all their lives. It was not perhaps the best training to fit them for the hard struggle that awaited them both; they were still so very young, when they had to go out into the world, and with what bitter melancholy, and with what inexpressible home-sickness did they long during many years for the sweet home in the little village on the heath.

Vincent came back there several times, and remained always in appearance the 'country boor', but Theo, who had become quite a refined Parisian, also kept in his heart something of the 'Brabant boy' as he laughingly liked to call himself.

Like Vincent once rightly observes: 'there will always remain in us something of the Brabant fields and heath', and when their father had died and mother had to leave the parsonage, he complains, 'now there is none of us left in Brabant'. When afterwards, in the hospital of Arles the faithful brother visited him and in tender pity laid his head on the pillow beside him, Vincent whispered: 'just like Zundert', and shortly after he writes: 'during my illness I have seen every room in the house at Zundert, every path, every plant in the garden, the fields around, the neighbours, the churchyard, the church, our kitchen garden behind it – and even the magpie's nest in the high acacia in the churchyard' [letter 573 of 23 January 1889].

So ineffaceable were those first sunny childhood's recollections. When Vincent was twelve years old he was sent to the boarding school of Mr Provily at Zevenbergen; about this period not a single particular has been found, except that one of the sisters afterwards writes to Theo: 'Do you remember how on mother's birthday Vincent used to come from Zevenbergen and what fun we had then?' Of friends in that time nothing is known.

When he was sixteen years old the choice of a profession became urgent and in this Uncle Vincent was consulted.

The latter, who meanwhile had acquired a large fortune as an art dealer, had been obliged by his feeble health to retire early from the strenuous business life in Paris – though still financially connected with the firm – and had settled at Princenhage, near his old father at Breda, and near his favourite brother at Zundert. Generally he passed the winter with his wife at Mentone in the south of France, and on his journey thither he always stayed some time at Paris, so that he remained in touch with the business. His beautiful country house at Princenhage had been enlarged by a gallery for his rare picture collection, and it was here that Vincent and Theo received their first impressions of the world of art. There was a warm cordial intercourse between the Zundert parsonage and the childless home of Princenhage; 'the carriage' from there was always loudly cheered by the children at Zundert, for it brought many surprises of flowers, rare fruits and delicacies, while on the other hand the bright, lively presence of the brother and sister from Zundert often cast a cheerful sunbeam on the life of the patient at Princenhage. These brothers, Vincent and Theo too, who differed but one year in age, were thoroughly attached to each other, and the fact of their wives being sisters made the attachment stronger still. What was more natural than that the rich art dealer destined the young nephew who bore his name as his successor in the firm – perhaps even to become his heir?

Thus in 1869 Vincent entered the house of Goupil & Co., at the Hague, as youngest employee under the direction of Mr Tersteeg, now a bright future seemed to lie in store for him. He boarded with the family Roos on the Beestenmarkt, where Theo afterwards lived also. It was a comfortable home where his material needs were perfectly provided for, but without any intellectual intercourse. This he found at the homes of various relations and friends of his mother, where he often visited, i.e. the Haanebeek's, the van Stockum's and aunt Sophy Carbentus with her three daughters, one of whom married our famous Dutch painter, A. Mauve, a second the less known painter, A. le Comte. Tersteeg sent to the parents good reports about Vincent's zeal and capacities, and like his grandfather in his time, he is 'the diligent studious youth' whom everybody likes.

When he had been at the Hague for three years, Theo, who is still at school at Oisterwijk (near Helvoirt, to which village their father has been called), comes to stay with him for a few days. It is after that visit in August 1872 that the correspondence between the two brothers begins, and from this, now faded, yellow, almost childish, little note it is carried on uninterruptedly until Vincent's death, when a half-finished letter to Theo was found on him, of which the desponding 'que veux-tu' (what can I say) at the end, seems like a gesture of resignation with which he parted from life.

The principal events of both their lives are mentioned in the letters and are completed in this biographical notice by particulars, either heard from Theo himself, or found in the correspondence of the parents with Theo, also preserved in full. (Vincent's letters to his parents were unfortunately destroyed.) They date from January 1873, when Theo then only fifteen years old, went to Brussels to be also brought up as an art dealer.

These letters, full of the tenderest love and care for the boy who left home at such a tender age – 'well Theo you are quite a man now at fifteen,' says his mother in one of her letters; the boy to whom they clung so fondly, because he, more than any of the other children, repays their love with never failing tenderness and devotion, and grows up to be 'the crowning glory of their old age,' as they were so fond of calling him – these letters tell of all the small events of daily life at the parsonage; what flowers were growing in the garden, and how the fruit trees bore, if the nightingale had been heard yet, what visitors had come, what the little sisters and brother were doing, what was the text of father's sermon, and among all this, many particulars about Vincent.

In 1873 the latter has been appointed to the firm in London. When leaving the Hague he gets a splendid testimonial from Mr Tersteeg, who also writes to the parents that at the gallery everybody likes to deal with Vincent – amateurs, clients, as well as painters – and that he certainly will succeed in his profession. 'It is a great satisfaction that he can close the first period of his career in that way, and withal he has remained just as simple as he was before,' writes mother. At first everything goes well with him in London; Uncle Vincent has given him introductions to some of his friends and he busies himself with great pleasure in his work; he earns a salary of £90 a year, and though living is expensive, he manages to lay by some money to send home now and then. Like a real business man he buys himself a top hat, 'you cannot be in London without one,' and he enjoys his daily trips from the suburbs to the gallery in Southampton Street in the city.

His first boarding-house is kept by two ladies, who own two parrots, the place is good but somewhat expensive for him, therefore he moves in August to the house of Mrs Loyer, a curate's widow from the south of France, who with her daughter Ursula keeps a day school for little children. Here he spends the happiest year of his life. Ursula makes a deep impression upon him – 'I never saw nor dreamt of anything like the love between her and her mother' he writes to one of his sisters, and: 'love her for my sake'.

He does not mention it to his parents, for he has not even confessed his love to Ursula herself, but his letters home are radiant with happiness. He writes that he enjoys his life so much – 'Oh fulness of rich life, your gift Oh God.'*

*The first line of a well-known Dutch poem.

In September an acquaintance is going over to London and undertook to carry a parcel for Vincent, and it is characteristic to hear that it contains, among other things, a bunch of grass leaves and a wreath of oak leaves, made at home during the holidays by Theo, who has meanwhile been appointed from Brussels to the House Goupil at the Hague. Vincent must have something in his room to remind him of the beloved fields and woods.

He celebrates a happy Christmas with the Loyers, and in those days he sends home now and then a little drawing, from his house and the street and from the interior of his room, 'so that we can exactly imagine how it looks, it is so well drawn,' writes his mother. In this period he seems to have weighed the possibility of becoming a painter; afterwards from Drenthe he writes to Theo: 'how often have I stood drawing on the Thames Embankment, as I went home from Southampton Street in the evening – and the result was nihil; had there been somebody then to tell me what perspective was, how much trouble would have been spared me, how much farther should I be now.'

At that time he now and then met Matthew Maris,[†] but was too bashful to speak out freely to him, and shut up all his longings and desires within himself – he had still a long road of sorrow to go ere he could reach his goal.

In January his salary is raised and until spring his letters remain cheerful and happy; he intends to visit Holland in July and before that time seems to have spoken to Ursula of his love. Alas it turns out that she is already engaged to somebody, who boarded with them before Vincent came. He tries all his influence to make her break this engagement but does not succeed, and with this first great sorrow there comes a change in his character; when he comes home for the holidays he is thin, silent, dejected, a changed being. But he *draws* a great deal. Mother writes: 'Vincent made many a nice drawing, he drew the bedroom window and the front door, all that part of the house, and also a large sketch of those houses in London upon which their window looks out; it is a delightful talent, that can be of great value to him.'

Accompanied by his eldest sister, who wants to find a situation, he returns to London; he takes furnished rooms in Ivy Cottage, 395 Kensington New Road, and there without any family life he grows more and more silent and depressed and also more and more religious.

His parents were glad he left the Loyers – 'there were too many

[†]A famous Dutch painter, living in London.

secrets and it was not a family like others; but it must have been a great disappointment to him that his illusions were not realized,' father writes, and mother complains, 'the evenings are so long already and his work finishes early, he must be lonely, if it only does not harm him'.

They feel uneasy and worried about his solitary, secluded life. Uncle Vincent also insists upon his mixing more with other people, 'that is just as necessary as to learn business'; but the depressed mood continues, letters home grow more and more scarce, and mother begins to think that the London fog depresses him and that even a temporary change might do him good – 'poor boy, he means so well, but I believe things are very hard for him just now'.

In October 1874, Uncle Vincent effects indeed a short removal to the firm in Paris, but Vincent himself is little pleased by this, in fact he is so angry that he does not write home, to the great grief of his parents. 'He is only in a bad temper,' his sister says, and Theo comforts, 'he is doing all right'.

Towards the end of December he returns to London where he takes the same rooms and leads the same retired life. Now for the first time the word *eccentric* is applied to him. His love for drawing has ceased, but he reads much and the quotation from Renan that closes the London period clearly shows what filled his thoughts and how he aimed even then at the high ideal: 'to sacrifice all personal desires, to realize great things, to obtain nobleness of mind, to surpass the vulgarity in which the existence of nearly all individuals is spent.' He did not know yet which way he had to go to reach that aim.

In May 1875, he is placed permanently in Paris and assigned especially to the picture gallery, where he feels himself quite out of place; he is more at home in his 'cabin', the little room at Montmartre where, morning and evening, he reads the Bible with his young friend, Harry Gladwell, than among the mondaine Parisian public.

His parents read from his letters that things are not going well, and when he comes home at Christmas and everything is talked over, father writes to Theo: 'I almost think that Vincent had better leave Goupil in two or three months; there is so much that is good in him, but yet it may be necessary for him to change his position, he is certainly not happy.' And they love him too well to persuade him to stay in a place where he would be unhappy; he wants to live for others, to be useful, to bring about something great, *how* he does not know as yet, but *not* in an art gallery. On his return from Holland he has the decisive interview with Mr Boussod (the son-in-law and successsor of Mr Goupil) that ends with his dismissal on the 1st of April, and he accepts it without bringing in any excuses for himself. One of the grievances against him was that he had gone home to Holland for Christmas and New Year, the busiest time for business in Paris.

In his letters he seems to take it rather lightly, but he feels how gloomily and threateningly the clouds begin to gather around him. At the age of twenty-three years he is now thrown out of employment, without any chance of a better career; Uncle Vincent is deeply disappointed in his namesake and washes his hands of him; his parents are well-meaning, but they cannot do much for him having been obliged to touch their capital for the education of their children. (The pastor's salary was about 820 guilders a year.) Vincent has had his share, now others must have theirs. It seems that Theo who becomes so soon the helper and adviser of all, has already at that time suggested Vincent's becoming a painter, but for the moment he will not hear of it. His father speaks of a position in a museum or advises him to open a small art gallery for himself, as Uncle Vincent and Uncle Cor have done before; he would then be able to follow his own ideas about art and be no longer obliged to sell pictures which he considered bad – but his heart again draws him to England and he plans to become a teacher.

Through an advertisement, in April 1876 he gets a position in Ramsgate at Mr Stokes', who moves his school in July to Isleworth. He received only board and lodging, but no salary, so he soon accepts another position at the somewhat richer school of Mr Jones, a Methodist preacher, where Vincent acts finally as a kind of curate.

His letters home are gloomy. 'It seems as if something were threatening me,' he writes, and his parents perceive full well that teaching does not satisfy him. They suggest his studying for a French or German college certificate, but he will not hear of it. 'I wish he could find some work in connection with art or nature,' writes his mother, who understands what is going on within him. With the force of despair he clings to religion, in which he tries to find satisfaction for his craving for beauty, as well as for his longing to live for others. At times he seems to intoxicate himself with the sweet melodious words of the English texts and hymns, the romantic charm of the little village church, and the lovely, holy atmosphere that envelops the English service. His letters in those days bear an almost morbid sensitiveness. Often and often he speaks about a position related to the church – but when he comes home for Christmas, it is decided that he will not go back to Isleworth, because there is absolutely no prospect for the future. He remains on friendly terms with Mr Jones, who afterwards comes to stay a few days at the Nuenen parsonage, and whom he later meets in Belgium. Once more Uncle Vincent uses his influence and procures for him a place in the bookshop of Blussé and Braam at Dordrecht. He accepts it, but without great enthusiasm. Characteristic are the words written to Theo by one of the sisters. 'You think that he is something more than an ordinary human being, but I think it would be much better if he thought himself just an ordinary being.' Another sister writes, 'His religion makes him absolutely dull and unsociable.'

To preach the Gospel still seems to him the only desirable thing, and at last an attempt is made to enable him to begin the study of Theology. The uncles in Amsterdam promised to give their aid; he can live with Uncle Jan van Gogh, Commandant of the Navy Yard, which will be a great saving of expenses: Uncle Stricker finds out the best teacher in the classical languages, the well-known Dr Mendes da Costa, and gives him some lessons himself; in the art gallery at Uncle Cor's he can satisfy his love for pictures and prints and so everybody tries to make it easy for him, all except Uncle Vincent, who is strongly opposed to the plan and will not help to forward it – in which he proved to be right after all. Full of courage Vincent sets to work, he must first prepare himself for a State examination before he can be admitted to the University; it will take him seven years ere he is ready; anxiously the parents ask themselves whether he will have the strength to persevere, and whether he who has never been used to regular study will be able to force himself to it at the age of twenty-four.

That period in Amsterdam, from May 1877 to 1878 is one long tale of woe. After the first half-year Vincent begins to lose ardour and courage; the writing of exercises and the study of grammar is not what he wants – he desires to comfort and cheer people by bringing them the Gospel – and surely he does not need so much learning for that! He actually longs for *practical* work, and when at last his teacher also perceives that Vincent never will succeed, he advises him to give up the study. In the *Handelsblad* of the 30th of November 1910, Dr Mendes da Costa writes his personal recollections of the afterwards so famous pupil, of whom he tells many characteristic particulars: his nervous, strange appearance, that yet was not without charm, his fervent intention to study well, his peculiar habit of self-discipline, self-chastisement, and finally his total unfitness for regular study. Not along that path was he to reach his goal! Openly he confesses that he is glad things have gone so far and that he can look towards his future with more courage than when he devoted himself hopelessly to Theological study, which period he afterwards called 'the worst time of his life'.

He will remain 'humble' and now wants to become an Evangelist in Belgium; for this no certificates are required, no Latin nor Greek; only three months at the school of Evangelisation at Brussels – where lessons are free and only board and lodging are charged for – and he can get his nomination. In July he travels thither with his father, accompanied by Mr Jones who on his way to Belgium has spent a few days with them at Etten, and together they visit the different members of the Committee of Evangelisation: the Rev. van den Brink from Rousselaere, Rev. Pietersen from Malines and Rev. de Jong from Brussels. Vincent explained his case clearly and made a very good impression. His father writes: 'His stay abroad and that last year at Amsterdam have not been quite fruitless after all, and when he takes the trouble to exert himself he shows that he has learned and observed much in the school of life,' and Vincent consequently is accepted as a pupil. But the parents regard this new experiment with fresh anxiety: 'I am always so afraid that wherever Vincent may be or whatever he may do, he will spoil everything by his eccentricity, his queer ideas and views on life,' his mother writes, and his father adds, 'It grieves us so when we see that he literally knows no joy of life, but always walks with bent head, whilst we did all in our power to bring him to an honourable position! It seems as if he deliberately chooses the most difficult path.'

In fact that was Vincent's aim – to humble himself, to forget himself, to sacrifice himself, 'mourir à soi-meme' (to sacrifice every personal desire), that was the ideal he tried to reach as long as he sought his refuge in religion, and he never did a thing by halves. But to follow the paths trodden by others, to submit to the will of other people, that was not in his character, he wanted to work out his own salvation. Towards the end of August he arrives at the school at Brussels, which had only been recently opened and counted but three pupils; in the class of Mr Bokma he certainly was the most advanced, but he does not feel at home at the school, he is 'like a fish out of water' he says, and is ridiculed for his peculiarities in dress and manners. He also misses the talent of extemporizing and is therefore obliged to read his lectures from manuscript; but the greatest objection against him is, 'he is not submissive', and when the three months have elapsed he does not get his nomination. Though he writes it [in letter 126 of 15 November 1878] in an off-hand way to Theo, he seems to have been greatly upset by it. His father receives a letter from Brussels, probably from the school, saying that Vincent is weak and thin, does not sleep, and is in a nervous and excited state, so that the best thing will be to come and take him home.

Immediately he travels to Brussels and succeeds in arranging everything for the best. Vincent goes at his own risk to the Borinage where he boards at 30 fr. a month with M. Van der Haegen, Rue de L'Eglise 39, at Paturages near Mons. He teaches the children in the evening, visits the poor and gives lectures from the Bible, and when in January the Committee meets, he will again try to get a nomination. The intercourse with the people there pleases him very well; in his leisure hours he draws large maps of Palestine, of which his father orders four at 10 fr. apiece, and at last, in January 1879, he gets a temporary nomination for six months at Wasmes at 50 fr. a month for which he must give Bible lectures, teach the children and visit the sick – the work of his heart. His first letters from there are very contented and he devotes himself heart and soul to his work, especially the practical part of it; his greatest interest is in nursing the sick and wounded. Soon, however, he falls back to the old exaggerations – he tries to put into practice the doctrines of Jesus, gives away everything, his money, clothes and bed, he leaves the good boarding-house at Denis, in Wasmes, and retires to a miserable hut where every comfort is wanting. Already they had written to his parents about it and when, towards the end of February, the Rev. Rochelieu comes for inspection, the bomb explodes, for so much zeal is too much for the committee and a person who neglects himself so cannot be an example to other people. The Church Council at Wasmes have a meeting and they agree that if he does not listen to reason he will lose his position. He himself takes it rather coolly. 'What shall we do now?' he writes, 'Jesus was also very calm in the storm, perhaps it must grow worse before it grows better.' Again his father goes to him, and succeeds in stilling the storm; he brings him back to the old boarding-house, advises him to be less exaggerated in his work, and for some time everything is all right, at least he writes that no reproofs are made. About that time a heavy mine explosion occurs and a strike breaks out, so Vincent can devote himself completely to the miners, and his mother in her naive religious faith writes, 'Vincent's letters that contain so many interesting things, prove that with all his singularities he yet shows a warm interest in the poor and that surely will not remain unobserved by God.' In that same time he also writes that he tries to *sketch the dresses and tools of the miners and will show them when he comes home.* In July bad tidings come again, 'he does not comply with the wishes of the committee and nothing will change him. It seems that he is deaf to all remarks that are made to him,' writes his mother, and when the six months of his temporary nomination are past, he is not appointed again, but they give him three months to look out for another position. He leaves Wasmes and travels on foot to Brussels to ask the Rev. Pietersen, who has moved thither from Malines, for advice. The latter paints in his leisure hours and has a studio, which probably was the reason why Vincent went to him for help. Tired and hot, exhausted and in a nervous condition he arrives there and so neglected was his appearance that the daughter of the house who opened the door for him was frightened, called for her father and ran away. The Rev. Pietersen received him kindly; procured him good lodgings for the night, invited him to his table the next day, showed him the studio, and as Vincent had brought some of his sketches of the miners, they probably talked as much about drawing and painting as about Evangelisation.

'Vincent gives me the impression of somebody who stands in his own light,' writes the Rev. Pietersen to his parents, and mother adds, 'how lucky it is that still he always finds somebody who helps him on, as now the Rev. Pietersen has.'

In accordance with the latter's advice, Vincent resolves to stay in the Borinage at his own expense, as he cannot be in the service of the committee, and that he will board with the Evangelist Frank, at Cuesmes. About the middle of August, at his parents' request, he visits them again at Etten. 'He looks well, except for his clothes, he reads Dickens all day and speaks only when he is addressed, about his future not a single word,' writes his mother. What could he say about his future? Did it ever look more hopeless than it did now? His illusion of bringing through the Gospel comfort and cheer into the miserable lives of the miners had gradually been lost in the bitter strife between doubt and religion, which he had to fight at that time, and which made him lose his former faith in God. (The Bible texts and religious reflections which became more and more rare in his last letters now stop entirely.)

No other thing has taken its place yet; he draws much and reads much, among others, Dickens, Beecher Stowe, Victor Hugo and Michelet, but it is all done without system or aim. Back in the Borinage he wanders about without work, without friends and very often without bread, for though he receives money from home and from Theo, they cannot give him more than is strictly necessary, and as it comes in at very irregular times and Vincent is a very poor financier, there are days, and even weeks when he is quite without money.

In October Theo, who has got a permanent position at Goupil's in Paris, comes to visit him on his journey thither and tries in vain to bring him to some fixed plan for the future; he is not yet ripe to take any resolution; before he becomes conscious of his real power he has still to struggle through the awful winter of 1879–80, that saddest, most hopeless time of his never very fortunate life. In these days he undertakes, with ten francs in his pocket, the hopeless expedition to Courrières, the dwelling place of Jules Breton, whose pictures and poems he so much admires, and with whom he secretly hopes to come in contact in some way or other. But the only thing that becomes visible to him is the inhospitable exterior of Breton's newly built studio and he lacks the courage to introduce himself. Disappointed in his hope, he has to undertake the long journey home; his money is all spent, generally he sleeps in the open air or in a hay loft. Sometimes he exchanges a drawing for a piece of bread, and he undergoes so much fatigue and want that his health always suffered from the consequences. In spring he comes once more to the vicarage of Etten and speaks again about going to London. 'If he really wants it, I shall enable him to go,' writes his father, but finally he returns again to the Borinage and lives that summer of 1880 at the house of the miner, Charles Decrucq at Cuesmes. There he writes in July a wonderfully touching letter (133) that tells of what is going on in his innermost self – 'My only anxiety is what can I do . . . could I not be of use, and good for something?' It is the old wish, the old longing to serve and comfort humanity, which made him write afterwards, when he had found his calling, 'And in a picture I wish to say something that would console as music does.' Now in the days of deepest discouragement and darkness at last the light begins to dawn. Not in books shall he find satisfaction, not in literature find his work, as his letters sometimes suggested, he turns back to his old love, 'I said to myself, I'll take up my pencil again, I will take up drawing, and from that moment everything has changed for me.' It sounds like a cry of deliverance, and once more, 'do not fear for me, if I can continue my work I will succeed.' At last he has found his work and herewith the mental equilibrium is restored; he no longer doubts of himself and however difficult or heavy his life may become, the inward serenity, the conviction of his own calling never more deserts him.

The little room in the house of the miner Decrucq, which he has to share with the children, is his first studio. There he begins his painter's career with the first original drawing of miners who go to work in the early morning. There he copies with restless activity the large drawings after Millet, and when the room is getting too narrow for him, he takes his work out into the garden.

When the cold autumn weather prevents his doing this, and as his surroundings at Cuesmes are getting too narrow for him, he moves in October to Brussels where he settles in a small hotel on the Bd du Midi 72. He is longing to see pictures again, but above all he hopes to become acquainted with other artists. Deep in his heart there was such a great longing for sympathy, for kindness and friendship, and though his difficult character generally prevented him from finding this and left him isolated in life, yet he always kept on longing for somebody with whom he could live and work.

Theo, who meanwhile had acquired a good position in Paris, could now assist him in word and deed. He brought Vincent into relation with the young Dutch painter van Rappard, who had worked some time in Paris and now studied at the academy at Brussels. At first the acquaintance did not progress, for the outward difference between the rich young nobleman and the neglected wanderer from the Borinage was too great to ripen the acquaintance at once into friendship; yet the artistic taste and opinions of both were too similar for them not to find each other; a friendship arose – perhaps the only one that Vincent ever had in Holland – it lasted for five years and then was broken through a misunderstanding, which van Rappard always regretted, though he acknowledged that intercourse with Vincent was very difficult.

'I remember as if it happened yesterday the moment of our first meeting at Brussels when he came into my room at nine o'clock in the morning, how at first we did not get on very well together, but so much the better after we had worked together a few times,' writes van Rappard to Vincent's mother after the latter's death. And again, 'whoever has witnessed this wrestling, struggling and sorrowful existence could not but feel sympathy for the man who demanded so much of himself, that it ruined body and mind. He belonged to the race that produces the great artists.

'Though Vincent and I had been separated the last years by a misunderstanding which I have often regretted – I have never ceased to remember him and the time we spent together with great sympathy.

'Whenever in the future I shall remember that time, and it is always a delight for me to recall the past, the characteristic figure of Vincent will appear to me in such a melancholy but clear light, the struggling and wrestling, fanatic, gloomy Vincent, who used to flare up so often and was so irritable, but who still deserved friendship and admiration for his noble mind and highly artistic qualities.'

Vincent's own opinion of van Rappard is clearly shown in his letters. A second acquaintance that Vincent made through Theo, with the painter Roelofs, was of less-during importance. Roelof's advice to enter the Academy was not followed by Vincent, perhaps they did not admit him because he was not far enough advanced, but probably he had had more than enough of academical institutions and theories, and in painting as well as in theology he preferred to go his own way; that is the reason he did not come into contact with other Dutch painters who were at that same time at the Academy at Brussels, for instance, Haverman.

He studied anatomy by himself, drew diligently from the living model, and from a letter to his father it seems that he took lessons in perspective from a poor painter at 1.50 fr. a lesson of two hours: it has not been possible to fix the name of the painter, it may have been Madiol.

At the end of the winter when van Rappard goes away, in whose studio he has often worked because his own little bedroom was too small, he longs for other surroundings, especially for the country; the expenses in Brussels are also somewhat heavy, and he thinks it will be cheapest to go to his parents at Etten where he has board and lodging free and can use all the money he receives, for his work.

He stays there for eight months, and this summer of 1881 is again a happy time for him. First, van Rappard comes to stay with him and he too always remembers with pleasure his stay at the vicarage, 'And my visit at Etten! I see you still sitting at the window when I came in,' he writes to Vincent's mother in the letter quoted above, 'I still enjoy that beautiful walk we all took together that first evening, through the fields and along the small path! And our excursions to Seppen, Passievaart, Liesbosch, I often look through my sketch books for them.'

In the beginning of August Theo comes over from Paris; shortly after Vincent makes an excursion to the Hague to consult about his work with Mauve, who firmly encourages him, so that he continues with great animation, and finally in those days he meets for the second time a woman who has great influence on his life. Among the guests who spent that summer at the vicarage at Etten was a cousin from Amsterdam – a young widow [referred to in his letters as 'K.'] with her little four-year-old son. Quite absorbed in her grief over the loss of her husband, whom she had loved so tenderly, she was unconscious of the impression which her beauty and touching sorrow made on the cousin, who was a few years her junior. 'He was so kind to my little boy,' she said when she afterwards remembered that time. Vincent who had great love for children, tried to win the heart of the mother by great devotion to the child. They walked and talked much together, and he has also drawn a portrait of her (which seems to have been lost), but the thought of a more intimate relation did not occur to her, and when Vincent spoke to her at last about his love, a very decided *no* was the immediate reply. She went back to Amsterdam and never saw him again. But Vincent could not abide by her decision, and with his innate tenacity he keeps on persevering and hoping for a change in her feelings for him; when his letters are not answered, he accuses both his and her parents of opposing the match, and only a visit to Amsterdam, where she refuses to see him, convinces him of the utter hopelessness of his love.

'He fancied that he loved me,' she said afterwards, but for him it was sad earnest, and her refusal becomes a turning point in his life. If she had returned his love it would perhaps have been a spur to him to acquire a social position, he would have had to provide for her and her child; as it is he loses all worldly ambition and in the future lives only for his work, without taking one step to make himself independent. He cannot bear to stay in Etten any longer, he has become irritable and nervous, his relations to his parents become strained, and after a violent altercation with his father, in December he leaves suddenly for the Hague.

The two years he spends there are, for his work, a very important period of which his letters give a perfect description. His low spirits rise at first, by the change of surroundings and the intercourse with Mauve, but the feeling of having been slighted and wronged does not leave him and he feels himself utterly abandoned. When he meets in January a poor neglected woman [referred to in the letters as 'Christine' and 'Sien'] approaching her confinement, he takes her under his protection, partly from pity but also to fill the great void in his life. 'I hope there is no harm in his so-called model. Bad connections often arise from a feeling of loneliness, of dissatisfaction,' writes his father to Theo, who is always the confidant of both parties and has to listen to all the complaints and worries; father is not far wrong. Vincent could not be alone, he wanted to live for somebody, he wanted a wife and children, and as the woman he loved had rejected him, he took the first unhappy woman who crossed his path, with children that were not his own. At first he feigns to be happy and tries to convince Theo in every letter how wisely and well he has acted, and the touching care and tenderness with which he surrounds the woman when she leaves the hospital after her confinement, strike us painfully when we think on whom that treasure of love was lavished. He prides himself now on having a family of his own, but when their living together has become a fact and he is continually associated with a coarse, uneducated woman, marked by smallpox, who speaks with a low accent and has a spiteful character, who is addicted to liquor and smokes cigars, whose past life has not been irreproachable, and who draws him into all kinds of intrigues with her family, he soon writes no more about his home life; even the posing, by which she won him (she sat for the beautiful drawing, *Sorrow*), and of which he had expected so much, soon ceases altogether. This unfortunate adventure deprives him of the sympathy of all in the Hague who took an interest in him. Neither Mauve nor Tersteeg could approve of his taking upon himself the cares of a family, and such a family!, while he was financially dependent on his younger brother. Acquaintances and relatives are shocked to see him walk about with such a slovenly woman; nobody cares to associate with him any longer and his home life is such that nobody comes to visit him. The solitude around him becomes greater and greater and as usual it is only Theo who understands and continues to help him.

When the latter comes to visit Vincent for the second time in the Hague, in the summer of 1883, and witnesses the situation – finds the household neglected, everything in bad condition and Vincent deeply in debt – he too advises to let the woman go her own way as she is not fit for a regulated life. She herself had already felt that things could not continue like that, because Vincent wants too much money for his painting to leave enough for the support of her and the children, and she was already planning with her mother to earn money in another way. Vincent himself feels that Theo is right, and in his heart he longs for a change of surroundings, and liberty to go where his work calls him, but it costs him a bitter struggle to give up what he had taken upon himself, and to leave the poor woman to her fate. Till the last he defends her, and excuses her for her faults with the sublime words, 'she has never seen what is good, so how can she be good?'

In those days of inward strife he allows Theo to read deeper than ever into his heart. These last letters from the Hague [letters 313 to 322] give the key to many things that were incomprehensible until now. For the first time he speaks openly about what has happened at the time of his dismissal from Goupil, for the first time he explains his strange indifference to show his own work or to try to make it productive, when he writes, 'it is so painful for me to speak to people. I am not afraid to do so, but I know I make a disagreeable impression; I am so much afraid that my efforts to introduce myself will do me more harm than good,' and how naively he adds, 'human brains cannot bear everything as is shown by van Rappard, who had brain fever and now has gone to Germany to recover.' As if he wanted to say: 'do not let me make efforts to know strange people, as the same thing might happen to me.' Once more he touches the old love story of Etten, 'a single word made me feel that nothing is changed in me about it, that it is and remains a wound, which I carry with me, but it lies deep and will never heal, it will remain in after years just what it was the first day.' And he expresses openly how different his life would have been without this disappointment in his love.

When at last he starts alone in September for Drenthe, he has made all possible provisions for the woman and the children, and there is a sorrowful parting, especially from the little boy to whom he had become attached as if it were his own child.

The trip to Drenthe proves a failure instead of doing him good. But some of his most beautiful letters date from those days. The season was too far advanced, the country too inhospitable, and what Vincent so ardently desired – to come into contact with some artists, for instance, Lieberman – was not realized.

Bitter loneliness and want of money put a too heavy strain on his nerves. He is afraid of falling ill, and in December 1883 hastens back to the parental vicarage, the only place where he can find a safe shelter.

His father had meanwhile left Etten and been nominated to Nuenen, a village in the neighbourhood of Eindhoven, and the new place and surroundings pleased Vincent so well that instead of paying a short visit, as first was his intention, he stays there for two years.

To paint the Brabant landscape and the Brabant types is now his aim, and to accomplish that aim he overlooks all other difficulties.

To live together with his parents was for him as well as for them a very difficult thing. In a small village vicarage, where nothing can happen without the whole village knowing it, a painter is obviously an anomaly; how much more a painter like Vincent, who had so completely broken with all formalities, conventionalities and with all religion, and who was the last person in the world to conform himself to other people. On both sides there must have been great love and great patience to put up with it so long. When his letters from Drenthe to his parents became more and more melancholy, his father anxiously had written to Theo, 'it seems to me that Vincent is again in a wrong mood. He seems to be in a melancholy state of mind; but how can it be otherwise? Whenever he looks back into the past and recalls to his memory how he has broken with all former relations, it must be very painful to him. If he had only the courage to think of the possibility that the cause of much which has resulted from his eccentricity lies in himself. I don't think he ever feels any self-reproach, only soreness against others, especially against the gentlemen at the Hague. We must be very careful with him for he seems to be in a fit of contrariness.'

And they *are* so careful. When he comes back to them of his own will, they receive him with so much love and try all in their power to make him comfortable; they are proud too of the progress in his work, of which it must be said they had no great expectations at first. 'Do you not like the pen drawings of the tower that Vincent sent you? It seems to come to him so easily,' writes his father in the first days of December to Theo, and then on the twentieth of December, 'You will be longing to know how things are getting on with Vincent. At first it seemed hopeless, but by and by things have arranged themselves, especially since we approved of his staying here for some time to make studies. He wanted the inner room fitted up for him; we did not think it a very fit abode for him, but we had a nice stove put there; as the room had a stone floor we had it covered with boards, and made it as comfortable as possible: we put a bed in it on a wooden stand, that it might not be too damp. Now we will make the room nicely warm and dry, so that it may turn out better than we expected. I proposed to have a large window made in it but he did not want that. In short, with real courage we undertake this new experiment and we intend to leave him perfectly free in his peculiarities of dress, etc. The people here have seen him anyhow, and though it is a pity he is so reserved in manner, we cannot change the fact of his being eccentric. . . .' 'He seems to occupy himself a great deal with your plans for the future, but you will be wise enough not to let yourself be influenced to do things that are not practical, for alas that certainly is his foible. One thing is certain, he works hard and finds here lots of subjects, he has made already several drawings, which we like very much.' Such is the feeling from their side; but Vincent is not satisfied with all that kindness and wants a deeper understanding of his innermost self than his parents can give, however much they try. When about the middle of January 1884 his mother meets with an accident and is brought home from Helmond with a broken leg, the relations become less strained. Vincent who has become an expert nurse in the Borinage, helps to nurse his mother with the greatest devotion, and in every letter of that time they praise him for his faithful help. 'Vincent is untiring, and the rest of his time he devotes to his painting and drawing with the greatest zeal.' 'The doctor praised Vincent for his ability and care.' 'Vincent proves an ideal nurse and at the same time he works with the greatest ambition.' 'I fervently hope that his work may find success for it is edifying to see how much he works,' is told in the letters of February.

Vincent's own letters at that time are gloomy and full of complaints and unjust reproaches to Theo that he never sells anything for him and does not even try to, ending at last with the bitter cry: 'A wife you cannot give me, a child you cannot give me, work you cannot give me – money yes, but what is the use of it when I must miss all the rest!' And Theo, who always understands him, never gives a sharp or angry answer to those reproaches: a light sarcasm is the only reply he sometimes gives to such outbursts. In May Vincent's spirits rise somewhat on his moving into a new, larger studio, two rooms in the house of the Sexton of the Catholic church. Shortly after, van Rappard comes to spend some time with him again, and besides, Vincent had during his mother's illness come more in contact with neighbours and friends of the village, who daily came to visit the patient, so that he writes in those days, 'I have had a much pleasanter time with the people here than at first, which is worth a great deal to me, for one must have some distraction now and then, and when one feels too lonely the work suffers from it.' But with a prophetic glance he continues, 'One must keep in mind however that these things do not always last.' Indeed, difficult times were approaching for him again. With one of his mother's visitors, the youngest of three sisters who lived next door to the vicarage, he had soon got into a more intimate relation; she was much older than he and neither beautiful nor gifted, but she had an active mind and a kind heart. She often visited the poor with Vincent; they walked much together, and on her part at least the friendship soon changed into love. As to Vincent, though his letters do not give the impression of any passionate feeling for her (the fact is he writes very little about it), yet he seems to have been inclined to marry her, but the family vehemently protested against the plan, and violent scenes took place between the sisters, which were not conducive to keep Vincent in a pleasant mood.

'Vincent works hard but he is not very sociable,' writes his mother in July, and it will get worse still, for the young woman, violently excited by the scenes with her sisters, tries to commit suicide, which fails, but shocks her health so much that she had to be nursed at a doctor's in Utrecht. She quite recovered and after half a year she came back to Nuenen, but their relations were broken for ever and the whole affair left Vincent in a gloomy, bitter mood.

For his parents the consequences were also painful, because the neighbours avoided the vicarage from that time, not wishing to meet Vincent, 'which is a great privation for me, but it is not your mother's way to complain,' the latter writes in October of that year. It is in those days that van Rappard once more comes to stay with them. 'He is not a talkative person, but a hard worker,' writes mother, and van Rappard himself writes in 1890, in the letter to her, quoted above, 'how often do I think of the studies of the weavers which he made in Nuenen, with what intensity of feeling did he depict their lives, what deep melancholy pervaded them, however clumsy the execution of his work may have been then. And what beautiful studies he made of the old church tower in the churchyard. I always remember a moonlight effect of it, which particularly struck me at that time. When I think of those studies in those two rooms near the church, it recalls to my mind so many memories, and reminds me of the whole surroundings, the cheerful hospitable vicarage with its beautiful garden, the family Begemann, our visits to the weavers and peasants, how I did enjoy it all.'

After van Rappard's visit Vincent has no other distraction than a few acquaintances in Eindhoven, with whom he has come into contact through the house painter, who furnishes his colours. They are a former goldsmith, Hermans, a tanner, Kersemakers, and also a telegraphist whose name is not mentioned, all of whom Vincent initiates into the art of painting. Mr Kersemakers has recorded his reminiscences of that time in the weekly *De Amsterdammer* of the 14th and 21st of April 1912, and gives among others the following description of Vincent's studio, which according to him looked quite 'Bohemian'.

'It was quite astonishing to see how crowded the place was with pictures, with drawings in water-colour and chalk; heads of men and women whose negro-like turned up noses, projecting jaw-bones and large ears were strongly accentuated, the fists callous and furrowed; weavers and weavers' looms, women driving the shuttle, peasants planting potatoes, women busy weaving, innumerable still-lives, at least ten studies in oil of the old church tower at Nuenen, of which he was so fond, and which he had painted in all seasons of the year and in all weathers (afterwards this old tower was demolished by the Nuenen Vandals, as he called them).

'Heaps of ashes around the stove, which never had seen brush or polish, a few frayed out rush-bottomed chairs, and a cupboard with at least thirty different birds' nests, all kinds of moss and plants brought from the heath, some stuffed birds, shuttles, spinning-wheel, bed-warmer, all sorts of farmers' tools, old caps and hats, dirty women's bonnets, wooden shoes, etc.' He also tells about their trip to Amsterdam (in the autumn of 1885) to see the 'Ryksmuseum', how Vincent in his rough ulster and his inseparable fur cap was calmly sitting painting a few small views of the town in the waiting room of the station; how they saw the Rembrandts in the museum, how Vincent could not tear himself away from the *Jewish Bride* and said at last, 'Do you know that I would give ten years of my life if I could sit here before this picture a fortnight, with nothing but a crust of dry bread for food.'

Dry bread was nothing unusual to him; according to Kersemakers, Vincent never ate it otherwise, in order not to indulge himself too much. His impression of Vincent's work is given as follows: 'At my first visit in Nuenen I could not understand it at all, it was so totally different from what I expected, it was so strong, so coarse and unfinished that I could not possibly admire it or see anything in it.

'At my second visit the impression was already much better, though I thought in my ignorance that he could not draw, or totally neglected the drawing of the figures, and I took the liberty of telling him straight out. I did not make him angry, he only laughed and said: "You will think differently about it later on."'

Meanwhile the winter days passed on gloomily enough at the vicarage. 'For Vincent I should wish that the winter were over, he cannot work out of doors and the long evenings are not profitable for his work. We often think that it would be better for him to be among people of his own profession, but we cannot dictate to him,' writes his father in December, and mother complains, 'how is it possible to behave so unkindly. If he has wishes for the future, let him exert himself, he is still young enough; it is almost impossible to bear it. I think he wants a change, perhaps he might find something that would give him inspiration, here it is always the same thing and he never speaks to anyone.' But still she finds one luminous point to mention: 'we saw that Vincent received a book from you, he seems to read it with much pleasure. I heard him say "that is a fine book", so you have given him great pleasure. I am glad that we regularly get books from the reading club; the illustrations in the magazines interest him most, and then there is the *Nouvelle Revue*, etc., every week something new is a great pleasure to him.' Incessantly Vincent continues his work in the gloomy cottages of peasants and weavers. 'I never began a year of a more gloomy aspect, in a more gloomy mood,' he writes on New Year's Day 1885. 'He seems to become more and more estranged from us,' complains his father, whose letters became more and more melancholy, as if he is not equal to the difficulties of living together with his gifted, unmanageable son, and feels himself helpless against his unbridled violence. 'This morning I talked things over with Vincent; he was in a kind mood and said there was no particular reason for his being depressed,' says the latter, 'may he meet with success anyhow,' are the last words he writes about Vincent in a letter of the 25th of March. Two days later, coming home from a long walk across the heath, he fell down on the threshold of his home and was carried lifeless into the house. Hard times followed in the vicarage; mother could remain there another year, but for Vincent it brought immediate changes. In consequence of several disagreeable discussions with the other members of the family, he resolved to live no longer at the vicarage, but took up his abode in the studio, where he stayed from May to November. Henceforth there is not a single thing to distract him from his aim – to paint the peasant life. He spends those months in the cottages of the weavers or with the peasants in the field. 'It is a fine thing to be right in the snow in the winter, right in the yellow leaves in autumn, in summer right in the ripe corn, in spring right in the grass, always with the peasant girls and reapers, in summer under the open skies, in winter near the open fireplace, and to know that it has always been so and will always be' [letter 425]. He is now in harmony with himself and his surroundings, and when he sends Theo his first great picture, *The Potato-Eaters*, he can say in good reason that it is 'from the heart of peasant life'.

An uninterrupted series of studies follow each other; the cottages of the old peasants and their witch-like wives, the old church tower of the cemetery, the autumn landscapes and the birds' nests, a number of still-lives and the strong drawings of the Brabant peasants. In Nuenen he also writes the beautiful passages about colour, in reference to Delacroix's laws of colours. It seems strange to hear him, who was called afterwards one of the first Impressionists, even Neo-Impressionists, declare, 'there is a school I think of Impressionists, but I do not know much about it' [letter 402], and in his usual spirit of contradiction he afterwards adds, 'from what you have told me about Impressionism I have learned that it is different from what I thought it was, but as to me I find Israëls for instance so enormous that I am little curious about or desirous of anything different or new. I think I shall change a great deal in touch and colour but I expect to become rather more dark than lighter.' As soon as he came to France he thought differently of it.

During the last days of his stay in Nuenen difficulties arise between him and the Catholic priest, who has long since looked askance at the studio next to his church, and now forbids his parishioners to pose for Vincent. The latter was already thinking about a change. He gives notice of leaving his studio the first of May, but starts for Antwerp, towards the end of November, leaving all his Brabant work behind. When in May his mother also leaves Nuenen, everything belonging to Vincent is packed in cases, left in care of a carpenter in Breda and – forgotten! After several years the carpenter finally sold everything to a junk dealer.

What Theo's opinion about his brother was at that time is shown in the letter to his sister of the 13th of October 1885, in which he writes: 'Vincent is one of those who has gone through all the experiences of life and has retired from the world, now we must wait and see if he has genius. I think he has . . . If he succeeds in his work he will be a great man. As to the worldly success, it will perhaps be with him as with Heyerdahl[*]: appreciated by some but not understood by the public at large. Those however who care whether there is really something in the artist, or if it is only outward shine, will respect him, and in my opinion that will be sufficient revenge for the animosity shown him by so many others.'

In Antwerp Vincent rents for 25 fr. a month a little room over a small paint-dealer's shop in the 'Rue des Images' 194. It is but a very small room but he makes it cosy with Japanese prints on the wall, and when he has rented a stove and a lamp, he feels himself safe and writes with profound satisfaction, 'no fear of my being bored I can assure you'. On the contrary he spends the three months of his stay in one feverish intoxication of work. The town life which he has missed so long fascinates him; he has not eyes enough to see, nor hands enough to paint: to make portraits of all the interesting types he meets is his delight, and in order to pay the models he sacrifices everything he has. As for food he does not bother. 'If I receive money my first hunger is not for food, though I have fasted ever so long, but the desire for painting is ever so much stronger, and I start at once hunting for models till there is nothing left,' he writes.

When he sees in January that he cannot go on like that, the expenses being too heavy, he becomes a pupil of the Academy, where the teaching is free and where he finds models every day. Hageman and de Baseleer were there among his fellow pupils and from Holland there was Briët. In the evening he worked again in the drawing class and after that, often till late at night, at a club where they also draw from life. His health cannot stand such a strain and in the beginning of February he writes that he is literally worn out and exhausted, according to the doctor it is complete prostration. He seems not to think about giving up his work, however, though he begins to make projects for a change, for the course at the Academy is almost finished and he has already had many disagreements with his teachers, for he is much too independent and self-willed to follow their guidance. Something must be done. Theo thinks it better for Vincent to go back

[*]Norwegian painter, then in Paris.

to Brabant, but he himself wants to go to Paris. Then Theo proposes to wait at least till June, when he shall have rented a larger apartment, but with his usual impetuosity Vincent cannot wait so long, and one morning in the end of February, Theo receives in his office at the Boulevard a little note written in chalk, that Vincent had arrived and awaits him in the Salon Carré of the Louvre. Probably he left all his work in Antwerp, perhaps his landlord the paint-dealer kept it for the unpaid rent of the room. Certain it is that none of the studies about which he writes, the view of the Park, of the Cathedral, Het Steen, etc., ever has been found again.

The meeting in the Louvre took place, and since then Vincent lived with Theo in the latter's apartment in the Rue de Laval. As there was no room for a studio he worked during the first month at Cormon's studio, which did not satisfy him at all, but when they moved in June to the Rue Lepic 54, on Montmartre, he had there a studio of his own and never went back to Cormon.

The new apartment on the third floor had three rather large rooms, a cabinet and a kitchen. The living room was comfortable and cosy with Theo's beautiful old cabinet, a sofa and a big stove, for both the brothers were very sensitive to the cold. Next to that was Theo's bedroom. Vincent slept in the cabinet and behind that was the studio, an ordinary sized room with one not very large window. Here he first painted his nearest surroundings – the view from the studio window, the Moulin de la Galette viewed from every side, the window of Madame Bataille's small restaurant where he took his meals, little landscapes on Montmartre which was at that time still quite countrified, all painted in a soft tender tone like that of Mauve. Afterwards he painted flowers and still-life and tried to renew his palette under the influence of the French 'plein air' painters such as Monet, Sisley, Pissarro, etc., for whom Theo had long since opened the way to the public. The change of surroundings and the easier and more comfortable life, without any material cares, at first greatly improved Vincent's health. In the summer of 1886 Theo writes to his mother, 'we like the new apartment very much; you would not recognize Vincent, he is so much changed, and it strikes other people more than it does me. He has undergone an important operation in his mouth, for he had lost almost all his teeth through the bad condition of his stomach. The doctor says that he has now quite recovered his health; he makes great progress in his work and has begun to have some success. He is in much better spirits than before and many people here like him . . . he has friends who send him every week a lot of beautiful flowers which he uses for still-life, he paints chiefly flowers, especially to make the colours of his next pictures brighter and clearer. If we can continue to live together like this, I think the most difficult period is past, and he will find his way.' To continue living together, that was the great difficulty, and of all that Theo did for his brother, there is perhaps nothing that proved greater sacrifice than his having endured living with him for two years. For when the first excitement of all the new attractions in Paris had passed, Vincent soon fell back to his old irritability; perhaps the city life did not agree with him either and overstrained his nerves. Whatever might be the cause, his temper during that winter was worse than ever and made life very hard for Theo, whose own health was not of the best at that time. Circumstances put too heavy a strain on his strength. His own work was very strenuous and exhausting, he had made the gallery on the Boulevard Montmartre centre of the Impressionists, there were Monet, Sisley, Pissarro and Raffaelli, Degas who exhibited nowhere else, Seurat, etc. But to introduce that work to the public, which filled the small entresol every afternoon from five until seven, what discussions, what endless debates, had to be held, and on the other hand how he had to defend the rights of the young painters against 'ces messieurs', as Vincent always called the heads of the firm. When he came home tired out in the evening he found no rest, but the impetuous, violent Vincent began to expound his own theories about art and art-dealing, which always came to the point that Theo ought to leave Goupil and open a gallery for himself. And this lasted till far into the night, ay sometimes he sat down on a chair before Theo's bed to spin out his last arguments. 'Do you feel how hard it sometimes is to have no other conversation than with gentlemen who speak about business, with artists whose life generally is difficult enough, but never to come in contact with women and children of your own sphere? You can have no idea of the loneliness in a big city,' writes Theo once to his youngest sister and to her he sometimes opens his heart about Vincent: 'my home life is almost unbearable, no one wants to come and see me any more, because it always ends in quarrels, and besides he is so untidy that the room looks far from attractive. I wish he would go and live by himself, he speaks sometimes about it, but if I were to tell him to go away, it would be just a reason for him to stay; as it seems I do him no good. I only ask him one thing, to do me no harm and by his stay he does so, for I can hardly bear it.' 'It seems as if he were two persons in one, one marvellously gifted, tender and refined, the other egoistic and hard-hearted. They present themselves in turns, so that one hears him talk first in one way, then in the other, and always with arguments on both sides. It is a pity that he is his own enemy, for he makes life hard not only for others but also for himself.' But when his sister advises him to 'leave Vincent for God's sake,' to himself, Theo answers, 'it is such a peculiar case. If he only had another profession I would long ago have done what you advise me, and I have often asked myself if I have not been wrong in helping him continually. I have often been on the point of leaving him to his own devices. After receiving your letter I have thought it over again, but I think in this case I must continue in the same way. He is certainly an artist and if what he makes now is not always beautiful, it will certainly be of use to him afterwards, and then his work will perhaps be sublime, and it would be a shame to keep him from his regular study. However unpractical he may be, if he succeeds in his work there will certainly come a day when he will begin to sell his pictures . . .

'I am firmly resolved to continue in the same way as till now, but I do hope that he will change his lodgings in some way or other.'

However, that separation did not take place. The old love and friendship which bound them together since childhood, did not fail them even now. Theo managed to restrain himself, and in the spring he wrote, 'as I feel much stronger than last winter I hope to be able to bring a change for the better in our relations; there will be no other change for the present and I am glad of it. We are already most of us so far from home that it would be no use to bring about still more separation.' And full of courage he continues to help Vincent bear the burden of his life.

With spring there came in all respects a better time. Vincent could again work in the open air and painted much at Asnières where he painted the beautiful triptych of *l'Isle de la grande Jatte*, the borders of the Seine with their gay, bright restaurants, the little boats on the river, the parks and gardens, all sparkling with light and colour. At that time he saw much of Emile Bernard, a young painter fifteen years younger than himself, whom he had met at Cormon's and who had a little wooden studio in his parents' garden at Asnières, where they sometimes worked together and where Vincent began a portrait of Bernard. But one day he fell into a violent quarrel with old Mr Bernard about the latter's projects for his son. Vincent could bear no contradiction, he ran away in a passion with the still wet portrait under his arm, and he never set foot again in the house of the Bernards. But the friendship with the young Bernard remained, and in his *Letters of Vincent van Gogh* (published at Vollard's in Paris), are the most beautiful pages written about Vincent.

In the winter of 1887–8, Vincent again paints portraits – the famous self-portrait before the easel, and many other self-portraits, as well as father Tanguy, the old merchant of colours in the Rue Clausel, in whose show-window his customers were allowed to exhibit their pictures by turns, and who unjustly sometimes has been described as a Mæcenas, the qualities for which were absolutely wanting in the poor old man, and even if he had possessed them, his shrewd wife would not have allowed him to use them. He sent, and justly too, very proper bills for the colours he furnished, and did not understand very much about the pictures that were exposed in his window.

From that time dates also the famous picture, *Interior with Lady by a Cradle*, and when Theo who has bought that winter a few pictures from young artists, to help them, and wants to do the same for Vincent, the latter paints for him the beautiful *Still Life in Yellow*, sparkling and radiant as from an inward glow, and with red letters he graves the dedication 'To my brother Theo'.

Towards the end of the winter he is tired of Paris, city life is too much for him, the climate too grey and chilly, in February 1888 he travels toward the south. 'After all the years of care and misfortune his health has not grown stronger and he decidedly wanted to be in a milder climate,' Theo writes. 'He has first gone to Arles to look around him, and then will probably go to Marseilles.

'Before he went away I went a few times with him to hear a Wagner concert; we both enjoyed it very much. It still seems strange that he is gone. He was so much to me the last time.' And Bernard tells how Vincent was busy that last day in Paris arranging the studio, 'So that my brother will think me still here.'

At Arles, Vincent reaches the summit of his art. After the oppressiveness of Parisian life he, with his innate love of nature, revives in sunny Provence. There follows a happy time of undisturbed and immense productivity. Without paying much attention to the town of Arles itself with its famous remains of Roman architecture, he paints the landscape, the glorious wealth of blossoms in Spring in a series of orchards in bloom, the cornfields under the burning sun at harvest time, the almost intoxicating richness of colours of the autumn, the glorious beauty of the gardens and parks, *The Poet's Garden*, where he sees as in a vision the ghosts of Dante and Petrarcha roaming about. He paints *The Sower, The Sunflowers, The Starlit Night*, the sea at Ste Marie: his creative impulse and power are inexhaustible. 'I have a terrible lucidity at moments, when nature is so glorious in those days I am hardly conscious of myself and the picture comes to me like in a dream,' and rapturously he exclaims, 'Life is after all enchanting.'

His letters henceforth, written in French, give a complete image of what passes within him. Sometimes when he has written in the morning, he sits down again in the evening to tell his brother how splendid the day has been. 'I never had such a chance, nature is extraordinarily beautiful here,' and a day later, 'I know that I wrote to you yesterday but the day has been again so glorious. My only regret is that you cannot see what I see here.'

Completely absorbed in his work as he is, he does not feel the burden of the great loneliness that surrounds him in Arles, for except a short acquaintance with MacKnight, Bock and the Zouave lieutenant Milliet, he has no friends whatever. But when he has rented a little house of his own on the Place Lamartine, and arranges it after his own taste, decorates it with his pictures, makes it a 'maison d'artiste', then he feels the old longing again, which he has already uttered at the beginning of his painting career in 1880, to associate himself with another artist, to live together and to work together. Just then he receives a letter from Paul Gauguin from Bretagne, who is in the greatest pecuniary embarrassment, and who tries in this roundabout way to ask Theo to try to sell some of his pictures for him: 'I wanted to write to your brother but I am afraid to bother him, he being so busy from morning until night. The little I have sold is just enough to pay some urgent debts and in a month I shall have absolutely nothing left. Zero is a negative force . . . I do not want to importune your brother, but a little word from you on this head would set my mind at ease or at least help me to have patience. My God, how terrible are these money questions for an artist.'

At once Vincent grasps at the idea of helping Gauguin. He must come to Arles and they will live and work together. Theo will pay the expenses and Gauguin will give him pictures in exchange. Again and again he insists on this plan with his innate perseverance and stubbornness, though Gauguin at first did not seem at all inclined to it. They had made each other's acquaintance in Paris, but it had been no more than a superficial acquaintance, and they were too different in talent and character ever to harmonize in the daily intercourse.

Gauguin, born in Paris in 1848, was the son of a Breton father, a journalist in Paris, and a Creole mother. His youth was full of adventures, he had gone to sea as cabin boy, had worked in a banker's office and had only painted in his leisure hours. Then after he had married and had a family, he devoted himself wholly to his art. His wife and children returned to her native city Copenhagen, as he was not able to provide for them, and he himself made a journey to Martinique where he painted, among others, his famous picture *The negresses*. He was now in Pont Aven in Brittany, without any source of income, so that the great need of money made him accept Vincent's proposition and come to Arles. The whole undertaking was a sad failure and had for Vincent a fatal end.

Notwithstanding the months of superhuman exertion which lay behind him, he strained every nerve in a last manifestation of power before the arrival of Gauguin. 'I am conceited enough to want to make a certain impression on Gauguin by my painting. I have finished as far as possible the things I had undertaken, pushed by the great desire to show him something new, and not to undergo his influence before I have shown him indisputably my own originality,' writes Vincent. When we know that to this last work belongs one of Vincent's most famous pictures, *la chambre à coucher*, and the series, *The Poet's Garden*, it makes us feel rather sceptical about Gauguin's later assertion that before his arrival Vincent had only been bungling a little, and that he only made progress after Gauguin's lessons. We know then what to think of Gauguin's whole description of the episode at Arles, which is such a mixture of truth and fiction.[*]

The fact is that Vincent was completely exhausted and overstrained, and was no match for the iron Gauguin with his strong nerves and cool arguing. It became a silent struggle between them, and the endless discussions held while smoking in the little yellow house were not fit to calm Vincent. 'Your brother is indeed a little agitated and I hope to calm him by and by,' Gauguin writes to Theo, shortly after his arrival at Arles. And to Bernard he tells more intimately how little sympathy there really is between Vincent and himself. 'Vincent and I generally

[*]'Paul Gauguin', by Chas. Morice, *Mercure de France*, 1903.

agree very little especially about painting. He admires Daudet, Daubigny, Ziem, and the great Rousseau, all people whom I cannot bear. And on the contrary he detests Ingres, Raphaël, Degas, all people whom I admire. I answer, "Brigadier, you are right", in order to have peace. He loves my pictures very much, but when I make them he always finds I am wrong in this or that. He is romantic and I rather inclined to the primitive state.'* And in later years when Gauguin again remembers this period he writes, 'between two beings, he and I, he like a Vulcan, and I boiling too, a kind of struggle was preparing itself . . .'† The situation in consequence becomes more and more strained. In the latter half of December Theo receives from Gauguin the following letter: 'Dear Mr van Gogh, – I would be greatly obliged to you for sending me a part of the money for the pictures sold. After all I must go back to Paris, Vincent and I simply cannot live together in peace, in consequence of incompatibility of temper, and he as well as I, we need quiet for our work. He is a man of remarkable intelligence, whom I highly respect and leave with regret, but I repeat it is necessary. I appreciate all the delicacy in your conduct towards me and I beg you to excuse my decision.' Vincent also writes, in letter 565, that Gauguin seems to be tired of Arles, of the yellow house, and of himself. But the quarrel is made up, Gauguin asks Theo to consider his return to Paris as an imaginary thing, and the letter he had written him as a bad dream. But it is only the calm before the storm.

The day before Christmas – Theo and I were just engaged to be married and intended to go together to Holland – (I was staying in Paris with my brother A. Bonger, the friend of Theo and Vincent) – a telegram arrived from Gauguin which called Theo to Arles. Vincent had on the evening of the 24th of December, in a state of violent excitement, 'un accès de fièvre chaude' (an attack of high fever), cut off a piece of his ear and brought it as a gift to a woman in a brothel. A big tumult had been raised. Roulin the postman had seen Vincent home, the police had interfered, had found Vincent bleeding and unconscious in bed, and sent him to the hospital. Theo found him there in a severe crisis, and stayed with him during the Christmas days. The doctor considered his condition very serious. 'There were moments while I was with him that he was well, but very soon after he fell back into his worries about philosophy and theology. It was painfully sad to witness,

*'Paul Gauguin', by Chas. Morice, *Mercure de France*, 1903.
†Emile Bernard, Paris, 1901, *Letters of V. van Gogh*.

for at times all his suffering overwhelmed him and he tried to weep but he could not; poor fighter and poor, poor sufferer; for the moment nobody can do anything to relieve his sorrow and yet he feels deeply and strongly. If he might have found somebody to whom he could have disclosed his heart, it would perhaps never have gone thus far,' Theo wrote to me after he had come back to Paris with Gauguin, and a day later, 'there is little hope, but during his life he has done more than many others, and he has suffered and struggled more than most people could have done. If it must be that he dies, be it so, but my heart breaks when I think of it.' The anxiety lasted a few more days. Dr Rey, the house doctor of the hospital, to whose care Theo had entrusted him so urgently, kept him constantly informed. 'I shall always be glad to send you tidings, for I too have a brother, I too have been separated from my family,' he writes the 29th of December when the tidings are still very bad. The Protestant clergyman, the Rev. Salles, also visits Vincent and writes to Theo about his condition, and then there is last but not least the postman, Roulin, who is quite dismayed at the accident that befell his friend Vincent, with whom he spent so many pleasant hours at the 'Café de la Gare' of Joseph Ginoux, and who has painted such beautiful portraits of him and his whole family! Every day he goes to the hospital for tidings and conveys them faithfully to Paris; as he is not a good penman, his two sons, Armand and Camille, serve him in turn as secretary. His wife too who posed for the *Berceuse* (Mme Ginoux was the original of the *Arlésiénne*) visits her sick friend, and the first sign of recovery is when Vincent asks her about little Marcelle, the handsome baby he had painted such a short time ago. Then there comes a sudden change for the better in his condition. The Rev. Salles writes on the 31st of December, that he had found Vincent perfectly calm, and that he is longing to start work again. A day later, Vincent himself writes a short note in pencil to reassure Theo, and on the second of January there comes another note from him, to which Dr Rey has added a word of reassurance. The 3rd of January an enthusiastic letter of Roulin's, 'Vincent has quite recovered. He is better than before that unfortunate accident happened to him,' and he, Roulin, will go to the doctor and tell him to allow Vincent to go back to his pictures. The following day they had been out and spent four hours together. 'I am very sorry my first letters were so alarming and I beg your pardon; I am glad to say I have been mistaken in this case. He only regrets all the trouble he has given you, and he is sorry for the anxiety he has caused.

You may be assured that I will do all I can to give him some distraction,' writes Roulin.

On the 7th of January Vincent leaves the hospital, apparently entirely recovered, but, alas, at every great excitement or fatigue, the nervous attacks return . . . they last longer or shorter, but leave him also periods of almost perfect health, during which he goes back to his work with the old vigour. In February he is taken back to the hospital for a short time, but after his return to his little house, the neighbours have grown afraid of him and send a petition to the mayor, saying that it is dangerous to leave him at liberty, in consequence of which he is actually again sent to the hospital on the 27th of February – this time without any cause. Vincent himself for a whole month keeps the deepest silence about this unhappy affair, but the Rev. Salles sends Theo a faithful report. On the 2nd of March he writes, 'The neighbours have raised a tumult out of nothing. The acts with which they have reproached your brother (even if they were exact), do not justify taxing a man with alienation or depriving him of his liberty. Unfortunately, the foolish act which necessitated his first removal to the hospital made people interpret in a quite unfavourable way every singular deed which the poor young man might perform; from anyone else it would remain unobserved, from him, everything takes at once a particular importance . . . As I told you yesterday, at the hospital he has won everybody's favour and after all it is the doctor and not the chief of police who has to judge in these matters.' The whole affair makes a deep impression on Vincent and again causes an attack from which he recovers with astonishing rapidity. It is again the Rev. Salles who tells Theo of Vincent's recovery. On the 18th of March he writes, 'Your brother has spoken to me with perfect calmness and lucidity of mind about his condition and also about the petition signed by his neighbours. The petition grieves him very much. "If the police," he says, "had protected my liberty by preventing the children and even the grown-ups from crowding around my house and climbing the windows as they have done (as if I were a curious animal), I should have more easily retained my self-possession, at all events I have done no harm to anyone." In short, I found your brother transformed, may God maintain this favourable change. His condition has something indescribable, and it is impossible to understand the sudden and complete changes which have taken place in him. It is evident that as long as he is in the condition in which I found him, there can be no question of interning him in an asylum; nobody, as far as I know, would have this sinister courage.' A day after this interview with the Rev. Salles, Vincent himself for the first time writes again to Theo and justly complains that such repeated emotions might become the cause of a passing nervous attack changing to a chronic evil. And with quiet resignation, he adds, 'to suffer without complaint is the only lesson we have to learn in this life.'

He soon recovers his liberty but continues to live in the hospital for a short time, until the Rev. Salles shall have found him new lodgings in a different part of the town. His health is so good that the Rev. Salles writes on the 19th of April, 'sometimes even no traces seem left of the disease which has affected him so vividly.' But when he was going to arrange with the new landlord, he suddenly avowed to the Rev. Salles that he lacked the courage to start again a new studio, and that he himself thought it best to go to an asylum for a few months. 'He is fully conscious of his condition, and speaks with me about his illness, which he fears will come back, with a touching openheartedness and simplicity,' writes the Rev. Salles. "I am not fit," he told me the day before yesterday, "to govern myself and my affairs. I feel quite different than I was before." The Rev. Salles had then looked around and advised the asylum of St Remy, situated quite near Arles; he adds that the doctors at Arles approve of it, 'given the state of isolation in which your brother would find himself upon leaving the hospital.'

It was that which troubled Theo mostly. 'Yes,' he wrote to me, shortly before our marriage, in answer to my question if Vincent would not rather return to Paris, or spend some time with his mother and sisters in Holland, as he was so alone in Arles, 'one of the greatest difficulties is, that whether in good or bad health his life is so barren of distraction. But if you knew him you would feel doubly how difficult is the solution of the question what must and can be done for him.

'As you know he has long since broken with what is called convention. His way of dressing and his manners show directly that he is an unusual personality and people who see him say, "he is mad". To me it does not matter, but for mother that is impossible. Then there is something in his way of speaking that makes people either like or dislike him strongly. He has always people around him, who sympathize with him, but also many enemies. It is impossible for him to associate with people in an indifferent way. It is either the one or the other, even to those who are his best friends it is difficult to remain on

1

good terms with him, as he spares nobody's feelings. If I had time for it, I would go to him and, for instance, take a walking tour with him. That is the only thing, I imagine, that would do him good. If I can find somebody among the painters who would like to do it, I will send him. But those with whom he would like to go, are somewhat afraid of him, a circumstance which the visit of Gauguin did not change, on the contrary.

'Then there is another thing which makes me afraid to have him come here. In Paris he saw so many things which he liked to paint, but again and again it was made impossible for him to do so. Models would not pose for him, he was forbidden to paint on the street, and with his irascible temper this caused many unpleasant scenes, which excited him so much that he became unapproachable to everybody and at last he got a great dislike of Paris. If he himself had wanted to come back here, I would not hesitate for a moment . . . but again I think I can do no better than to let him follow his own wishes. A quiet life is impossible for him, except alone with nature or with very simple people like the Roulins, for wherever he passes he leaves the trace of his passing. Whatever he sees that is wrong he must criticize and that often occasions strife.

'I hope that he will find, some time, a wife who will love him so much that she will share his life but it will be difficult to find one who would be fit for that. Do you remember that girl in *Terre Vierge* by Tourgenief,[*] who is with the nihilists and brought the compromising papers across the frontiers? I imagine she should be like that, somebody who has gone through life's misery to the bottom . . . It pains me not to be able to do something for him, but for uncommon people uncommon remedies are necessary and I hope these will be found where ordinary people would not look for them.'

When Vincent himself now resolves to go to St Remy, Theo's first impression is that this may be a kind of self-sacrifice so as to be in nobody's way, and he writes to him once more asking with emphasis, whether he would not rather go to Pontaven or go to Paris.

But as Vincent sticks to his resolution Theo writes to him: 'I do not consider your going to St Remy a retreat as you call it, but simply as a temporary rest cure which will make you come back with renewed strength. I for my part attribute your illness principally to the fact that your material existence has been too much neglected. In an establish-

[*] Turgenev, *Virgin Soil*.

ment like that of St Remy there is a great regularity in the hours for meals, etc., and I think that regularity will do you no harm, on the contrary.' When Theo has arranged everything with the director of the establishment, Dr Peyron, a free room for Vincent and a room where he can paint, and as much liberty as possible to wander about as he likes, Vincent leaves for St Remy on the 8th of May accompanied by the Rev. Salles who writes to Theo the next day: 'Our voyage to St Remy has been accomplished under the most excellent conditions; Monsieur Vincent was perfectly calm and himself has explained his case to the director as a man who is fully conscious of his condition. He remained with me till my departure and when I took leave of him he thanked me warmly and seemed somewhat moved, thinking of the new life he was going to lead in that house. Monsieur Peyron has assured me that he will show him all the kindness and consideration which his condition demands.' How touching sounds that, 'somewhat moved', at the departure of the faithful companion! His leave-taking broke the last tie that united Vincent with the outer world and he stayed behind in what was worse than the greatest loneliness, surrounded by neurotics and lunatics, with nobody to whom he could talk, nobody who understood him. Dr Peyron was kindly disposed, but he was a reserved silent character, and the monthly letters by which he keeps Theo informed of the situation are not full of the warm sympathy which the doctors in the hospital at Arles showed him.

A full year Vincent spent amid these cheerless surroundings, struggling with unbroken energy against the ever returning attacks of his illness, but continuing his work with the old restless zeal, which alone can keep him living now that everything else has failed him. He paints the desolate landscape which he sees from his window at sunrise and sunset, he undertakes long wanderings to paint the wide fields, bordered by the range of hills of the Alps, he paints the olive orchards with their dismally twisted branches, the gloomy cypresses, the sombre garden of the asylum, and he painted also the *Reaper*, 'that image of death as the great book of Nature represents it to us'.

It is no longer the buoyant, sunny, triumphant work from Arles; there sounds a deeper sadder tone than the piercing clarion sound of his symphonies in yellow of the last year: his palette has become more sober, the harmonies of his pictures have passed into a minor key.

'To suffer without complaint,' well had he learned that lesson; and when in August the treacherous evil attacks him again, just when he had hoped to be cured for good, he only utters a desponding sigh, 'I can see no possibility of again having hope or courage.'

Having painfully struggled through the winter, in which however he paints some of his most beautiful works, the *Piéta* after Delacroix, the *Resurrection of Lazarus*, and the *Good Samaritan* after Rembrandt, the *Quatre heures du jour* after Millet; a few months follow during which he is not able to work, but now he feels that he would lose his energy for ever if he stayed longer in those fatal surroundings, he *must* get away from St Remy. For some time Theo had been looking around for a opportunity – near Paris and yet in the country – where Vincent could live under the care of a physician, who would at the same time be a friend to him, and when he had found this at last, by the recommendation of Pissarro at Auvers sur Oise, an hour by train from Paris, where lived Dr Gachet who had been in his youth a friend of Cézanne, Pissarro and the other Impressionists, then Vincent returns from the south on the 17th of May 1890. First he was going to spend a few days with us in Paris; a telegram from Tarascon informed us that he was going to travel that night and would arrive at ten in the morning. Theo could not sleep that night for anxiety – if anything happened to Vincent on the way, he had but scarcely recovered from a long and serious attack and had refused to be accompanied by anyone. How thankful we were when it was at last time for Theo to go to the station!

From the Cité Pigalle to the Gare de Lyon is a long distance, it seemed an endless time before they came back and I began to be anxious that something had happened, when I saw at last an open fiacre enter the Cité, two merry faces nodded to me, two hands waved – a moment later Vincent stood before me.

I had expected to see a patient and there stood before me a strong, broad-shouldered man, with a healthy colour, a smile on his face and an expression of great resoluteness in his whole appearance; from all the self-portraits the one before the easel is most like him at that period. Apparently there had again come such a sudden puzzling change in his state as the Rev. Salles had already observed to his great surprise at Arles.

'He seems perfectly well, he looks much stronger than Theo,' was my first thought.

Then Theo drew him to the room where was the cradle of our little boy, that had been named after Vincent; silently the two brothers looked at the quietly sleeping baby – both had tears in their eyes. Then Vincent turned smilingly to me and said, pointing to the simple crotcheted cover on the cradle: 'Do not cover him too much with lace, little sister.'

He stayed with us three days and was all the time cheerful and lively. St Remy was not mentioned. He went out by himself to buy olives which he used to eat every day and which he insisted on our eating too; the first morning he was up very early and was standing in his shirt-sleeves looking at his pictures of which our apartment was full; the walls were covered with them – in the bedroom the *Blooming Orchards*, in the dining-room over the mantelpiece *The Potato Eaters*, in the sitting-room (salon was too solemn a name for the cosy little room) the great *Landscape from Arles*, and the *Night View on the Rhône*, besides to the great despair of our *femme de ménage*, there were under the bed, under the sofa, under the cupboards, in the little spare room, huge piles of unframed canvases, that were now spread out on the ground and studied with great attention.

We had also many visitors, but Vincent soon perceived that the bustle of Paris did him no good and he was longing to set to work again. So he started the 21st of May for Auvers, with an introduction to Dr Gachet, whose faithful friendship was to become his greatest support during the short time he was to spend at Auvers. We promised to come and see him soon, and he also wanted to come back to us in a few weeks to paint our portraits. In Auvers he took up his lodgings at an inn and immediately set to work.

The hilly landscape with the sloping fields and thatched roofs of the village pleased him, but what he enjoyed most was to have models again, and again to paint figures. One of the first portraits he painted was that of Dr Gachet, who immediately felt great sympathy for Vincent, so that they spent most of their time together and became great friends – a friendship not ended by death, for Dr Gachet and his children continued to honour Vincent's memory with rare piety, that became a form of worship, touching in its simplicity and sincerity. 'The more I think of it the more I think Vincent was a giant. Not a day passes that I do not look at his pictures, I always find there a new idea, something different each day . . . I think again of the painter and I find him a colossus. Besides he was a philosopher. . .'

So Gachet wrote to Theo shortly after Vincent's death and speaking of the latter's love for art he says: 'The word love of art is not exact, one must call it *faith*, a faith to which Vincent fell a martyr!' None of his contemporaries had understood him better.

It was curious to note that Dr Gachet himself somewhat resembled Vincent physically (he was much older) and his son Paul – then a boy of fifteen years – resembled Theo a little.

Their house, built on a hill, was full of pictures and antiques, which received but scanty daylight through the small windows; before the house there was a splendid terraced flower-garden, behind, a large yard where all kinds of ducks, hens, turkeys and peacocks walked about in the company of four or five cats; it was the home of an original, but an original of great taste.

The doctor no longer practised in Auvers, but had an office in Paris where he gave consultations a few days a week, the rest of the time he painted and etched in his room, that looked most like the workshop of an alchemist of the Middle Ages. Soon after, the 10th of June, we received an invitation from him to come with the baby and spend a whole day in Auvers. Vincent came to meet us at the train and he brought a bird's nest as a plaything for his little nephew and namesake. He insisted upon carrying the baby himself and had no rest until he had shown him all the animals in the yard, where a too-loudly crowing cock made the baby red in the face for fear and made him cry, whilst Vincent cried laughingly, 'the cock crows cocorico,' and was very proud that he had introduced his little namesake to the animal world. We lunched in the open air and after lunch took a long walk; the day was so peacefully quiet, so happy, that nobody would have suspected how tragically a few weeks later our happiness was to be destroyed for ever. In the first days of July, Vincent visited us once more in Paris; we were exhausted by a serious illness of the baby – Theo was again considering the old plan of leaving Goupil and setting up his own business, Vincent was not satisfied with the place where the pictures were kept, and our removal to a larger apartment was talked of; so those were days of much worry and anxiety. Many friends came to visit Vincent, among others, Aurier, who had written recently his famous article about Vincent,[*] and who now came again to look at the pictures with the painter himself, and Toulouse Lautrec who stayed for lunch with us and made many jokes with Vincent about an undertaker they had met on the stairs. Guillaumin was also expected to come, but it became too much for Vincent, so he did not wait for this visit but

[*]'Les Isolés', *Mercure de France*, January 1890.

hurried back to Auvers – overtired and excited, as his last letters and pictures show, in which the threatening catastrophe seems approaching like the ominous black birds that dart through the storm over the cornfields.

'I hope he is not getting melancholy or that a new attack is threatening again, everything has gone so well lately,' Theo wrote to me the 20th of July, after he had taken me with the baby to Holland and himself had returned to Paris for a short time, till he also should take his holidays. On the 25th he wrote to me, 'there is a letter from Vincent which seems very incomprehensible; when will there come a happy time for him? He is so thoroughly good.' That happy time was never to come for Vincent; fear of the again threatening attack or the attack itself, drove him to death.

On the evening of the 27th of July, he tried to kill himself with a revolver. Dr Gachet wrote that same evening to Theo the following note, 'With the greatest regret I must bring you bad tidings. Yet I think it my duty to write to you immediately. At nine o'clock in the evening of today, Sunday, I was sent for by your brother Vincent who wanted to see me at once. I went there and found him very ill. He has wounded himself . . . as I did not know your address and he refused to give it to me, this note will reach you through Goupil.' The letter reached Theo in consequence only the next morning and he immediately started for Auvers. From there he wrote to me the same day, the 28th of July: 'This morning a Dutch painter* who also lives in Auvers brought me a letter from Dr Gachet that contained bad tidings about Vincent and asked me to come. Leaving everything I went and found him somewhat better than I expected. I will not write the particulars, they are too sad, but you must know dearest, that his life may be in danger . . .

'He was glad that I came and we are together all the time . . . poor fellow, very little happiness fell to his share and no illusions are left him. The burden grows too heavy for him, at times he feels so alone. He often asks for you and the baby, and said that you would not imagine there was so much sorrow in life. Oh! if we could give him some new courage to live. Don't make yourself too anxious, his condition has been so hopeless before, but his strong constitution deceived the doctors.' That hope proved idle. Early in the morning of the 29th of July Vincent passed away.

Theo wrote to me, 'one of his last words was: "I wish I could die
*Hirschig.

now," and his wish was fulfilled. A few moments and all was over. He had found the rest he could not find on earth . . . The next morning there came from Paris and elsewhere eight friends who decked the room where the coffin stood with his pictures, which came out wonderfully. There were many flowers and wreaths. Dr Gachet was the first to bring a large bunch of sunflowers, because Vincent was so fond of them . . . He rests in a sunny spot amidst the cornfields . . .'

From a letter of Theo's to his mother: 'One cannot write how grieved one is nor find any comfort. It is a grief that will last and which I certainly shall never forget as long as I live; the only thing one might say is, that he himself has the rest he was longing for . . . life was such a burden to him; but now, as often happens, everybody is full of praise for his talents . . . Oh! mother he was so my own, own brother.'

Theo's frail health was broken. Six months later, on the 25th of January 1891, he had followed his brother.

They rest side by side in the little cemetery between the cornfields of Auvers.

J. VAN GOGH-BONGER
December 1913

Going Nowhere

These early letters begin in 1873 when Vincent was just twenty and his younger brother Theo still at school. Through his Uncle Vincent, who had formerly headed the firm, Vincent was employed as a clerk by Goupil's, the art dealers, first at the Hague and then in London and Paris. Goupil's had a thriving business in art reproductions, and also a dealership in painters of the Barbizon school and The Hague school, for whom Vincent shows tremendous enthusiasm in his letters. But, when Vincent joined the firm, the Impressionists were still too new and too controversial for Goupil's to want to handle them.

After a while, however, it became obvious that Vincent was not cut out to be a dealer. He had developed an intense interest in religion which may have been interfering with his work. He then found work teaching French, German and Arithmetic in a boys' school first in Ramsgate and then in Isleworth where the head of the school, a Methodist minister, fired Vincent's enthusiasm for preaching. (Vincent himself preached in chapels in Turnham Green, Richmond and Petersham.) Seeing that Vincent's career was leading nowhere, his family found him a job in a bookshop in Dordrecht, but Vincent showed no enthusiasm to become a bookseller either. He had decided he wanted to follow in his father's footsteps as a Protestant minister.

The Hague, 17 March 1873

. . . I am longing very much to see London, as you can imagine, but still I am sorry to leave here; now that it is decided that I shall go away, I feel how much I am attached to the Hague. Well it cannot be helped, and I intend not to take things too hard. It will be splendid for my English, I can understand it well enough, but I cannot speak it as well as I should wish . . . *Be sure to tell me more about the pictures you see.* A fortnight ago I was in Amsterdam to see an exhibition of the pictures that go from here to Vienna.

It was very interesting, and I am curious to know what figure the Dutch artists will cut in Vienna. I am also curious to see the English painters, we see so little of them, as almost everything remains in England. In London Goupil has no gallery, but sells only directly to art dealers . . .

Theo, I must strongly advise you to smoke a pipe, that is a remedy against the blues, which I happen to have now and then of late . . .

The first year of Vincent's stay in London was perhaps the most happy, and the most carefree of his life. His salary was large enough to live on, he felt great interest in his work and in all the new attractions that London offered him, and from August 1873, he found a delightful home at Mrs Loyer's, the widow of a curate from the south of France, who with her daughter Ursula kept a small day school and had a few paying guests. Vincent felt great sympathy for the mother, fell in love with the daughter and spent with them a happy time, as the cheerful tone of his letters clearly shows.

But Ursula was already secretly engaged, and though Vincent when he heard this tried his influence to break the engagement, he did not succeed. No mention, however, is made in his letters.

✳ ✳ ✳

To Theo (9)
London, 13 June 1873

My address is c/o Messrs Goupil & Co., 17 Southampton Street, Strand, London . . .

. . . you must tell me what pictures you have seen lately and also if some new etchings or lithographs have been published. Tell me as much as you can about these things, for here I do not see much of them as it is only a wholesale house. Considering the circumstances I am doing pretty well here.

The boarding-house where I stay pleases me so far. There are also three Germans, who are very fond of music and play the piano and sing, so we spend very pleasant evenings together. I am not so busy here as I was in the Hague, as I work only from nine until six, and on Saturdays we close at four o'clock. I live in one of the suburbs of London, where it is comparatively quiet . . . Life is very expensive here, my boarding house costs me 18 shillings a week, washing excepted, and then I have still to take my dinner in the city. Last Sunday I went to the country with Mr Obach, my principal, to Boxhill, that is a high hill about six hours by road from London, partly of chalk and overgrown with box and at one side a wood of high oak trees. The country is beautiful here, quite different from Holland or Belgium. Everywhere you see charming parks with high trees and shrubs. Everyone is allowed to walk there . . .

✳ ✳ ✳

To Theo (10)
London, 20 July 1873

. . . At first English art did not seem very attractive to me, one must get used to it. But there are clever painters here, among others, Millais, who has painted the *Huguenot, Ophelia*, etc., of which I think you know the engravings; his things are beautiful. Then there is Boughton of whom you know the *Puritain allant à l'église* in our Galerie Photographique; I have seen very beautiful things by him. Then among the old painters Constable, he is a landscape painter who lived about thirty years ago, he is splendid, his work reminds me of Diaz and Daubigny; and Reynolds and Gainsborough, who have especially painted very beautiful ladies' portraits, and then Turner whose engravings you must have seen.

Some good French painters are living here, among others Tissot, of whose work there are several photographs in our Galerie Photographique; also Otto Weber and Heilbuth . . .

Thanks for what you wrote me about pictures. If you happen to see anything by Lagye, de Braekeleer, Wauters, Maris, Tissot, George

Saal, Jundt, Ziem, Mauve, you must not forget to tell me, those are the painters I am very fond of and of whom you probably will see something . . .

✳ ✳ ✳

To Theo   (11)
London, 13 September 1873

. . . Oh, lad, I should like to have you here to show you my new lodgings, of which you certainly have heard. I now have a room such as I always longed for, without a slanting ceiling and without blue paper with a green border. I live with a very amusing family now, they keep a school for little boys.

One Saturday some time ago I went boating on the Thames with two Englishmen. That was very beautiful. Yesterday, I saw an exhibition of Belgian art, where I noticed many of the same pictures that were at the Brussels exhibition.

There were several beautiful things by Alb. and Julien de Vriendt, Cluysenaer, Wauters, Coosemans, Gabriel, de Schampheleer, etc.

Have you ever seen anything of Terlinde's, if so tell me. It was a real pleasure to see those Belgian pictures, the English ones are with a few exceptions very bad and uninteresting. Some time ago I saw one which represented a kind of fish or dragon, six yards long. It was awful. And then a little man, who came to kill the dragon above mentioned. I think the whole represented, *The Archangel Michael, killing Satan* . . .

✳ ✳ ✳

To Theo   (12)
London, 19 November 1873

. . . Lately we have had here many pictures and drawings, and we sold a great many, but it is not enough yet; it must become something more during and solid. I think there is still much work to do in England, but it will not succeed at once, and of course the first thing necessary is to have good pictures, and that will be very difficult . . . But it is a pleasure to see how well the photographs sell, especially the coloured ones, and there is a big profit in them . . .

5

Vincent's enthusiasm for the Dutch Hague school and for the Barbizon school and their precursors is very evident in the next letter. This group of artists who settled in the village of Barbizon in the forest of Fontainebleau and formed a colony of artists, who loved landscape and painted out of doors, would, for Vincent, remain an ideal throughout his life. And Millet, son of a peasant and a leading painter in this group, would remain his idol throughout his life.

❋ ❋ ❋

To Theo   (13)
London, January 1874

. . . From your letter I see that you have a great love for art, that is a good thing, lad. I am glad you like Millet, Jacque, Scheyer, Lambinet, Frans Hals, etc., for like Mauve says, 'that's the stuff'.

Yes, that picture by Millet, *The Angelus*, that's the thing, that is beauty, that is poetry. How I should like to talk with you about art, but now we must write about it often; *admire* as much as you can, *most people do not admire enough*. Here follow some names of painters whom I like especially, Scheffer, Delaroche, Hebert, Hamon, Leys, Tissot, Lagye, Boughton, Millais, Thys Maris, de Groux, de Braekeleer Jr, Millet, Jules Breton, Feyon-Perrin, Eugene Feyen, Brion, Jundt, George Saal, Israëls, Anker, Knaus, Vautier, Jourdan, Compte-Calix, Rochussen, Meissonier, Madrazzo, Ziem, Boudin, Gerome, Fromentin, Decamps, Bonington, Diaz, Th. Rousseau, Troyon, Dupré, Corot, Paul Huet, Jacque, Otto Weber, Daubigny, Bernier, Emile Breton, Chenu, César de Cock, Mlle Collart, Bodmer, Koekkoek, Schelfhout, Weissenbruch and last but not least, Maris and Mauve. But I might go on like that for I don't know how long, and then there are the old masters, and I am sure I have forgotten some of the best modern ones.

Try to walk as much as you can and keep your love for nature, for that is the true way to learn to understand art more and more.

Painters understand nature and love her and *teach us to see her* . . .

❋ ❋ ❋

London, 13 April 1874

. . . I walk as much as I can, but I am very busy. It is very beautiful here (though it is in the city). In every garden the lilacs and hawthorn and laburnums are in bloom and the chestnut trees are beautiful.

If one really loves nature, one can find beauty everywhere. But still I sometimes long for Holland and especially for home.

I am very busy gardening and have sown a little garden full of poppies, sweet peas and mignonette . . .

I enjoy the walks from home to the office and in the evening from the office home. It takes me about three-quarters of an hour . . .

The apple trees have blossomed beautifully; I think everything is earlier here than in Holland . . .

❊ ❊ ❊

To Theo (17)
London, 16 June 1874

Thanks for your letter. I intend to leave here Thursday the 25th, or Saturday the 27th of June, if nothing prevents. I am longing so much for everybody and for Holland. I long also to have a good talk with you about art . . .

In the Royal Academy there are beautiful things this year. Tissot has three pictures there. Of late I took up drawing again, but it did not amount to much . . .

Before he went to Holland he declared his love to Ursula Loyer, but heard that she was already engaged to be married, so he returned there in a melancholy mood. From that time, there is a change in his character, he inclines more and more toward a religious fanaticism, he leads a secluded life, living alone in rooms and seeing nobody, he rarely writes home, which gives his parents great anxiety. 'Poor boy he does not take life easily,' writes mother, and father says, 'His living at the Loyer's with all those secrets has done him no good, I am glad he left there, but it must have been a bitter disappointment to him, that his hopes were not realized.'

In October Uncle Vincent uses his influence to get his nephew a temporary transfer to the house in Paris, hoping that the change will do him good, but the removal has no effect, and in the same depressed mood he returns to London in January 1875, where he stays till May of the same year.

✳ ✳ ✳

To Theo (20)
London, 31 July 1874

I am glad you have read Michelet [*L'Amour*] and that you understand him so well. Such a book teaches us that there is much more in Love than people generally suppose.

That book has been a revelation to me as well as a Gospel at the same time, 'no woman is old'. (That does not mean that there are no old women, but that a woman is not old as long as she loves and is loved.) . . .

That a woman is quite a different being than a man, and a being that we do not yet know, at least only quite superficially, as you said, yes, I am sure of it. And that man and wife can be one, that is to say one whole and not two halves, yes, I believe that too . . .

Since I am back in England my love for drawing has stopped, but perhaps I will take it up again some day or other. I am reading a great deal just now . . .

✳ ✳ ✳

To Theo (23)
London, 6 March 1875

Bravo, Theo. Your appreciation of that girl in *Adam Bede* is very good. That landscape – in which the fallow, sandy path runs over the hill to the village, with its clay or white-washed cottages, with mossgrown roofs, and here and there a black thorn-bush, on either side the brown heath, and a gloomy sky over it, with a narrow white streak at the horizon – it is from Michel.

But there is a still purer and nobler sentiment in it than in Michel. Today I enclose in the box we send, the little book containing poetry I spoke of. Also *Jesus* by Renan and *Joan of Arc* by Michelet and also a portrait of Corot from the *London News*, which hangs in my room too . . .

✳ ✳ ✳

London, 18 April 1875

Enclosed I send you a little drawing. I made it last Sunday, the morning when the little daughter of my landlady died, she was thirteen years old. It is a view on Streatham Common, a large grassy plain with oak trees and gorse.

It had been raining over night and the ground was soaked and the young spring grass was fresh and green . . .

✳ ✳ ✳

To Theo (26)
London, 8 May 1875

. . . Ay, lad, 'What shall we say?' C. M. [Vincent's uncle, an art dealer in Amsterdam] and Mr Tersteeg [head of Goupil's in The Hague] have been here and left again last Saturday. In my opinion they have been too often to the Crystal Palace and other places with which they had nothing to do. I think they might just as well have come to see the place where I lived. I hope and trust that I am not what many people think me to be just now, we shall see, some time must pass; probably they will say the same of you a few years hence, at least if you remain what you are: my brother in every sense . . .

'To act well in this world one must give up all selfish aims. The people who become the missionary of a religious thought, have no other fatherland than this thought.

Man is not on this earth only to be happy, he is not only there to be simply honest, he is there to realize great things for humanity, to attain nobility and to surpass the vulgarity in which the existence of almost all individuals drags on.'

Renan.

About the middle of May, Vincent was sent to Paris, first for six or eight weeks, but in June it is decided that he will stay there until further notice. It is against his will; his letters home are melancholy, he no longer wants to be an art dealer, and at last his parents also begin to understand that it would perhaps be better for him to change his position, though he does not yet know what to choose instead.

✳ ✳ ✳

To Theo (27)
Paris, 31 May 1875

. . . Yesterday I saw the exhibition of Corot. There was among others, the picture, *The Garden of Olives*, I am glad he has painted that.

To the right a group of olive trees, dark against the glimmering blue sky, on the background, hills covered with shrubs and a few large, ivy grown trees over which the evening star shines . . .

Of course I have also seen the Louvre and the Luxembourg.

The Ruysdaels at the Louvre are splendid, especially *Le Buisson*, *L'Estacade* and *Le Coup de Soleil*.

I wish you could see the little Rembrandts there, *The Pilgrims of Emmaus*, and its counterpart, *The Philosophers* . . .

❊ ❊ ❊

To Theo (28)
Paris, 19 June 1875

I had hoped to see her [his cousin Annette] before her death, but it might not be. God leads us and we must follow . . .

I do not know how long I shall stay here, but before I go back to London I hope to go to Helvoirt [where his cousin had lived], I hope you will be there also. I will pay for the journey.

I am sure you will not forget her or her death but keep it to yourself.

This is one of those things that make us as time goes on 'sorrowful but always glad,' that is what we have to learn . . .

❊ ❊ ❊

To Theo (29)
Paris, 29 June 1875

. . . There has been a sale here of drawings by Millet, I do not know whether I have already written to you about it.

When I entered the hall of the Hotel Drouot, where they were exhibited, I felt like saying: 'Take off your shoes for the place where you are standing is Holy Ground.' . . .

Paris, 6 July 1875

. . . I have taken a little room on Montmartre which I am sure you would like. It is small but it overlooks a little garden full of ivy and wild vine.

   I will tell you what engravings I have on the wall:

Ruysdael,	*The Bush.*
	The Bleacheries.
Rembrandt,	*Bible Lecture.* (A large old-fashioned Dutch room at evening, a candle on the table, where a young mother is sitting reading the Bible, beside the cradle of her baby. An old woman is sitting listening, it is a thing that reminds you of, 'Again, I say to you, where two or three are gathered together in my name, there am I in the midst of them.' It is an old copper engraving as large as *The Bush*, splendid.)
Ph. de Champaigne,	*Portrait of a Lady.*
Corot,	*Evening.*
Bodmer,	*Fontainebleau.*
Bonington,	*A Road.*
Troyon,	*The Morning.*
Jules Dupré,	*The Evening.*
Maris,	*A Woman Washing.*
	The Christening.
Millet,	*The Hours of the Day.* (Wood-cuts, four pages.)
V. d. Maaten,	*Burial in the Corn Fields.*
Daubigny,	*The Dawn.* (*Crowing Cock.*)
Charlet,	*Hospitality.* (Farm, surrounded by pine trees, in winter in the snow, a peasant and a soldier before the door.)
Ed. Frère,	*The Seamstress.*
	The Barrel-Maker.

✳ ✳ ✳

To Theo (31)
Paris, 15 July 1875

Uncle Vincent has been here again, I have been with him pretty often and talked things over. I asked him if there was any chance of getting you here in Paris. At first he wouldn't hear of it and said it was much better for you to stay in the Hague. I insisted, however, and you may be sure he will keep it in mind. When he comes to the Hague he probably will talk about it to you; be as calm as you can and let him say whatever he likes, it will do you no harm and probably you will want his help later on. You must not speak about me, if you can avoid it . . .

※ ※ ※

To Theo (32)
Paris, 24 July 1875

A few days ago we received a picture by de Nittis, a view of London on a rainy day, Westminster Bridge and the House of Parliament. I used to pass Westminster Bridge every morning and every evening and know how it looks when the sun sets behind Westminster Abbey and the House of Parliament, and how it looks early in the morning, and in winter in snow and fog.

When I saw the picture I felt how much I loved London. Still I think that it is better for me that I left it . . .

George Michel (1763–1843), for whom Vincent shows great enthusiasm, was a landscape painter and a precursor of the Barbizon school.

※ ※ ※

To Theo (36)
Paris, 4 September 1875

. . . I have bought the book about Michel, with etchings from his pictures; as soon as I have finished it I will send it to you.

Yet Michel is not so beautiful, by far, as that landscape described in

12

Adam Bede, that impressed us both so much. There is a painting by Bonington also which is almost it, but *not quite* . . .

✳ ✳ ✳

To Theo   (38)
Paris, 17 September 1875

A feeling, even a keen one for the beauties of Nature is not the same as a religious feeling, though I think these two stand in close relation to one another.

Almost everybody has a feeling for nature, one more, the other less, but there are few who feel God is a spirit and whoever worships Him must worship Him in spirit and in truth. Our parents belong to those few; I think Uncle Vincent too.

You know that there is written: 'This world passes and all its magnificence.' And that there is on the contrary also mentioned 'a good part that shall not be taken from us,' and, 'a well of water springing up into everlasting life'. Let us also pray that we become rich in God . . .

Let us ask that our part in life should be to become the poor in the kingdom of God, God's servants. We are still far from it; let us pray that our eye may become single and then our whole body shall be full of light . . .

✳ ✳ ✳

To Theo   (42)
Paris, 11 October 1875

. . . As you know I live on Montmartre. In the same house lives a young Englishman, employee of the house, eighteen years old, son of an art dealer in London, who probably will enter his father's business later on. He had never been from home before, and, especially the first week that he was here, he was very uncouth; for instance, he ate every morning, afternoon and evening, four or six pieces of bread (bread is very cheap here), adding in addition several pounds of apples and pears, etc. He is notwithstanding that as thin as a stick, with two rows of strong teeth, full red lips, glittering eyes, a pair of large, generally red, projecting ears, close cropped head, black hair, etc., etc. I can assure you quite a different being than the *Lady* by Ph. de Champaigne. At first everybody laughed at him, even I. Later on I grew to like him, and now I assure you I am glad to have his company in the evening.

He has quite a naïve and unspoiled heart and is very good at his work. Every evening we go home together, eat something in my room and the rest of the evening I read aloud, generally from the Bible. We intend to read it through. In the morning, usually between five and six, he comes to wake me; we breakfast in my room and about eight o'clock we go to the office. Lately he is less greedy at his meals and has begun to collect prints, in which I help him. Yesterday we went together to the Luxembourg and I showed him the pictures I liked best, and indeed the simple minded know many things that the wise ignore . . .

✳ ✳ ✳

To Theo (45)
Paris, 15 November 1875

. . . My dear Englishman prepares oatmeal every morning, of which his father sent him twenty-five pounds. How I wish you could taste it with us. I am so glad that I met this boy. I have learned from him and in return have been able to show him a danger that threatened him.

He had never been away from home, and though he did not show it, he had a sickly (though noble) longing for his father and his home.

He longed for them with a longing that belongs only to God and to Heaven. Idolatry is not love. He who loves his parents must follow their footsteps in life. He understands this now clearly . . .

✳ ✳ ✳

To Theo (46)
Paris, 4 December 1875

. . . Is it as cold in Holland as it is here? Gladwell [the Englishman] and I are very comfortable in the morning and in the evening with our little stove.

I have taken to smoking a pipe again and I enjoy it as of old . . .

In January, 1876, follows the episode of Vincent's dismissal from Goupil.

❃ ❃ ❃

To Theo (50)
Paris, 10 January 1876

Since we saw each other, I have not written to you; something
happened to me during that time that did not come quite unexpectedly. When I saw Mr Boussod again, I asked him if he approved of my
being employed at the house for another year, and said that I hoped he
had no serious complaints against me. But the latter was indeed the
case, and in the end he forced me, as it were, to say that I would leave
the first of April, thanking the gentlemen for all that I might have
learned in their house.

When the apple is ripe a soft breeze makes it fall from the tree, so it
is here; I have done things that have been very wrong in one way and
therefore I have but little to say . . .

*We do not know precisely why he was dismissed, but it may have been something to
do with his increasing attraction towards religion and his loathing for the materi-
alism of the art world.*

❃ ❃ ❃

To Theo (51)
Paris, January 1876

In the first box that goes to the Hague you will find a few parcels, will
you be so kind as to deliver them.

First there is one for yourself in which is *Felix Holt* . . . It is a book that
impressed me very much and I am sure it will be the same with you . . .

You are right in taking English lessons, you will not be sorry for it. I
should like to send you a Longfellow and Andersen's *Fairy Tales*. I shall
try to get them; if I send them read especially Longfellow's *Evangeline*,
Miles Standish, *King Robert of Sicily*, etc. . . . .

To Theo (52)
Paris, 1876

... Gladwell has decided to move without thinking much about it. I am
very sorry he is going, it will probably be soon, toward the end of the
month. We have these last days a mouse in our 'cabin', you know that
is the name of our room. Every evening we put down some bread and
the mouse already knows quite well where to find it.

I am reading the advertisements in the English papers and have
already answered some. Let us hope for success ...

✳ ✳ ✳

To Theo (54)
Paris, 7 February 1876

... Yesterday I went to an English church here, it was a pleasant sensation to assist once more at the English service, it is so simple and beautiful. The text of the sermon was, 'The Lord is my Shepherd, I shall not
want.'

✳ ✳ ✳

To Theo (55)
Paris, 19 February 1876

... In the next box you will find Longfellow. Yesterday evening Gladwell
was with me, he comes every Friday and we read poetry together.

I have not read *Hyperion* yet, but I have heard that it is very beautiful,
I have just read a very beautiful book by Eliot, three tales, *Scenes from
Clerical Life*, especially the last story, *Janet's Repentance*, struck me very
much. It is the life of a clergyman who lives chiefly among the inhabi-
tants of the dirty streets of a town, his study looks out on the gardens
with litter, etc., and on the red roofs and smoking chimneys of poor
tenements. For his dinner he usually had nothing but underdone
mutton and watery potatoes. He died at the age of thirty-four and
during his long illness he was nursed by a woman who was a drunkard,
but by his teaching, and leaning as it were on him, she had conquered
her weakness and found rest for her soul. At his burial they read the

chapter which says, 'I am the resurrection and the life, he that believeth in Me though he were dead yet shall he live.' And now it is again Saturday evening, for the days pass so quickly and the time for my departure will soon be here . . .

✳ ✳ ✳

To Theo   (57)
Paris, 23 March 1876

. . . Gladwell has got my place at the gallery and is there already to become familiar with his work before I leave . . .

✳ ✳ ✳

To Theo   (59)
Etten, 4 April 1876

On the morning before I left Paris, I got a letter from a schoolmaster at Ramsgate who proposes that I should go there for a month (without salary) and at the end of that time he will decide whether I am fit for the position.

You can imagine I am glad to have found something. At all events I have board and lodging free.

Yesterday I went with father to Brussels; we found Uncle Hein in a very sad state. In the train father and I spoke much about pictures, among others about the pictures by Rembrandt at the Louvre and the portrait of the *Burgomaster Six*, and particularly about Michel.

Gladwell saw me off at the station last Friday night; on my birthday he came at half-past six in the morning and brought me a beautiful etching after Chauvel, an autumn landscape with a herd of sheep on a sandy road . . .

Now that Vincent has broken for ever with his career as an art dealer – which has proved a greater shock to him than he shows now – there follows a long and diffi-cult time of experiments. It seems afterwards that the idea of becoming a painter has occurred to him even then. Theo also seems to have mentioned it, but Vincent is too much taken up with religious fanaticism and thinks he will be most useful as a teacher, especially as a Bible teacher. With the force of despair, he clings to religion as his sole support and his letters prove clearly the almost morbid sensitiveness of that time.

✳ ✳ ✳

To Father and Mother (60)
Ramsgate, 17 April 1876

. . . In thought we will stay together today. What do you think is better . . . the joy of meeting or the sorrow of parting? We have often parted already, this time there was more sorrow in it than there used to be, but also more courage, because of the firmer hope, the stronger desire for God's blessing. And was not Nature feeling with us, everything looked so grey and dull a few hours ago.

Now I am looking across the far stretching meadows and everything is so quiet and the sun disappears again behind the grey clouds but sheds a golden light over the fields . . .

On the steamer I thought so often of Anna [his sister, who had previously stayed for a while with him in London], everything reminded me of our journey together.

The weather was clear and especially on the river it was beautiful, and also the view of the dunes dazzling white in the sun as viewed from the sea. The last thing I saw of Holland was a little grey church spire. I stayed on deck until sunset, but then it became too cold and rough.

Next morning in the train from Harwich to London it was beautiful to see at dawn the black fields and green meadows with sheep and lambs and here and there a thorn bush and a few large oak trees with dark twigs and grey moss-grown trunks. The glimmering blue sky with still a few stars, and a bank of grey clouds at the horizon. Before sunrise I already heard the lark. When we were near the last station before London, the sun rose. The bank of grey clouds had disappeared and there was the sun, as simple and grand as ever I saw it, a real Easter sun. The grass sparkled with dew and night frost. But still I like better that grey hour when we parted. Saturday afternoon I stayed on deck till the sun had set. As far as one could see the water was fairly dark blue with rather high white-crested waves. The coast had already disappeared from sight.

The sky was one vast light blue without a single little cloud.

And the sunset cast a ray of glittering light on the water.

It was indeed a grand and majestic sight, but still the simpler, more quiet things touch one so much more deeply.

Arrived in London the train started for Ramsgate two hours later. That is still about four and a half hours by train. It is a beautiful road, for instance we passed one part that was quite hilly. At the foot the hills are covered with scanty grass and at the top with oak woods. That reminded me of our dunes. Between the hills was a village with a grey church overgrown with ivy like most of the houses. The orchards were in full bloom and the sky was light blue with grey and white clouds.

We also passed Canterbury, a city with many medieval buildings, especially a beautiful cathedral, surrounded by old elm trees. I had often seen pictures representing it.

You can imagine I was looking out of the window for Ramsgate a long time before we got there.

At one o'clock I arrived at Mr Stokes', he was absent from home but will come back tonight. During his absence his place was taken by his son (23 years old, I think), a teacher in London. I saw Mrs Stokes at dinner. There are twenty-four boys from ten to fourteen years. (It is a pleasant sight to see them at their dinner.) So the school is not large. The window looks out on the sea. After dinner we took a walk out on the shore, it was very beautiful. The houses on the shore are generally built in simple Gothic style of yellow stone, and have gardens full of cedars and other dark evergreens. There is a harbour full of ships, shut in between stone dykes, where one can walk. And then there is the sea in its unspoiled state and that is very beautiful. Yesterday everything was grey. In the evening we went with the boys to church. On the wall of the church was written: 'Lo, I am with thee always, even unto the end of the world.'

At eight o'clock the boys go to bed and they rise at six.

There is another assistant teacher of seventeen years. He, four boys and myself sleep in another house near by, where I have a little room that is waiting for some prints on the wall . . .

✳ ✳ ✳

To Theo   (62)
Ramsgate, 21 April 1876

. . . Today Mr Stokes has come home. He is a man of medium height, with bald head and whiskers, the boys seem to respect him and yet to like him. A few hours after his homecoming he was playing at marbles with them; we often go to the beach. This morning I helped the boys to make a fortress of sand, as we did in the garden at Zundert . . .

✳ ✳ ✳

To Theo (63)
Ramsgate, 28 April 1876

. . . Now I am going to tell you about a walk we took yesterday. It was to an inlet of the sea, and the road thither led through fields of young corn and along hedges of hawthorn, etc.

Arrived there, we saw to our left a high steep ridge of sand and stone as high as a house of two stories. On the top of it were old, gnarled hawthorn bushes, whose black and grey moss-grown stems and branches were all bent to one side by the wind, there were also a few elder bushes.

The ground on which we walked was covered all over with big grey stones, chalk and shells.

To the right lay the sea, as calm as a pond and reflecting the light of the transparent grey sky where the sun was setting.

The tide was out and the water very low . . .

✳ ✳ ✳

To Theo (64)
Ramsgate, 1 May 1876

. . . Yesterday there blew such a violent wind that Mr Stokes would not let the boys go out. But I asked for permission to go for a little walk with six of the elder boys. We went to the beach, it was high tide and it was a tough job to walk against the wind, we saw the lifeboat brought in by a tug, returning from an expedition to a ship that had been stranded on a sandbank far away, but they brought nothing with them . . .

✳ ✳ ✳

Ramsgate, 12 May 1876

Thanks for your letter; I am also so fond of that, 'Tell me the old, old story'. I heard it for the first time in Paris one night in a little church where I often went. I am sorry indeed that I did not hear Moody and Sankey when they were in London. There is such a longing for religion among the people in the large cities. Many a labourer in a factory or shop has had a pious childhood. But city life sometimes takes away the 'early dew of morning'. Still the longing for the 'old, old story remains; whatever is in the bottom of the heart, stays there. [George] Eliot describes in one of her novels the life of factory workers who have formed a small community and held their services in a chapel in Lantern Yard and she calls it the 'Kingdom of God on earth', no more or less. There is something touching in seeing those thousands of people crowding to hear these evangelists . . .

❋ ❋ ❋

Ramsgate, 31 May 1876

. . . Did I tell you about the storm I saw lately? The sea was yellowish especially near the shore; at the horizon a streak of light and above it the immense dark grey clouds from which the rain poured down in slanting streaks. The wind blew the dust from the little white path on the rocks into the sea and swayed the blooming hawthorn bushes and wallflowers that grow on the rocks. To the right, were fields of young green corn and in the distance the town that looked like the towns that Albrecht Dürer used to etch.

. . . That same night I looked from the window of my room on the roofs of the houses that can be seen from there and on the tops of the elm trees, dark against the night sky. Over those roofs, one single star, but a beautiful, large friendly one. And I thought of you all and of my own past years and of our home, and in me arose the words and the feeling: 'Keep me from being a son who makes ashamed, give me your blessing, not because I deserve it but for my mother's sake. Thou art love, cover all things. Without Thy continued blessings we succeed in nothing.'

Enclosed is a little drawing of the view from the window of the school, through which the boys wave goodbye to their parents after a visit when they are going back to the station.

None of us will ever forget the view from the window. *You ought to have seen* it this week when we had rain, especially in the twilight when the lamps are lit and their light is reflected in the wet street.

Mr Stokes was often in a bad temper, and when the boys made more noise than he liked, it sometimes happened that they had to go without their supper.

I wish you could have seen them then looking from the window, it was rather melancholy; they have so little else except their meals to look forward to and to help them pass their days. I also should like you to see them going from the dark stairs and passage to the dining-room. But there the bright sun is shining.

Another curious place is the room with the rotten floor, where are six washing basins in which they have to wash themselves and where a dim light flows through the window with its broken panes on the wshing-stand . . .

✻ ✻ ✻

To Theo   (69)
Welwyn, 17 June 1876

Last Monday I started from Ramsgate to London, it is a long walk and when I left it was very hot and it stayed so until the evening when I arrived in Canterbury. That same evening I went still a little farther, till I arrived at a few large beech and elm trees near a little pond where I rested for a while. At half-past three in the morning the birds began to sing at sight of dawn and I started again. It was fine to walk then.

In the afternoon I arrived at Chatham, where one sees in the distance between partly flooded low meadows, with elm trees here and there, the Thames full of ships; I believe it is always grey weather there. There I met a cart that brought me a few miles further but then the driver went into an Inn and I thought that he would stay there a long time, so I continued my way and arrived towards evening in the familiar suburbs of London and walked to the city along the long, long 'Roads'. I stayed two days in London and have been running from one part to another to see different persons, among others, a clergyman to whom I wrote.

. . . One night I stayed at Mr Reid's and the next day at Mr Gladwell's, where they were very very kind. Mr Gladwell kissed me goodnight that evening and it did me good, may it be given to me to prove now and then my friendship to his son in the future.

I wanted to go back that very evening to Welwyn; but they kept me back literally by force because of the pouring rain. However when it began to stop, about four o'clock in the morning, I set off for Welwyn.

First a long walk from one end of the city to the other. In the afternoon at five o'clock I was with our sister [Anna] and was very glad to see her . . .

The letter to the clergyman contained a potted history of Vincent's life and his express wish to find 'a situation in connection with the church'.

The school of Mr Stokes at Ramsgate is moved in June to Isleworth. As Mr Stokes cannot or will not give him any salary, he leaves on 1 July for the school of Mr Jones, a Methodist clergyman to whom Vincent serves as a kind of curate.

✳ ✳ ✳

To Theo   (70)
Isleworth, 5 July 1876

. . . It seems to me of late that there are no other situations in the world but those of schoolmaster and clergyman, with all that lies between these two; such as missionary, especially a London Missionary, etc. I think it must be a peculiar profession to be a London Missionary, one must go around among the labourers and the poor to preach the Bible, and if one has some experience talk with them, find foreigners who are looking for work or other persons who are in difficulties and try and help them, etc., etc. Last week I went to London two or three times to find out if there was a chance of becoming one of them, as I speak several languages, and have mixed, especially in Paris and London, with people of the lower class and foreigners; being a foreigner myself, it might be that I was fit for it and might become so more and more.

However one must be at least twenty-four years old and at all events I have to wait another year.

Mr Stokes says that he decidedly cannot give me any salary because he can get teachers enough for just board and lodging, and that is true. But will it be possible for me to continue in this way? I am afraid not, it will be decided soon enough.

. . . Last week I was at Hampton Court to see the beautiful gardens and long avenues of chestnut and lime trees, where many crows and rooks have their nests, and to see also the palace and the pictures. There are among others many portraits by Holbein which are very beautiful and two splendid Rembrandts (the portrait of his wife, and of a rabbi) and also beautiful Italian portraits by Bellini, Titian, a picture by Leonardo da Vinci, cartoons by Mantegna, a beautiful picture by S. Ruysdael, a still-life of fruit by Cuyp, etc. I wish you had been there with me, it was a pleasure to see pictures again.

And involuntarily, I thought of the persons who had lived there at Hampton Court, of Charles I and his wife (it was she who said, 'I thank Thee my God! for having made me queen, but an unhappy queen') and at whose grave Bossuet spoke from the fullness of his heart . . .

Enclosed a feather from one of the rooks there . . .

✳ ✳ ✳

To Theo   (72)
Isleworth, 7 August 1876

. . . Yesterday Mr Jones and his family came home. I had decorated the boys' dining-room with 'Welcome Home', on the wall, of holly and evergreen, and large bouquets on the table . . .

I suppose the boys will now soon arrive . . .

. . . the sea is very beautiful; there were many bugs at Mr Stokes, but the view from the school window made one forget them . . .

✳ ✳ ✳

To Theo   (73)
Isleworth, 18 August 1876

Yesterday I went to see Gladwell who is home for a few days; something very sad happened to his family: his sister, a girl full of life, with dark eyes and hair, seventeen years old, fell from her horse on

Blackheath, she was unconscious when they lifted her and died five hours later without returning to consciousness.

As soon as I heard what happened and that Gladwell was at home, I went there. Yesterday morning at eleven o'clock I started from here and had a long walk to Lewisham, the road ran from one end of London to another; at five o'clock I was with Gladwell.

They had all just come back from the funeral, it was indeed a house of mourning and it was good to be with them. I felt a kind of shyness and shame on witnessing that great impressive sorrow . . .

✳ ✳ ✳

To Theo   (75)
Isleworth, 3 October 1876

From home I heard that you are ill, Poor lad, how I should like to be with you. Yesterday night I walked to Richmond, and all the way over I was thinking of you, it was a beautiful grey evening, you know that I go there every Monday night, to the Methodist Chapel; last evening I spoke a few words about: 'Nothing pleaseth me but in Jesus Christ, and in Him everything pleaseth me.'

. . . Last Saturday week, I made a long trip to London, and heard there about a position, that perhaps might do for me sometime. The clergymen at seaports like Liverpool and Hull often want assistants, who can speak several languages, to work among the sailors and the foreigners and also to visit the sick, some salary would be attached to such a position.

In the morning I left here early at four o'clock, it was beautiful in the park here with the dark avenues of elm trees and the wet road through it, and a grey rainy sky over it all, in the distance there was a thunderstorm.

At daybreak I was in Hyde Park and there the leaves were already failing from the trees and the Virginia creeper against the houses was beautifully red, and there was a mist. At seven o'clock I was at Kensington, and rested a little in a church there where I used to go so many Sunday mornings.

In London I visited some friends and was also at the gallery of Messrs Goupil & Co., and saw there the drawings that van Iterson had brought with him, and it was delightful to see once more the Dutch

25

towns and meadows in that way. That picture by Artz; the *Mill on the Canal*, I think very fine.

❋ ❋ ❋

To Theo (76)
Isleworth, 7 October 1876

. . . Last Wednesday we took a long walk to a village an hour's distance from here. The road led through meadows and fields, along hedges of hawthorn, full of blackberries and clematis, and here and there a large elm tree. It was so beautiful when the sun set behind the grey clouds, and the shadows were long. By chance we met the school of Mr Stokes, where there are still several of the boys I knew.

The clouds retained their red hue long after the sun had set and the dusk had settled over the fields, and we saw in the distance the lamps lit in the village. While I was writing to you, I was called to Mr Jones, who asked if I would walk to London to collect some money for him. And when I came home in the evening, hurrah there was a letter from father with tidings about you. How I should like to be with you both, my boy. And thank God, there is some improvement, though you are still weak . . .

Now I am going to tell you about my walk to London. I left here at twelve o'clock in the morning and reached my destination between five and six. When I came into that part of the town where most of the picture galleries are, around the Strand, I met many acquaintances: it was dinner-time, so many were in the street, leaving the office or going back there. First I met a young clergyman who once preached here, and with whom I then became acquainted, and then the employee of Mr Wallis, and then one of the Messrs Wallis himself, whom I used to visit now and then at his house, now he has two children; then I met Mr Reid and Mr Richardson, who are already old friends. Last year about this time Mr Richardson was in Paris and we walked together to Père Lachaise . . .

In the City I went to see Mr Gladwell and to St Paul's Church. And from the City to the other end of London, where I visited a boy who had left the school of Mr Stokes because of illness and I found him quite well playing in the street. Then to the place where I had to collect the money for Mr Jones. The suburbs of London have a peculiar charm, between the little houses and gardens are open spots covered with grass and generally with a church or school or workhouse in the middle between the trees and shrubs, and it can be so beautiful there, when the sun is setting red in the thin evening mist.

Yesterday evening it was so, and afterwards I wished you could have seen those London streets when the twilight began to fall and the lamps were lit, and everybody went home; everything showed that it was Saturday night and in all that bustle there was peace, one felt the need of, and the excitement at the approaching Sunday.

In the City it was dark, but it was a beautiful walk along the row of churches one has to pass. Near the Strand I took a bus that took me quite a long way, it was already pretty late. I passed the little church of Mr Jones and saw in the distance another one, where at that hour a light was still burning, I entered and found it to be a very beautiful little Catholic church, where a few women were praying. Then I came to that dark park about which I have written you already and from there I saw in the distance the lights of Isleworth and the church with the ivy, and the churchyard with the weeping willows towards the Thames.

Tomorrow I shall get for the second time, some small salary for my new work, and with it buy a pair of new boots and a new hat. And then, with God's will, I shall again start on my way . . .

✳ ✳ ✳

To Theo   (79)
Isleworth, undated [1876]

. . . Theo, your brother has preached for the first time, last Sunday, in God's dwelling, of which is written, 'In this place, I will give peace.' May it be the first of many more.

It was a clear autumn day and a beautiful walk from here to Richmond, along the Thames, in which the great chestnut trees with their load of yellow leaves, and the clear blue sky were mirrored, and through the tops of the trees one could see that part of Richmond which lies on the hill, the houses with their red roofs and uncurtained windows, and green gardens, and the grey spire high above them, and below the long grey bridge with the tall poplars at each side, over which the people passed like little black figures.

When I was standing in the pulpit I felt like somebody who,

27

emerging from a dark cave under ground comes back to the friendly daylight, and it is a delightful thought that in the future wherever I shall come, I shall preach the Gospel . . .

✳ ✳ ✳

To Father and Mother (81)
Isleworth, 17 November 1876

. . . And so the weeks go by and we are approaching winter and a merry Christmas. Tomorrow I must be in the two remotest parts of London, in Whitechapel, that very poor part about which you have read in Dickens, and then across the Thames in a little steamer and from there to Lewisham. The children of Mr Jones have recovered, but now three of the boys have got the measles.

This week I had to go with one of the boys, for Mr Jones to Acton Green, that grass plot which I saw from the sexton's window.

It was very muddy there, but it was a beautiful sight, when it grew dark and the fog began to rise and one saw the light of a little church in the middle of the plain, and to our left was the railroad on a rather high dyke, and a train just passed and that was a beautiful sight, the red glow of the engine and the row of lights in the carriages in the twilight. To our right a few horses were grazing in a meadow surrounded by a hedge of hawthorn, crossed by blackberries . . .

✳ ✳ ✳

To Theo (82)
Isleworth, 25 November 1876

. . . In the morning it was so beautiful on the road to Turnham Green, the chestnut trees, and the clear blue sky, and the morning sun mirrored in the water of the Thames, the grass was sparkling green and all around one heard the sound of the church bells. The day before I made a long tramp to London. I left here at four o'clock in the morning, and at half-past six was in Hyde Park, there the dew was lying on the grass and the leaves were falling from the trees, in the distance one saw the pale lights of the lamps which had not yet been put out, and the towers of Westminster Abbey and the Houses of

Parliament, and the sun rose red in the morning mist – from there to Whitechapel, the poor part of London, then to Chancery Lane and Westminster, then to Clapham to visit Mrs Loyer again, who had her birthday the day before. I was also at Mr Obach's to see his wife and the children again.

Then from there to Lewisham, where I arrived at half-past three at the Gladwells' . . . At half-past ten in the evening I was back here, I partly returned by underground railway. I had been lucky enough to collect some money for Mr Jones.

When he comes home next Christmas, it is decided that he will not go back to England as there are no prospects whatever for the future.

✳ ✳ ✳

To Theo   (83)
Etten, 31 December 1876

. . . As to the religious work, I still do not give it up. Father is so broad-minded and so many-sided and I hope in whatever circumstances [it] may be something of that will unfold in me. The change will be that instead of teaching the boys, I shall work in a bookshop . . .

✳ ✳ ✳

To Theo   (85)
Dordrecht, undated [1877]

. . . There may be a time in life when one is tired of everything and feels as if all one does is wrong, and there may be some truth in it – do you think this is a feeling one must try to forget and to banish, or is it 'the longing for God', which one must not fear, but cherish to see if it may bring us some good? Is it 'the longing for God' which leads us to make a choice which we never regret? . . .

. . . After church I took alone a beautiful walk on a dyke along the mills, there was a splendid sky over the meadows, mirrored in the wet ditches. In other countries there are some curious things, for instance on the French coast I saw at Dieppe – the rocks were covered with green grass – and the sea and the sky, the harbour with the old boats were like a painting by Daubigny, with brown nets and sails, the little houses, among which are a few restaurants with white curtains and green pine branches in the window . . . the carts with white horses, harnessed with blue halters and red tassels, the drivers with their blue blouses, the fishermen with their beards and oilskins, and the French women with pale faces, dark, often deep-set eyes, black dresses and white caps, and then too the London streets in the rain with the lanterns, and the night spent there on the steps of a little old grey church, as it happened to me this summer, after that excursion to Ramsgate, there are in other countries also some curious things . . . but as I walked last Sunday alone on that dyke, I thought how good it was to feel the Dutch soil under my feet, and I felt something like, 'Now it is in mine heart to make a covenant with the Lord God', for I recalled all our childhood memories, how often we walked, in those last days of February with father to Rysbergen, and heard the lark over the black fields with young green corn, the radiant blue sky with the white clouds over it – and then the stony path with the beech trees – Oh, Jerusalem, Jerusalem! or rather, Oh, Zundert! Oh, Zundert! . . .

✳ ✳ ✳

To Theo (89)
Dordrecht, 22 March 1877

. . . Coming home I found a letter from Etten. Father was not well last Sunday, and the Rev. Kam preached for him; I know his heart is burning within him that something may happen to enable me to follow him in his profession, father always expected it from me, oh, that it may happen and God's blessing rest upon it. In writing to you what my intentions are, my thoughts become more clear and definite . . .

In our family, which is a Christian family in the full sense of the word, there has always been, as far as one can remember, from generation to generation, one who preached the Gospel. Why should not a member of that family feel himself called to that service now . . .

✳ ✳ ✳

To Theo (91)
Etten, 3 April 1877

. . . as you see I write you from Etten. Yesterday morning I received a letter from home, in which father wrote to me that Aerssen was dying, and that he had been to see him, as Aerssen had expressed the wish that father should visit him.

When I heard that, my heart was drawn so strongly towards Zundert that I longed to go there also.

Saturday night I took the last train from Dordrecht to Oudenbosch, and walked from there to Zundert. It was so beautiful on the heath; though it was dark one could distinguish the heath, and the pine woods, and moors extending far and wide, it reminded me of the print by Bodmer, that hangs in father's study. The sky was overcast, but the evening star was shining through the clouds, and now and then more stars appeared: It was very early when I arrived at the churchyard in Zundert, where everything was so quiet, I went over all the dear old spots, and the little paths, and awaited the sunrise there. You know the story of the Resurrection, everything reminded me of it that morning, in the quiet graveyard . . .

✳ ✳ ✳

To Theo (92)
Dordrecht, 16 April 1877

. . . Oh! might I be shown the way to devote my life more than is possible at present, to the service of God, and the gospel. I keep praying for it and I think I shall be heard, I say it in all humility. Humanly speaking, one would say it cannot happen, but when I think seriously about it and penetrate under the surface of what is impossible to man, then my soul is in communion with God, for it is possible to Him, who speaketh and it is; who commandeth and it stands, and stands firm.

Oh! Theo, Theo boy, if I might only succeed in this, if that heavy depression because everything I undertook failed, that torrent of reproaches which I have heard and felt, if it might be taken from me, and if there might be given to me, both the opportunity and the strength needed to come to full development and to persevere in that course for which my father and I would thank the Lord so fervently . . .

PART TWO

'Homesick for the Land of Pictures'

Amsterdam May 1877–July 1878 – Etten, Brussels and
The Borinage July 1878–July 1880

Vincent's wish to follow in his father's footsteps and preach is now taken seriously. But before he attends university to study theology, he must first pass the state examination. This demands a preparatory study of at least two years. His whole family rallies. His uncle Jan, Commandant of the Navy Yard in Amsterdam provides him with lodgings. His uncle Stricker finds him a tutor in Latin and Greek, and in his Uncle Cor's art gallery in the Leidschestraat he can now and then indulge his love for pictures to his heart's content. At the age of twenty-four he finds academic study too gruelling, and finally does succeed in finding a place where he can exercise his evangelist zeal: in the poverty-stricken coal-mining district of the Borinage in Belgium. But as in everything else he will do, he applies too much zeal in following Christ's original principles. He gives away all his possessions and lives in poverty alongside the peasants.

But, ultimately, will this prove to be what Vincent really wants to do?

To Theo (95)
Amsterdam, 19 May 1877

. . . A Jewish bookseller who procures me the Latin and Greek books I
want, had a large number of prints and I could choose from them very
cheaply, thirteen pieces for 70 cents, I took some for my little room, to
give it the right atmosphere, for that is necessary to get new thoughts
and new ideas . . .

I have a lot of work to do, and it is not very easy, but patience will
help me through, I hope to remember the ivy, 'which stealeth on
though he wears no wings', as the ivy creeps along the walls, so the pen
must crawl over the paper.

Every day I take a long walk, lately I came through a very nice part
of the town, I went along the Buitenkant to the Dutch railroad station,
there I saw men working with sand-carts near the [River] Y, and I
passed through many narrow streets with gardens of ivy. It reminded
me somehow of Ramsgate.

Near the station I turned to the left, where all the mills are, along a
canal with elm trees, everything there reminds one of the etchings by
Rembrandt . . .

✳ ✳ ✳

To Theo (98)
Amsterdam, 30 May 1877

. . . There was a sentence in your letter that struck me, 'I wish I were
far away from everything, I am the cause of all, and bring only sorrow
to everybody, I alone have brought all this misery on myself and
others.' These words struck me because that same feeling, just the
same, not more nor less, is also on my conscience . . .

When I was standing beside the corpse of Aerssen the calmness and
dignity and solemn silence of death contrasted with us living people to
such an extent, that we all felt the truth of what his daughter said in her
simplicity: 'he is freed from the burden of life, which we have to carry
on still.' And yet we are so much attached to the old life, because next
to our despondent moods we have our happy moments, when heart
and soul rejoice, like the lark that cannot keep from singing in the
morning, even though the soul sometimes sinks within us and is full of

fears. And the memories of all we have loved, stay and come back to us in the evening of our life. They are not dead but they sleep, and it is well to gather a treasure of them . . .

✳ ✳ ✳

To Theo (102)
Amsterdam, 15 July 1877

. . . Mendes told me last week about a very interesting part of the city, namely, the outskirts that extend from the Leidsche Poort, that is near the Vondel Park, to the Dutch railroad station. It is full of mills and sawmills, workmen's cottages with little gardens, also old houses, everything, and it is very populous, and the quarter is cut through by many small canals and waterways full of boats and all kinds of picturesque bridges, etc. It must be a splendid thing to be a clergyman in such a quarter.

The study is very difficult, boy, but I must keep on . . .

If you can get *John Halifax* read it over again, though we read it with melancholy yet we must not say 'that is nothing for me', for it is good to keep your faith in everything that is good and noble. I heard that not long ago the man died whose life and character inspired the author of this book, his name was Harper and he was the head of a large publishing firm in London.

Once I met on the street in London the painter Millais, just after I had been so lucky as to see several of his pictures. And that noble figure reminded me of John Halifax . . .

✳ ✳ ✳

To Theo (103)
Amsterdam, 27 July 1877

. . . Mendes has given me hope that at the end of three months we shall have accomplished what he had planned we should, if everything went well, but Greek lessons in the heart of Amsterdam, in the heart of the Jewish quarter, on a very close and sultry summer afternoon, with the feeling that many difficult examinations await you, arranged by very learned and cunning professors, I can tell you they make one feel more oppressed than the Brabant cornfields, that are beautiful on such a day . . .

✻ ✻ ✻

To Theo   (104)
Amsterdam, 3 August 1877

Thanks for your last letter which made me very happy, many thanks. So you have been at [Anton] Mauve's [his relative by marriage and an artist of the Hague school] and had a good time, did you make any drawing while you were there? I was once at the studio of Weissenbruch, a few days before my first departure for London, and the memory of what I saw there, the studies and pictures, is still as vivid as that of the man himself. When you write again tell me something about the exhibition that opened yesterday; how many subjects for pictures the artists could find here on the wharf . . .

✻ ✻ ✻

To Theo   (106)
Amsterdam, 18 August 1877

. . . Aunt Mina had her birthday last Sunday, and being there that evening Uncle Stricker asked me a few things about my work, and did not seem dissatisfied . . . I feel that I have made some progress. Thursday I had a nice morning; Uncle Jan had gone to Utrecht, and I had to be at Stricker's at 7 o'clock, because Jan went to Paris and I had promised to see him off. So I got up early and saw the workmen arrive in the Yard, while the sun was shining brightly. You would enjoy that curious sight, that long line of black figures, big and small, first in the narrow street, where the sun just peeps in, and afterwards in the Yard. Then I breakfasted on a piece of dry bread and a glass of beer, that is what Dickens advises for those who are on the point of committing suicide, as being very fit to keep them, at least for some time, from that purpose. And even if one is not in such a mood, it is right to do so now and then, while thinking of, for instance Rembrandt's picture, *The Pilgrims of Emmaus*. Before I went to Stricker, I walked through the Jewish quarter and along the Buitenkant, the old Teertuinen, Zeedyk,

Warmoes Straat, and around the Oudzyds Chapel and the Old and the South church, through all kinds of old streets with forges and coopers' shops etc., and through narrow alleys, like the Niezel, and canals with narrow bridges, like those we saw that evening at Dordt. It was curious to notice the starting of the new day's work there.

I have written a composition in which all the parables are arranged in proper order, and the miracles, etc. I am doing the same in English and French, expecting to be able to write it afterwards in Latin and Greek too. In the daytime I have to prepare for Mendes and so I do this late in the evening, or for instance as today, deep in the night or early in the morning. Having been so long in England and France, it would not be right if I did not acquire a thorough mastery of these languages at last, or at least kept them up; there is written, 'polissez-le sans cesse et le repolissez' and also 'travaillez prenez de la peine'. . .

❊ ❊ ❊

To Theo (108)
Amsterdam, 4 September 1877

. . . I am . . . copying the whole of the *Imitation of Jesus Christ* from a French edition, which I borrowed from Uncle Cor, that book is sublime and he who wrote it must have been a man after God's own heart. It is a peculiar book, that of Thomas à Kempis, there are words in it so deep and serious that one cannot read them without emotion and almost fear . . .

How I should love to show you several things here in the Jewish quarter, and also in other places, I often think of de Groux, there are interiors, with wood-choppers, carpenters, grocery stores; forges, drug-gists, etc. etc., which would have delighted him, I saw this morning a big dark wine cellar and warehouse, with doors standing open; for a moment I saw an awful vision in my mind, you know what I mean, in the dark vault men with lights were running to and fro, it is true that is a thing you can see daily, but there are moments when the daily common things make an extraordinary impression and have a deep significance and a different aspect . . .

❊ ❊ ❊

To Theo (109)
Amsterdam, 7 September 1877

It was a delightful sensation to hear Gladwell's voice in the hall, while I sat working in my room upstairs, and to see him come in a moment later, and to shake hands with him. Yesterday we took a long walk through the principal streets and past most of the churches, and this morning we got up before five o'clock to see the workmen enter the Yard, and then we walked to Zeeburg, and have been twice to the Trippenhuis . . .

He gave me Bunyan's *Pilgrim's Progress*, which is as great an acquisition as Bossuet's *Oraisons Funèbres*, which I bought very cheaply sometime ago, and the *Imitation* of Thomas à Kempis in Latin, which Vos gave me and which I hope to be able to read in the original some day.

We talked about many things, and what we said to each other was this: many people arriving at the moment in life when they must make a choice, have chosen for their part, 'the love of Christ and poverty', or rather 'give me neither poverty nor riches, feed me with bread convenient for me'. I for my part am thankful from the depth of my heart, that it has been given me to see him again, and to find in him still what first attracted me . . .

* * *

To Theo (110)
Amsterdam, 18 September 1877

. . . This week Mendes is out of town, spending a few days with the Rev. Schröder at Zwolle, a former pupil of his. So having some leisure I could carry out an old plan to go and see the etchings by Rembrandt in the Trippenhuis . . . Blessed twilight, when two or three are gathered in His name and He is in the midst of them, and blessed he who knows these things and follows them too.

Rembrandt knew that, for from the rich treasure of his heart he brought forth among other things that drawing in sepia, charcoal, ink, etc. which is at the British Museum, representing the house in Bethany. In that room twilight has fallen, the figure of our Lord, noble and impressive, stands out serious and dark against the window through which the evening twilight is falling. At the feet of Jesus sits Mary who has chosen the good part, that will not be taken away from her, and Martha is in the room busy with something or other, if I remember well she trims the fire or something like it. That drawing I hope never to forget nor what it seems to tell me: 'I am the light of the world, whosoever follows Me will not walk in darkness, but will have the light of life.' . . .

❉ ❉ ❉

To Theo (112)
Amsterdam, 30 October 1877

. . . Lad, the study of Latin and Greek is very difficult, but still it makes me feel happy, and I am doing what I longed to do. I may not sit up so late in the evening any more, Uncle has strictly forbidden it, still I keep in mind what is written under the etching by Rembrandt: 'In medio noctis vim suam lux exerit' (In the middle of the night the light diffuses its radiance), and I keep a small gaslight burning low all night and in 'medio noctis' I often lie looking at it, planning my work for the next day and thinking how to arrange my studies as well as possible.

❉ ❉ ❉

To Theo (113)
Amsterdam, 19 November 1877

. . . I have been looking for a teacher in Algebra and Mathematics and have found one, a cousin of Mendes, Teixeira de Mattos, teacher at the Jewish pauper school. He gives me hope that we shall be ready about October of next year.

The preparatory studies (that precede the real theological studies and the practice in preaching and reciting) consist of History, Grammar and the Geography of Greece, Minor Asia, and Italy, so I have to study these also, with the same tenacity with which a dog gnaws at a bone, and I should also like to know the Grammar, History and Geography of the northern countries, namely those that border on the North Sea and the Channel . . .

❉ ❉ ❉

Amsterdam, 10 February 1878

. . . As you know, father has been here . . . You can imagine the days flew by, and when I had seen father off at the station, and had looked after the train as long as it was in sight, even the smoke of it, and came home to my room and saw father's chair still standing near the little table on which the books and copy-books of the day before were still lying, though I know that we shall see each other again pretty soon, I cried like a child . . .

✳ ✳ ✳

To Theo (119)
Amsterdam, 18 February 1878

. . . Last evening I saw at Uncle Cor's a whole volume of that magazine, *L'Art*, of which you have the number with the woodcuts after Corot. I was especially struck by woodcuts after drawing – by Millet, among others *The Falling Leaves*, *The Ravens' Wedding*, *Donkeys in a Marsh*, *The Woodcutters*, *Housewife Sweeping her Room*, *A Farm Courtyard* (night effect), etc. Also an etching after Corot: *The Dune*, and after Breton: *St John's Eve*, and others by Chauvin, and another after Millet: *The Beans* . . .

✳ ✳ ✳

To Theo (120)
Amsterdam, 3 March 1878

. . . how I should have liked to be with you today, it was such beautiful weather here, and one feels spring approaching. In the country I suppose the lark is already heard, but in the city that is impossible, unless one hears the sounds of the lark in the voice of some old clergyman, whose words come from a heart that is tuned like that of the bird.

Have you read a good book lately? Be sure you read the books by George Eliot, you will not regret it, *Adam Bede*, *Silas Marner*, *Felix Holt*, *Romola* (Savonarola's history), *Scenes from Clerical Life*.

When I have time again for reading, I shall certainly read them over again. Have you ever seen an etching by Millet himself, a man who carries dung in a wheelbarrow in a garden, on a day like today, in the beginning of Spring, and remember also that he has made an etching, *Les Bêcheurs*, if you ever happen to see that, you will not soon forget it. I thought today of the former when Uncle Stricker was looking this morning for texts in which the word dung appears, for example 'Let it alone this year also, till I shall dig about it and dung it.' . . .

Vincent began full of courage – but his father and mother question, with anxiety, if one who has never been used to regular study, can acquire this habit, when in his twenty-fourth year. The result has proved negative in this case. But Vincent tried hard, and for a whole year struggled with his Latin exercises, until it became too much for him at last; he longed for more practical work. In the summer of 1878 he gives up the study at Amsterdam, with his parents' permission, and returns to the parsonage at Etten.

Although it now has been proved that Vincent has no aptitude for study, he does not give up his ideal, which is to bring comfort to the poor through the Gospel. After a month spent in Etten at his parents' home, he leaves in August 1878 for the training school for Evangelists in Brussels, under the direction of Master Bokma. There he is the most advanced of the pupils, but cannot comply with what is required of him; one of his fellow-pupils says, 'he did not know what submission was'.

✸ ✸ ✸

To Theo (123)
Etten, 22 July 1878

. . . We [Vincent and his father] saw the Flemish training school, it has a course of three years, while as you know in Holland the study would last for six years more at the shortest. And they do not even require that you quite finish the course, before you can apply for a place as Evangelist. What is wanted is the talent to give popular and attractive lectures for the people, rather short and interesting than long and learned. So they require less knowledge of the ancient languages and of the theological study (though all one knows about them, is a great recommendation) but they take more account of the fitness for practical work, and of the faith that comes from the heart. Still there are many obstacles to overcome, in the first place, one does not acquire at once, but only by long practice, the talent of speaking to the people, with seriousness and feeling, with fluency and ease, and what one has to say must have a meaning, and a purpose, and some persuasion to rouse one's hearers, so that they will try to root their convictions in truth.

In short, one must be a popular orator to succeed over there. Ces messieurs in Brussels wanted me to come there for three months to become better acquainted, but that would again cause too many expenses, and this must be avoided as much as possible . . .

When we drove back from Zundert that evening across the heath, father and I got out and walked awhile, the sun was setting red behind the pine trees, and the evening sky was reflected in the pools; the heath and the yellow and white and grey sand were so full of harmony and sentiment – see, there are moments in life when everything, within us too, is full of peace and sentiment, and our whole life seems to be a path through the heath, but it is not always so . . .

✻ ✻ ✻

To Theo   (124)
Etten, beginning of August 1878

. . . The fields here are now so beautiful, they are reaping the corn, and the potatoes are getting ripe and their leaves begin to wither, and the buck-wheat is full of beautiful white blossoms . . .

✻ ✻ ✻

To Theo   (126)
Laeken [nr Brussels], 15 November 1878

On the evening of the day we spent together, which passed only too quickly for me, I want to write to you again. It was a great joy for me to see you again and to talk with you, and it is a blessing that such a day, that passes in a moment, and such a joy that is of so short duration, stays in our memory and will never be forgotten. When we had taken leave I walked back, not along the shortest way but along the tow-path. Here are workshops of all kinds that look picturesque, especially in the evening with the lights, and to us who are also labourers and workmen, each in his sphere and in the work to which he is called,

43

they speak in their own way, if we only listen to them, for they say: Work while it is day, the night cometh when no man can work.

It was just the moment when the street cleaners came home with their carts with the old white horses. A long row of these carts were standing at the so-called Terme des boues, at the beginning of the towpath. Some of these old white horses resemble a certain old aquatint engraving, which you perhaps know, an engraving that has no great art value, it is true, but which struck me, and made a deep impression upon me. I mean the last from that series of prints called *The Life of a Horse*. It represents an old white horse, lean and emaciated, and tired to death by a long life of heavy labour, of too much and too hard work. The poor animal is standing on a spot utterly lonely and desolate, a plain scantily covered with withered dry grass, and here and there a gnarled old tree broken and bent by the storm. On the ground lies a skull, and at a distance in the background a bleached skeleton of a horse, lying near a hut where lives a man who skins horses. Over the whole is a stormy sky, it is a cold, bleak day, gloomy and dark weather . . . Involuntarily I was reminded of that engraving, when I saw tonight those horses of the ash-carts.

As to the drivers themselves with their dirty filthy clothes, they seemed sunk and rooted still deeper in poverty than that long row or rather group of poor people, that Master de Groux has drawn in his *The Bench of the Poor*. It always strikes me and it is very peculiar, that when we see the image of indescribable and unutterable desolation – of loneliness, of poverty and misery, the end of all things, or their extreme – then rises in our mind the thought of God.

. . . I should like to begin making rough sketches from some of the many things that I meet on my way, but as it would probably keep me from my real work, it is better not to begin it.

That little drawing *Au Charbonnage* is nothing remarkable indeed, but the reason I made it is that one sees here so many people that work in the coal mines, and they are rather a characteristic kind of people. This little house stands not far from the road, it is a small inn attached to the big coal shed, where the workmen come to eat their bread and drink their glass of beer during the lunch hour.

When I was in England I applied for a position as Evangelist among the miners in the coal mines, but then they paid no heed to it, and said I had to be at least twenty-five years old.

Experience has taught that those who walk in the darkness, in the centre of the earth, like the miners in the black coal mines for instance, are very much impressed by the words of the Gospel, and believe it too. Now there is in the south of Belgium, in Hainault, in the neighbourhood of Mons, up to the French frontiers, aye, even far across it, a district called the Borinage, that has a peculiar population of labourers who work in the numerous coal mines . . . I should very much like to go there as an Evangelist . . .

The three months' trial demanded of me by the Rev. Jong and the Rev. Pietersen, have almost passed . . .

There are already in the Borinage many little Protestant communities and certainly schools also. I wish I could get a position there as Evangelist, preaching the Gospel to the poor, that means those who need it most and for whom it is so well suited, and then during the week devoting myself to teaching . . .

When the three months' time of trial had passed he received no nomination, to his great disappointment. With his father's consent he goes to the Borinage, a mining district in Belgium, at his own expense, and lives in Paturages with a hawker, van der Haegen, whose children he teaches in the evening. Besides he practises Bible reading and visiting the sick, and at last in January, 1879, he gets after all a temporary nomination for six months as Evangelist in the Borinage. All the misery of the miner's life which he witnesses there, a serious mine accident takes place, and a strike breaks out, shows him more and more clearly that Bible texts and sermons are of little use there, religion gives way more and more to practical work – such as nursing the sick and wounded; he gives away all he possesses, clothes, money, even his bed; he lives no longer in a boarding house, but in a small miner's hut, where even the strict necessities are wanting, in this way he tries to follow literally Jesus' teaching.

✳ ✳ ✳

To Theo   (127)
Petites Wasmes, the Borinage, 26 December 1878

. . . here in the Borinage there are no pictures; speaking in general one does not even know what a picture is. So of course I have not seen anything in the way of art since I left Brussels. But notwithstanding this the country is very picturesque and very peculiar here, everything *speaks* as it were, and is full of character. Of late in these dark days before Christmas, the ground was covered with snow; everything then reminded one of the medieval pictures of the Peasant Breughel for instance, and of so many others who have known how to express so remarkably well that peculiar effect of red and green, black and white. At every moment I am reminded here of the work of Thys Maris or of Albrecht Dürer. There are hollow roads, grown over with thorn bushes, and old gnarled trees with their fantastical roots, which perfectly resemble that road on the etching by Dürer, *Death and the Knight*. So, a few days ago, it was a curious sight to see the miners go home in the white snow in the evening at twilight. Those people are quite black. When they come from the dark mines into daylight they look exactly like chimney-sweeps. Their houses are very small and might rather be called huts; they are scattered along those hollow roads, and in wood, and on the slope of the hills. Here and there one sees moss-covered roofs, and in the evening the light shines kindly through the small-paned windows.

As we have in our Brabant the underbrush of oak, and in Holland the willows, so you see here the black thorn hedges around the gardens, fields and meadows. With the snow it makes just now an effect as of black characters on white paper, like the pages of the Gospel.

I have already spoken in public here several times, in rather a large room, especially arranged for religious meetings, as well as at the meetings they used to hold in the evenings in the miners' cottages, which may be called Bible lectures. I spoke among others, about the parable of the mustard seed, the barren fig tree, the blind-born man. On Christmas, of course about the stable in Bethlehem and peace on earth. If with God's blessing I might get a permanent appointment here, I shall be very, very happy . . .

❊ ❊ ❊

To Theo (129)
Wasmes, April 1879

. . . Not long ago I made a very interesting expedition, namely I was for six hours in a mine.

It was one of the oldest and most dangerous mines in the neighbourhood, called Marcasse. That mine has a bad reputation, because many perish in it, either in descending or ascending, or by the poisoned air, or by gas explosion, or by the water in the ground, or by the

collapse of old tunnels, etc. It is a gloomy spot, and at first sight everything around looks dreary and desolate.

Most of the miners are thin and pale from fever and look tired and
emaciated, weather beaten and aged before their time, the women, as
a whole, faded and worn. Around the mine are poor miners' huts with
a few dead trees black from smoke, and thorn hedges, dung-hills, and
ash dumps, heaps of useless coal, etc. . . .

I had a good guide, a man who has already worked for 33 years
there . . .

So we went down together, 700 metres deep, and explored the most
hidden corners of that underworld. The 'maintenages' or 'gredins'
(cells where the miners work) which are situated farthest from the exit
are called 'des caches'.

This mine has five floors, the three upper ones are exhausted and
abandoned, and they no longer work there, because there is no more
coal. If anyone would try to make a picture of the 'maintenages' that
would be something new and unheard of, or rather never seen.
Imagine a row of cells in a rather narrow and low passage supported
by rough timber. In each of those cells a miner, in a coarse linen suit,
filthy and black like a chimney-sweep, is busy cutting coal by the pale
light of a small lamp. In some of those cells the miner stands erect, in
others he lies on the ground; (□□□□□ tailles à droit, □□□
tailles à plat). The arrangement is more or less like the cells in a
beehive, or like a dark gloomy passage in a prison underground, or like
a row of small weaving looms, or rather more like a row of bakers'
ovens such as the peasants have, or like the partitions in a vault. The
tunnels themselves are like the big chimneys of the Brabant peasants.

In some the water leaks through, and the light of the miner's lamp
makes a curious effect, and is reflected like in a grotto of stalactite.
Some of the miners work in the 'maintenages', others load the cut coal
in small carts, that are run along rails, like a tramway, this is done
especially by children, boys as well as girls. There is also a stable yard
down there, 700 metres underground, with about seven old horses that
transport a great many of those carts and bring them to the so-called
'accrochage', that is the place where they are pulled up to the surface.
Other miners are repairing the old passages to prevent their tumbling
down, or they are making new passages in the coal vein. As the
mariners ashore are homesick for the sea, notwithstanding all the
dangers and troubles that threaten them, so feels the miner, he would

rather be underground than above it. The villages here look desolate and dead and forsaken, because life is going on underground instead of above . . .

People here are very ignorant and untaught, most of them cannot read, but at the same time they are intelligent and quick in their difficult work, brave and frank, of small stature but square shouldered with melancholy deep-set eyes. They are handy in many things, and work terribly hard. They have a nervous temperament, I do not mean weak, but very sensitive. They have an innate, deeply rooted hatred, and a deep mistrust of everybody who would try to domineer over them. With the charcoal-burners one must have a charcoal-burner's character and temperament, and no pretentious pride or mastery, or one would never get on with them or gain their confidence . . . there have been many cases of typhoid and malignant fever, of what they call 'la sotte fièvre', that gives them bad dreams like nightmare, and makes them delirious. So there are again many sickly and bedridden people, emaciated, weak and miserable . . .

To descend in a mine is a very unpleasant sensation, one goes in a kind of basket or cage, like a bucket in a well, but in a well of 500–700 metres deep, so that in looking upward from the bottom one sees daylight about the size of a star in the sky.

✳ ✳ ✳

To Theo   (130)
Wasmes, June 1879

. . . A few days ago we had a very heavy thunderstorm here at about eleven o'clock in the evening; quite near our house there is a spot from where one can see far below in the distance a great part of the Borinage, with the chimneys, the mounds of coal, the little miners' cottages, the scurrying to and fro of the little black figures by day, like ants in a nest, far away in the distance dark pine woods with little white cottages silhouetted against them, a few church spires a way off, an old mill, etc. Generally there is a kind of haze hanging over all, or there is a fantastic effect of light and dark formed by the shadows of the clouds, that reminds one of the pictures of Rembrandt, or Michel or Ruysdael.

But during that thunderstorm, in the pitch dark night there was a curious effect made by the flashes of lightning, which now and then rendered everything visible for a moment. Near by the large gloomy buildings of the mine, Marcasse, standing alone, isolated in the open field, reminding one indeed that night of the huge bulk of Noah's Ark, as it must have looked in the terrible pouring rain and the darkness of the Flood, illuminated by a flash of lightning.

I often read *Uncle Tom's Cabin*, these days – there is so much slavery still in the world – and in that remarkably wonderful book that important question is treated with so much wisdom, so much love, and such zeal and interest for the true welfare of the poor oppressed, that one comes back to it again and again, and always finds new things in it.

I still can find no better definition for the word Art, than this, 'L'art c'est l'homme ajouté à la nature', nature, reality, truth, but with a significance, a conception, a character, which the artist brings out in it, and to which he gives expression, 'qu'il dégage', which he disentangles, and makes free and clears up . . .

Following Jesus's teaching by living in abject poverty was not to the liking of the committee – there was too much zeal, and not of the right kind, in their estimation – and after six months, in July 1879, Vincent gets his dismissal. The days that now follow are the most bitter of his life; he wanders about full of cares, without faith, without work, without any prospects, without any friends. Few facts about that time are known, but the strikingly beautiful letters then written give an idea of what passed within him.

✳ ✳ ✳

To Theo (131)
Cuesmes, 5 August 1879

. . . Did you ever read Dickens's *Hard Times*? . . . It is excellent, there is a figure in it of a working man, Stephen Blackpool, who is most striking and sympathetic . . .

Lately I have been at a studio again, namely at the Rev. Pietersen's who paints in the manner of Schelfhout or Hoppenbrouwers, and has good ideas about art.

He asked me for one of my sketches, a miner type. Often I am drawing until late in the night, to keep some souvenirs, and to strengthen the thoughts raised involuntarily by the aspect of things here . . .

. . . When I saw you again, and walked with you, I had the selfsame feeling, which I used to have, more than now, as if life were something good and precious, which one must value, and I felt more cheerful and alive than I had done for a long time, because gradually life has become less precious, much more unimportant and indifferent to me, at least it seemed so. When one lives with others and is united by a feeling of affection, one is aware of a reason for living, and one perceives that one is not quite worthless and superfluous, but perhaps good for something, because we need each other, and make the same journey as travelling-companions; but that feeling of proper self-esteem also depends very much on our relations to others.

Like everyone else I feel the need of relations and friendship, of affection, of friendly intercourse, and I am not made of stone, or of iron, like a street pump or a lantern pole, so I cannot miss these things without feeling, like any other intelligent and honest man, a void and deep need. I tell you this to let you know how much good your visit has done me.

And as I hope that we too will not be estranged from each other, I hope the same may be true in regard to all at home.

But for the moment I do not feel very much like going back there and I am strongly inclined to stay here. But perhaps the fault is mine, and you may be right, that I do not see it well; so it may be, that notwithstanding my strong repugnance, and notwithstanding that it will be a hard road to take, I will go to Etten for at least a few days . . .

How fresh lies in my memory that time spent in Amsterdam. You were there yourself, so you know how things were planned and discussed, argued and considered, talked over with wisdom, with the best intentions, and yet how miserable was the result, how ridiculous the whole undertaking, how utterly foolish. I shudder still when I think of it.

It is the worst time I ever lived through. How desirable and attractive have become the difficult days, full of care here in this poor country, in these uncivilized surroundings, compared to that. I fear a similar thing will be the result of following wise advice given with the best intentions.

Such experiences are too dreadful, the harm, the sorrow, the afflic-tion is too great, not to try on either side to become wiser by this dearly bought experience. If we do not learn from this, then from what shall we learn? . . .

I would rather die a natural death than to be prepared for it by the Academy, and I sometimes have had a lesson from a hay-mower that was of more use to me than one in Greek . . .

❅ ❅ ❅

To Theo (133)
Cuesmes, July 1880

It is rather with reluctance that I write to you, not having done so since so long, for many reasons.

To a certain degree you have become a stranger to me, and I have become the same to you, more than you may think; perhaps it would be better for us not to continue this way. It is likely I would not have written to you even now, if I were not under the obligation and the necessity of doing so, if you yourself had not given me cause. I learned at Etten that you had sent fr. 50 for me, well I have accepted them. Certainly with reluctance, certainly with a rather melancholy feeling, but I am up against a stone wall, and in a sort of mess. How can I do otherwise? So it is to thank you for them that I write to you.

Perhaps you know I am back in the Borinage; father would rather have me stay in the neighbourhood of Etten; I refused, and I think I acted in this for the best.

Involuntarily, I have become in the family more or less a kind of impossible and suspect personage, at least somebody whom they do not trust, so how could I in any way be of any use to anybody?

Therefore above all, I think the best thing and the most reasonable for me to do, is to go away, and keep at a convenient distance, so that I cease to exist for you all.

What moulting time is for the birds – the time when they change their feathers – so adversity or misfortune is the difficult time for us human beings. One can stay in it, in that time of moulting, one can also come out of it renewed, but anyhow it must not be done in public and it is not at all amusing, therefore the only thing to do is to hide oneself. Well, be it so.

Now, though it is a very difficult and almost impossible thing to regain the confidence of a whole family, that is not quite free from prejudices, and other qualities as fashionable and honourable, yet I do not quite despair of the fact that by and by, slowly but surely, a cordial understanding may be renewed between some of us.

And in the very first place, I should like to see that 'cordiale entente' not to put it stronger, re-established between father and me, and I desire no less to see it re-established between us two.

'Entente cordiale' is infinitely better than misunderstandings. Now I must bore you with certain abstract things, but I hope you will listen patiently to them. I am a man of passions, capable of and subject to doing more or less foolish things, of which I happen to repent, more or less, afterwards. Now and then I speak and act too quickly, when it would have been better to wait patiently . . . Must I consider myself a dangerous man, incapable of anything? I do not think so. But the question is to try by all means to put those selfsame passions to a good use. For instance, to name one of the passions, I have a more or less irresistible passion for books, and I want continually to instruct myself, to study if you like, just as much as I want to eat my bread. *You* certainly will be able to understand this. When I was in other surroundings, in the surroundings of pictures and things of art, you know how I then had a violent passion for them, that reached the highest pitch of enthusiasm. And I do not repent it, for even now, *far from that land, I am often homesick for the land of pictures.*

You remember perhaps that I knew well (and perhaps I know it still) who Rembrandt was, or Millet, or Jules Dupré or Delacroix or Millais or M. Maris. Well – now I do not have those surroundings any more – yet that thing that is called soul, they say it never dies, but it lives always, and goes on searching always and always and forever. So instead of giving way to this homesickness I said to myself: that land, or the fatherland is everywhere. So instead of yielding to despair, I chose the part of active melancholy, in so far as I possessed the power of activity, in other words I preferred the melancholy that hopes and aspires, and seeks, to that which despairs in stagnation and woe. So I studied more or less seriously the books within my reach like the Bible, and the *French Revolution* by Michelet, and last winter, Shakespeare and a few of Victor Hugo and Dickens, and Beecher Stowe, and lately *Eschylus*, and then several others, less classical, several great 'little masters'. You know that among those 'little masters' are people like Fabritius or Bida.

Now he who is absorbed in all this, is sometimes 'choquant', shocking to others, and unwillingly sins more or less against certain forms and customs and social conventions.

It is a pity however when this is taken in bad part. For instance you know that I have often neglected my appearance, this I admit, and I admit that it is shocking. But look here, poverty and want have their share in the cause, and then a deep discouragement comes in too for a part and then it is sometimes a good way to assure oneself the necessary solitude for concentration on some study that preoccupies one . . .

Now for more than five years already, I do not know exactly how long, I am more or less without employment, wandering here and there; you say: since a certain time you have gone down, you have deteriorated, you have not done anything. Is this quite true?

It is true that now and then I have earned my crust of bread, now and then a friend has given it to me in charity. I have lived as I could, as luck would have it, haphazardly, it is true that I have lost the confidence of many, it is true that my financial affairs are in a sad state, it is true that the future is only too sombre, it is true that I might have done better, it is true that just for earning my bread I've lost time, it is true that even my studies are in a rather sad and hopeless condition, and that my needs are greater, infinitely greater than my possessions.

But on the path I have taken now I must keep going; if I don't do anything, if I do not study, if I do not go on seeking any longer, then I am lost. Then woe is me.

That is how I look at it; to continue, to continue, that is what is necessary. But you will ask: What is your definite aim? That aim becomes more definite, will stand out slowly and surely, as the rough draught becomes a sketch, and the sketch becomes a picture, little by little, by working seriously on it, by pondering over the idea, vague at first, over the thought that was fleeting and passing, till it gets fixed . . .

Now for the moment it seems things go very badly with me, and this has been so already for a considerable time, and it may continue so in the future for a while; but after everything seemed to go wrong, there will perhaps come a time when things will go right. I do not count on it, perhaps it will never happen, but in case there comes a change for the better, I would consider it so much gain, I would be contented, I would say: at last! you see *there was something after all!* . . .

And men are often prevented by circumstances from doing things, a prisoner in I do not know what horrible, horrible, most horrible cage. There is also, I know it, the deliverance, the tardy deliverance. A just or unjustly ruined reputation, poverty, fatal circumstances, adversity, that is what makes men prisoners.

One cannot always tell what it is, that keeps us shut in, confines us, seems to bury us, but, however, one feels certain barriers, certain gates, certain walls. Is all this imagination, fantasy? I do not think so. And then one asks: 'My God! is it for long, is it for ever, is it for eternity!' Do you know what frees one from this captivity? It is every deep serious affection. Being friends, being brothers, love, that is what opens the prison by supreme power, by some magic force. But without this one remains in prison.

There where sympathy is renewed, life is restored.

And the prison is also called prejudice, misunderstanding, fatal ignorance of one thing or another, distrust, false shame.

But to speak of other things, if I have come down in the world, you on the contrary have risen. If I have lost sympathies, you on the contrary have gained them. That makes me very happy, I say it in all sincerity, and it will always do so. If you were but little serious, and with but little depth, I would fear that it would not last, but as I think you are very serious and of great depth, I believe that it will last. But I should be very glad if it were possible for you to see in me something else than an idle man of the worst type.

Then if ever I can do anything for you, be of some use to you, know that I am at your disposal. If I have accepted what you have given me, you might, in case I could render you some service, ask it of me; it would make me happy, and I would consider it a proof of confidence. We are rather far apart, and we have perhaps different views on some things, but nevertheless there may come an hour, there may come a day, when we may be of service to one another.

For the present I shake hands with you, thanking you again for the help you have given me . . .

PART THREE

'I Will Go On With My Drawing'

The Borinage (Cuesmes) July–October 1880 –
Brussels October 1880–April 1881 – *Etten* April–August 1881

At last Vincent realises that he cannot resist his impulse to draw. From the moment he takes up drawing again, he becomes conscious of his true vocation, and finally we hear a new confident voice when he writes once more to Theo in August 1880. However, life will be no easier. In the Borinage, he continues to live with a peasant family and in dire poverty.

Then, in October 1880, he moves to Brussels with the intention of studying art at the Academy, which is free. Here he continues copying reproductions and plaster casts and studying anatomy, but also finds models among working people. His intention now is to become a professional illustrator, but he finds few outlets for his work. In Brussels he meets a rich, young, aristocratic painter, Anton van Rappard, with whom he will form a friendship and with whom he can have longed-for discussions on art. But, only a few months later, in April 1881, he is disillusioned, as once more he is overcome by poverty and obliged to return to his father's vicarage at Etten (to the north of Antwerp).

Cuesmes, the Borinage, 20 August 1880

If I am not mistaken you must still have *Les Travaux des Champs*, by Millet.

Would you be so kind as to lend them to me for a short time, and send them by mail?

I must tell you that I am busy copying large drawings after Millet, and that I have already finished, *Les Heures de la Journée* as well as *Le Semeur*.

Well, perhaps if you saw them, you would not be altogether dissatisfied with them. Now if you would send me *Les Travaux des Champs*, you might perhaps add some other prints by, or after, Millet, Breton, Feyen Perrin, etc. Do not buy them on purpose, but lend me what you have.

Send me what you can and do not fear for me. If I can only continue my work, get on my feet once more, I will rise up again. But by doing this you will help me a great deal. If sooner or later you may take a trip to Holland, I hope that you will not pass by here without coming to see the sketches.

I write to you while I am busy drawing, and I am in a hurry to go back to it, so good night, and send me the prints as soon as possible . . .

. . . I have sketched a drawing representing miners, men and women, going to the shaft in the morning through the snow, by a path along a hedge of thorns; shadows that pass, dimly visible in the twilight. In the background the large constructions of the mine, and the heaps of clinkers, stand out vaguely against the sky.

I send you a hasty sketch, so that you can see what it is like. But I feel the need of studying the drawing of figure from masters, like Millet, Breton, Brion, or Boughton, or others. What do you think of the sketch, do you think the idea good? . . .

✳ ✳ ✳

To Theo   (135)
Cuesmes, 7 September 1880

The prints, etchings, etc., which you sent me sometime ago, I received in good order, and I thank you very much.

You did me a great service by sending them . . . I sketched the ten pages *Travaux des Champs* by Millet (almost the size of a page of *Cours de Dessins Bargue*), and that I have quite finished one. I should have done more but I wanted to make first the *Exercices au Fusain*, by Bargue, which Mr Tersteeg has kindly lent me, and I have now finished the sixty pages . . .

As to [Millet's] *The Sower* I have already drawn it five times, twice in small size, three times in large, and I will take it up again, I am so entirely absorbed by that figure. When sooner or later you write to me (which by way of distraction would be very welcome) could you tell me something about the etchings by A. Legros. If I remember well I saw a dozen of them when in England, and they were very beautiful . . .

* * *

To Theo   (136)
Cuesmes, 24 September 1880

. . . What you say in your letter about Barbizon is quite true . . . I have not seen Barbizon, but though I have not seen that, last winter I saw Courrières. I had undertaken a walking tour, mostly in the Pas de Calais, not la Manche, but the department or province. I had undertaken that trip, hoping perhaps to find there if possible some kind of work. I would have accepted anything. But after all perhaps I went involuntarily, I cannot exactly tell you why. I had said to myself, you must see Courrières. I had only fr. 10 in my pocket, and having started by taking the train, I was soon out of money, and as I was on the road for a week, I had a long weary walk of it. Anyhow I saw Courrières, and the outside of M. Jules Breton's studio. The outside of the studio was rather disappointing, as it was quite newly built of bricks, of a Methodist regularity, of an inhospitable, chilly and irritating aspect. If I could only have seen the interior, I would certainly not have given a thought to the exterior, I am sure of that . . .

[But] I lacked the courage to enter and introduce myself. I looked elsewhere in Courrières for any traces of Jules Breton, or some other artist; the only thing I was able to discover was his picture at a photographer's, and in a dark corner of the old church a copy of Titian's *Burial of Christ*, which in the shadow seemed to me to be very beautiful and of wonderful tone. Was it by him? I do not know, as I was unable to discern any signature.

But of any living artist, no trace; there was only a café called Café des Beaux-Arts, also built of new bricks, equally inhospitable, chilly and repelling . . .

But I have at least seen the country around Courrières, the haystacks, the brown earth or almost coffee coloured clay, with white spots here and there where the marl appears . . .

Then the French sky seemed to me very much more clear and limpid, than the smoky and foggy sky of the Borinage. Besides there were farms and sheds which, the Lord be praised, still retained their moss-grown thatched roofs, I also saw flocks of crows made famous by the pictures of Daubigny and Millet. Not mentioning in the first place, as I ought to have done, the characteristic and picturesque figures of the different travellers, diggers, woodcutters, peasants driving horses, and here and there a woman's silhouette in a white cap. Even in Courrières there was a charbonnage or mine. I saw the day shift coming up in the twilight, but there were no women in men's clothes as in the Borinage, only miners, with tired and miserable faces, blackened by the coal dust, clad in tattered miners' clothes, and one of them in an old soldier's cape. Though this trip was almost too much for me, and I came back from it overcome by fatigue, with sore feet, and in a more or less melancholy condition . . . I earned some crusts of bread along the road here and there, in exchange for some drawings which I had in my valise. But when the fr. 10 were all gone I had to spend the last nights in the open air, once in an abandoned wagon, which was white with frost the next morning – rather a bad resting place – once in a pile of fagots, and once, that was a little better, in a hay-stack . . .

Well, it was even in that deep misery that I felt my energy revive and that I said to myself: in spite of everything I shall rise again, I will take up my pencil, which I have forsaken in my great discouragement, and I will go on with my drawing; and from that moment everything seems transformed for me; and now I have started, and my pencil has become somewhat docile, becoming more so every day. It was the too long and too great poverty which had discouraged me so much, that I could not do anything.

. . . Poverty prevents growth, that is the old proverb of Palissy, which has some truth in it . . . it is sure that I cannot go on very much longer in the little room where I am now. It is already a small room, and then there are two beds, one for the children and one for me . . .

Though every day difficulties come up and new ones will present themselves, I cannot tell you how happy I am to have taken up drawing again. I have been thinking of it for a long time, but I always considered the thing impossible and beyond my reach. But now, though I feel my weakness and my painful dependency in many things, I have recovered my mental balance, and day by day my energy increases . . .

✳ ✳ ✳

To Theo   (137)
Brussels, 15 October 1880

You see it is from Brussels that I write to you. For I thought it better to change my domicile for the present. And that for more than one reason.

In the first place it was urgently necessary, because the little room where I was lodged and which you saw last year, was so narrow, and the light there was so bad, that it was very inconvenient to draw there.

. . . I went to see Mr Schmidt here at Brussels and told him about the affair, that is to say I asked him if he could not help me to enter into relation with some artist, so that I could continue my study in a good studio for I feel that it is absolutely necessary to have good things to look at and also to see artists at work . . .

It is already a long time since I have seen enough pictures or drawings, etc., and the very sight of some good things here in Brussels has given me new inspiration and has strengthened my desire to make things with my own hands.

Will you do what I ask you to that effect, that is write a little note to Mr Schmidt? I have made another pen drawing after the Woodcutter of Millet (the woodcut that you sent me). I think pen drawing is a good preparation, if one should afterwards want to learn etching. The pen is also very useful in accentuating pencil drawings but one does not succeed in it at once . . .

But for the moment my aim must be to learn to make as soon as possible some drawings that are presentable and saleable, so that I can begin to earn something directly through my work. For that is the necessity that is forced upon me . . .

Once having mastered my pencil or water-colouring, or etching, I can go back to the country of the miners or weavers, and work better from nature than I can do now, but first I must learn more of the technique . . .

I think that a somewhat better lodging and perhaps better food than that of the Borinage will also help to set me right again. For I have undergone some misery in the Belgian 'black country', and my health has not been very good lately, but if I can succeed some day in learning to draw well what I want to express, I will forget all that . . .

❊ ❊ ❊

To Theo (138)
Brussels, 1 November [1880]

. . . I have been to see Mr Roelofs, the day after receiving your letter, and he has told me that in his opinion from now on I must draw principally from nature, that is from either cast or model, but not without the guidance of someone who knows it well. And he and others too have advised me so earnestly to go and work at the Academy, either here or at Antwerp or wherever I can, that I have felt obliged to try to get admission to the said Academy, though I do not think it so very agreeable. *Here in Brussels the teaching is free of charge* (in Amsterdam, for instance, I hear it costs fr. 100 a year) and one can work in a well-heated and well-lighted room, which is a good thing, especially in winter . . .

I intend to get from the veterinary school, the pictures of the anatomy, for instance, of a horse, a cow, or sheep, and to draw them likewise, as I did the anatomy of the human body.

There are laws of proportion, of light and shadow, of perspective, which one *must know* in order to be able to draw well; without that knowledge it always remains a fruitless struggle, and one never brings forth anything. Therefore I think I was right . . .

I have also been to see Mr van Rappard who now lives at Rue Traversière 6a and had a talk with him. He is a fine looking man; of his work I saw only a few small landscape pen drawings. But judging from his way of living, he must be wealthy, and I do not know whether he is the person with whom I might live and work, because of financial reasons. But I certainly shall go and visit him again. The impression he made upon me was that he takes things seriously . . .

You must not imagine that I live richly here, for my chief food is dry bread and some potatoes or chestnuts, which people sell here on the corners of the streets, but by having a somewhat better room and taking now and then a somewhat better meal in a restaurant, whenever I can afford it, I shall get on very well. But for almost two years I have had a hard time in the Borinage, that was no pleasure trip I assure you. The expenses here will be somewhat more than fr. 60, which cannot be helped. Drawing materials, studies to copy, for instance for anatomy, all that costs money, and yet they are strictly necessary things . . .

✳ ✳ ✳

To Theo   (140)
Brussels, January 1881

. . . these last days there has been a change for the better. I have finished at least a dozen drawings or rather sketches in pencil, and pen and ink, which seem to me to be somewhat better. They vaguely resemble certain drawings by Lançon, or certain English woodcuts, but they are more clumsy and awkward as yet. They represent a porter, a miner, a snow shoveller, a walk in the snow, old women, type of an old man ('Ferragus' from Balzac's *History of the Thirteen*), etc. I send you two small ones: *En Route* and *Devant les Tisons*. I see perfectly well that they are not good, but it begins to look like something.

I have a model almost every day, an old porter, or some working man, or some boy, that poses for me. Next Sunday I shall perhaps have one or two soldiers that will sit for me. And because I am now no longer in a bad humour, I have quite a different and better opinion of you, and of the whole world in general. I have also made again a drawing of a landscape; a heath, a thing I had not done for a long time . . .

✳ ✳ ✳

To Theo   (142)
Brussels, 4 February 1881

. . . From father I hear that without my knowing it you have sent me money for a long time, in this way helping me effectually to get on. Receive my hearty thanks for it I firmly believe that you will not regret it; in this way I learn a handicraft, and though it certainly will not make me rich, I will at any rate earn my fr. 100 a month, which is the least one needs to live on, as soon as I become a better draughtsman and get some regular work . . .

This winter I have spent let us say fr. 100 a month, though in reality it has scarcely been as much. And from that I spent a great deal on drawing materials and also got myself some clothes. I bought, namely, two workmen's suits of rough black velvet, of that material known as veloutine. That looks well, and one can appear everywhere in it; besides they will be of use to me afterwards, because I shall want a great many workman's clothes, as I already do now for my models, which of course I need like everybody else. By and by, I must make a collection to that effect, of all kinds of dresses, second-hand if necessary, men's as well as women's; but of course I need not do all this at once, though I have started it, and go on with it . . .

Uncle Cor so often helps other draughtsmen, would it be so unnatural now if some day, when I needed it, he would show me his goodwill? I do not say this however to get some financial help from him. In quite another way than by giving money, he would be able to help me, for instance, if it were possible to bring me in contact with persons from whom I could learn many things, or for instance to help me to get regular work for some magazine. In this way I talked it over with father; I noticed that people talked about the strange and unaccountable fact, that I was so hard up, and yet belonged to such and such a family . . .

So I wait for your reply . . . and in the meantime I work with Rappard.

Rappard has painted some good studies, among others a few after the models at the Academy, which are well done. A little more fire and passion would do him no harm, a little more self-confidence and more courage . . .

✳ ✳ ✳

To Theo (143)
Brussels, 12 April 1881

As I heard from father that there is a chance of your being in Etten next Sunday, and that it would be well for me to be there also, I start thither today.

So I hope to meet you soon, and am longing for it very much, also because I have sketched two drawings at Rappard's, *The Lamp Bearers*, and *The Bearers of the Burden*, and I should like to consult with you how to go on with them. To finish them I must have somehow, the necessary models, and then I trust the result will be good, that is I shall have a few compositions to show to Smeeton Tilly, or to the editors of the *Illustration* or the like.

So I leave today and tell you this, so that you will not look out for me at Brussels. I should like to make a few sketches of the heath at Etten, that is the reason I start a few days earlier.

So I hope to meet you soon, and now shake hands with you in thought . . .

Vincent would stay at his father's vicarage at Etten for six months, daily practising his drawing and growing in confidence.

✳ ✳ ✳

To Theo (146)
Etten, undated [Summer 1881]

. . . You must know that Rappard has been here for about twelve days, and now he is gone. Of course he sends you his best regards. We have taken many long walks together, have been, for instance, several times to the heath, near Seppe, to the so-called Passievaart, a big swamp. Rappard painted there a large study (1 metre by 50), it was not bad. Besides that he has made about ten small sepias, also in the Liesbosch.

While he was painting I made a drawing in pen and ink, from another spot in the swamp, where all the water-lilies grow (near the road to Roozendaal) . . .

I bought Cassagne: *Traité d'Aquarelle*, and am studying it; even if I should not make any water-colours I shall probably find many things in it, for instance, about sepia and ink. For until now I have exclusively drawn in pencil accented by the pen, sometimes a reed pen, which has a broader stroke.

What I have been drawing lately demanded that way of working, because the subjects required much *drawing*, drawing in perspective too, for instance, a few workshops in the village here, a forge, a carpenter's shop and sabot-maker's.

To Theo (148)
Etten, undated [Summer 1881]

. . . It would not be right, if in drawing from nature I took up too many details and overlooked the great things. And that was too much the case in my last drawings I thought. And therefore I want to study again the method of Bargue (who gives only great lines and forms, and simple delicate outlines). And for the moment I leave off drawing outdoors. When I shall go back to it shortly, I shall have a better view of things than before.

I do not know if you ever read English books, if so I can strongly recommend you to read *Shirley* by Currer Bell [Charlotte Brontë], author of another book called *Jane Eyre*. It is as beautiful as are the pictures by Millet or Boughton or Herkomer . . .

I think I shall find a good model here in Piet Kaufman, the gardener, but I think it will be better to let him pose with a spade or plough or something like that, not here at home, but either in the yard or in his own home or in the field. But what a tough job it is to make people understand how to pose. Folks are desperately obstinate in this respect, and it is hard to make them yield on this point; they only want to pose in Sunday clothes, with impossible folds in which neither knees, nor elbows, nor omoplates, nor any other part of the body have left their characteristic dents or bumps. Indeed that is one of the *petites misères de la vie d'un dessinateur* . . .

✳ ✳ ✳

To Theo (149)
Etten, undated [Summer 1881]

I just came back from a trip to the Hague . . .

I went to see Mr Tersteeg, Mauve and de Bock. Mr Tersteeg was very kind, and said he thought I had made progress. As I had again copied the whole series *Exercices au Fusain* [by Bargue], 1–60, I had brought them with me, and it was especially in reference to these that he made the remark . . .

With Mauve I spent an afternoon and part of an evening, and saw many beautiful things in his studio. My own drawings seemed to interest Mauve more. He has given me a great many hints, which I was glad to get, and I have arranged with him to come back to see him, in a relatively short time, when I shall have new studies.

He has shown me a whole lot of his studies and explained them to me, not sketches for drawings or pictures, but real studies, seemingly of little importance. He thinks I should now start painting.

I enjoyed meeting de Bock; I was at his studio. He is painting a large picture of the dunes that has much that is fine in it. But the fellow must practise figure drawing, and then he will produce still better things I think . . .

❋ ❋ ❋

To Theo (150)
Etten, August 1881

. . . there has come a change in my drawing, in my technique as well as in its results. In reference also to some things Mauve told me, I have begun to work from the living model again . . .

Five times over I have drawn a man with a spade, *Un Bêcheur*, in different positions, twice a sower, twice a girl with a broom. Then a woman with a white cap who is peeling potatoes, and a shepherd leaning on his staff, and finally an old sick farmer sitting on a chair near the hearth, with his head in his hands, and his elbows on his knees. And of course I shall not stop at that, when a few sheep have crossed the bridge the whole flock follows. Diggers, sowers, ploughers, male and female, that is what I must draw continually. I have to observe and to draw everything that belongs to country life . . .

From the Hague I brought some crayon in wood (like pencil) and that is what I use most just now. I also begin to touch up my work with a brush and stump, with a little sepia and India ink, and now and then with a little colour. It is a fact that the drawings I have made lately resemble very little those I used to make until now . . .

Above all I should like to have a woman pose with a seed basket, to draw that little figure which I showed you last spring, and which you see in the foreground of the last sketch.

Well, as Mauve calls it, 'the factory is in full swing'.

❋ ❋ ❋

To Theo
Etten, August 1881

. . . I will tell you now what I have been doing since I wrote you last.

In the first place two large drawings, (crayon and a little sepia) pollard-willows.

If one draws a willow as if it were a living being, and it really is so after all, then the surroundings follow in due course, if one has only concentrated all one's attention on that same tree, and does not give up until one has brought some life into it . . .

PART FOUR

Passion and Duty

Etten September–December 1881 – *The Hague* December
1881–September 1883

While Vincent spends the summer of 1881 at his parents' vicarage at Etten, and is working hard on his drawing, a cousin from Amsterdam comes to stay with them. She is Cornelia Adriana Vos-Stricker (referred to as 'K.' in his letters). She is a young widow with a small son. She is beautiful and attractive and grateful for the attention Vincent shows her little boy. So a kind of friendship arises which on Vincent's side becomes a passionate love, not in the least returned by K, for she is too much engrossed in her recent loss to think of a new love.

This disappointment, which Vincent never recovers from, brings a great change in his life. Etten becomes an unbearable place and, at the end of the year, he moves to the Hague.

Here he has valuable advice and lessons from his relative by marriage Anton Mauve, an artist and member of the Hague school of painters. Vincent perseveres with his artistic work, but his kind-heartedness brings him endless problems. He becomes involved with his model, a charwoman and part-time prostitute, Clasina Maria Hoornik (referred to in his letters as Christine, Sien and lastly 'the woman'). She has an illegitimate child and another on the way. Vincent takes her in, and while he enjoys the domesticity of family life, his finances become increasingly strained as do relations with his family – his father, his Uncle Mauve and even his brother Theo – and artist friends of his own class, as well as Mr Tersteeg, his former employer at Goupil's, on whom he relies for advice and contacts. At one point he is admitted to hospital with – as later biographers suspect – venereal disease. Finally he has to make a choice between 'the woman' and his art.

Etten, 3 September 1881

There is something in my heart that I must tell you; perhaps you know about it already and it is not new for you. I want to tell you that this summer a deep love has grown in my heart for K., but when I told her this, she answered me that, to her, past and future remained one, so she never could return my feelings.

Then there was a terrible indecision within me what to do. Should I accept her 'no, never never', or considering the question as not finished or decided, should I keep some hope and not give up?

I chose the latter. And up to now I do not repent of that decision, though I am still confronted by that 'no, never never'. Of course since that time I have met with many 'petites misères de la vie humaine' . . .

However, until now I am glad that I left the resignation of the 'how not to do it' system to whoever may like it, and for myself kept some courage.

One of the reasons why I did not write to you about it before is that my position was so vague and undecided, that I could not explain it to you. But now we have reached the point where I have spoken about it, besides to her, to father and mother, to Uncle and Aunt S., and to Uncle and Aunt at Prinsenhage.

The only one who told me, but very officiously and in secret, that there really was some chance for me, if I worked hard and had some success, was somebody from whom I did not expect it in the least: Uncle Vincent. He had rather liked the way in which I took K.'s 'no, never never' – not taking it too seriously, but rather in a humorous way. Well, I hope to continue to do so, and to keep melancholy and depression far from me, meanwhile working hard, and since I have met her I get on much better with my work.

I told you that my position has become more sharply outlined; I think I shall have the greatest trouble with the elder persons, who consider the question as settled and finished, and will try to force me to give it up. For the present I believe they will be very considerate to me, and keep me dangling and put me off with fair promises, until the silver wedding of Uncle and Aunt takes place in December. Then I fear measures will be taken to cut me off.

K. herself thinks she will never change her mind, and the elder people try to convince me that she cannot, yet they are afraid of that change. The elder people will only change in this affair, not when K. changes her mind, but when I have become somebody who earns at least fr. 1000 a year. Again forgive me the harsh outlines in which I draw things. You will perhaps hear it said about me, that I try to force the situation, and similar expressions, but who would not understand that forcing is absurd in love. No, that intention is far, very far from me. But it is no unreasonable or unjust desire to wish that K. and I might see each other, speak to each other, and write to each other, in order to become better acquainted, and in this way to get a better insight into whether we are suited for each other or not.

A year of free intercourse with each other would be beneficial for both of us, but the elder people are really obdurate on that point.

But now you understand that I hope not to leave a single thing undone, that may bring me nearer to her, and it is my intention:

> To love her so long
> Till she'll love me in the end.

Theo, are you perhaps in love too? I wish you were, for believe me, even the little miseries of it have their value . . .

✳ ✳ ✳

To Theo (154)
Etten, 7 September 1881

This letter is for you alone, you will keep it to yourself, will you not?

In the first place I must ask you, if it astonishes you in the least that there is a love serious and passionate enough, not to be chilled by many 'no, never nevers'?

I suppose far from astonishing you, this will seem very natural and reasonable.

For love is something positive, so strong, so real that it is as impossible for one who loves to take back that feeling, as it is to take his own life. If you answer this by saying: 'But there are people who put an end to their own life,' I simply answer you this: 'I really do not think I am a man with such inclinations'.

Life has become very dear to me, and I am very glad that I love. My life and my love are one. 'But you are confronted by a "no, never

72

never"', is your reply. And my answer to that is: 'Old boy, for the present I consider that "no, never never" as a block of ice that I press to my heart to thaw it.'

Do you think it considerate of the family to insinuate that I must be prepared to hear soon, that she has accepted another richer suitor, that she has become quite handsome, and will no doubt be asked in marriage, that she has a positive dislike to me, if I go further than 'brother and sister' (that was the utmost limit), that it would be such a pity if 'meanwhile (!!!) I let a better chance go by (!!!) . . .'

But she has loved another, and her thoughts are always in the past, and she seems to have conscientious scruples, even at the thought of a possible new love. But there is a saying, and you know it: 'Il faut avoir aimé, puis désaimé, puis aimer encore.'

'Aimez encore: ma chère, ma trois fois chère, ma bien aimée – '

I saw that she always was thinking of the past and buried herself in it with devotion. Then I thought: though I respect that feeling and though it touches and moves me, that deep grief of hers, yet I think there is some fatalism in it.

So it must not weaken my heart, but I must be resolute and firm, like a steel blade. I will try to raise 'something new', which does not take the place of the old, but has a right to a place of its own.

And then I began, at first crudely, awkwardly, but still firmly, and I finished with the words: K. I love you as myself – then she said: 'no never never' . . .

Then in that inexpressible anguish of soul, rose a thought in me like a clear light in the night, namely this: whosoever can resign himself, let him do so, but he who has faith let him believe! Then I arose, not resigning but believing, and had no other thought than 'she, and no other' . . .

So I remain calm and confident through all this, and that influences my work, which attracts me more than ever, just because I feel I shall succeed. Not that I shall become anything extraordinary, but 'ordinary', and then I mean by ordinary, that my work will be sound and reasonable, and will have a right to exist, and will serve to some end. I think that nothing awakens us to the reality of life so much as a true love . . .

❋ ❋ ❋

. . . Father and mother are very good at heart, but have little understanding of our inward feelings, and of your real circumstances as little
as of mine. They love us with all their hearts – you especially, and we
both, I as well as you, love them very much indeed, but alas, practical
advice they cannot give us in many cases, and there are cases where
with the best intentions they do not understand us. That is not our fault
or theirs, but it is the difference in age and difference in opinion, and
difference in circumstances . . . But that our home is and remains our
resting-place, come what may, and that we must appreciate it, and
from our side respect that home, there I quite agree with you, though
perhaps you did not expect such a candid declaration from me . . .

Now it is one of the little miseries of human life for me, that I cannot
go once in awhile to see her, or write to her, and that some people, who
might have a good influence to undermine that 'no, never never', on
the contrary further that 'no, never never'. I wish that she found no
sympathy anywhere for her 'no, never never', and that everyone would
join in efforts to bankrupt that 'no, never never'. That they would quite
reduce it to a monument of warning to other 'no, never never'-saying
ladies, and to the encouragement of those that say: 'aimer encor'. But
we have not arrived as far as that.

I should like it very much if you could persuade father and mother
to less pessimism, and to more good courage and humanity, for they
are awfully pessimistic, and call what I did this summer 'premature and
indelicate' . . .

They want me to stop all correspondence, for instance with Uncle
and Aunt, of course I cannot promise such a thing, and even if I might
stop writing for some time, I would certainly start again with new
vigour afterwards.

She refuses to read my letters but – but – but the frost and the winter
cold are too bitter to last very long . . .

Since I really love there is more reality in my drawings, and I sit
writing to you now in the little room with quite a collection around me
of men, women and children from the 'Heike', etc. . . .

✻ ✻ ✻

To Theo   (156)
Etten, undated [Autumn 1881]

. . . Since the beginning of this love I felt, that unless I gave myself up
to it entirely, without afterthought, without any restriction, with all my
heart, entirely and for ever, there was no chance for me whatever, and
even so my chance is slight. But what is it to me whether my chance is
slight or great? I mean must I consider this when I love? No – no reckoning, one loves because one loves.

To love – *quelle chose!* . . .

I sent you a few drawings, because, I thought you might find something of Brabant in it.

Now tell me why they do not sell, and how can I make them
saleable? For I should like to earn now and then some money for a railroad ticket so as to go and fathom that 'no, never never' . . .

Theo, all fathers of girls possess a thing which is called the key to the
front door. A very terrible weapon, which can open and shut the front
door before mentioned, like Peter and Paul open the gates of heaven.
Well, does this instrument also fit the heart of the respective daughters
in question? Does that open or shut with the key of the front door? I
think not, but God and love alone can open or shut a woman's heart.
Will hers ever open, brother, will she ever let me in? – God knows, I
cannot tell . . .

✳ ✳ ✳

To Theo   (157)
Etten, 12 November 1881

. . . Theo, if you were in love with the same sort of love as I, and, boy,
why should you ever have another kind of love, then you would
discover something quite new in yourself. Such as you and I, who as a
rule generally associate with men, and you in a large way and I in a
small, attend business of some kind, well, we are used to do most of our
work with our brains – with a certain diplomacy, with a certain sharp
calculation. But now fall in love, and look here, you will perceive to
your astonishment that there is still another force that urges us on to
action, that is the heart.

We are sometimes rather inclined to ridicule it, but it cannot be denied to be true, that especially when in love one says: I do not go to my head to ask my duty in this case, I go to my heart.

What kind of love was it I felt when I was twenty? It is difficult to define, my physical passions were very weak then, perhaps because of a few years of great poverty and hard work. But my intellectual passions were strong and I mean thereby that without asking anything in return, without wanting any pity, I only wanted to give, but not to receive. Foolish, wrong, exaggerated, proud, rash, for in love one must not only give, but also take, and reversing it, one must not only take but also give. Whoever deviates either to the right or to the left, he falls, there is no help for it. So I fell, but it was a wonder that I got up again. What helped me more than anything else to recover my balance was the reading of practical books on physical and moral diseases. I got a deeper insight into my own heart and also into that of others. By and by I began to love my fellow-men again, myself included, and more and more my heart and soul revived, that for a time through all kinds of great misery, had been withered, blighted and stricken. And the more I turned to reality, and mingled with people, the more I felt new life reviving in me, until at last I met *her* . . .

If I had had other motives when I proposed to her, she would have despised me, and now she does not despise me. But my third page is almost full and I have still something to ask. Boy, I must see her face again, and speak to her once more; if I do not do so soon, something will happen at the silver wedding that would perhaps do me great harm. Do not ask me to define what. If you were in love too, you would understand it; because you are not in love I would not be able to make it clear to you.

Theo, I want money for the trip to Amsterdam; if I have but just enough I go. Father and mother have promised not to oppose me in this, if I only leave them out of the matter, as it were. Brother, if you will send it to me, I will make lots of drawings for you from the Heike, and whatever you want . . .

✳ ✳ ✳

To Theo   (158)
Etten, 18 November 1881

If I could not give vent to my feelings now and then, I think the boiler would burst.

I must tell you something which if I had to keep it to myself would perhaps upset me, but if I can make a clean breast of it it will perhaps not be so bad. As you know father and mother on one side and I on the other do not agree about what must be done or not done in regard to a certain 'no, never never'.

Well, after having heard for some time the rather strong expressions, 'indelicate and untimely' (just fancy that you were in love and they called your love indelicate, would you not have proudly resented it, and said: stop), this had ceased at my emphatic request not to use those expressions any more, but another term came up.

They say now 'that I am breaking up family ties'.

The fact that I 'wrote letters' was the real grievance against me. But when they persisted in using so rashly and recklessly that miserable expression 'breaking up family ties', I did the following.

For a few days I did not speak a word or take any notice of father and mother. Against my wish, but I wanted to make them feel how it would be if those family ties were really severed.

Of course they were astonished at my behaviour, and when they asked me about it I answered: See, *that is how it would be* if there were no tie of affection between us, but happily it does exist and will not soon be broken so easily. But I beg you, consider now how miserable that expression, 'breaking up of ties' is, and do not use it any more.

But the result was that father grew very angry, ordered me out of the room with a curse, at least it sounded exactly like it! When father gets in a passion he is used to having everyone give in to him, even I, but now I was quite determined to let him rage for once. In anger father also said something, that I had better leave the house and go elsewhere; but because it was said in a passion I do not attach much importance to it . . .

✳ ✳ ✳

To Theo   (159)
Etten, Friday evening, Autumn 1881

. . . No, no, no, there is something wrong, it cannot be right that they want to put me out of the house just at this moment. There is no excuse for it and it would thwart me in my work. So I cannot allow it to go on. What would she think if she knew what happened this morning? She is

77

so tender and kind that it pains her to say one unkind word, but if one so soft, so tender, so loving as she is roused – *piquées au vif!* then woe to those who are the cause of this anger.

May it not be against me her anger is roused, dear brother. I think she begins to understand that I am neither thief nor criminal, but, on the contrary, am inwardly more quiet and sensible than I outwardly appear. She did not understand that in the beginning, at first she really had an unfavourable impression of me, but now I do not know why, while the sky becomes clouded and overcast with quarrels and curses, there rises light from her side . . .

✳ ✳ ✳

To Theo   (161)
Etten, 23 November 1881

. . . Now in regard to the 'case in question' as Uncle S. calls what happened between K. and me, I must tell you that I have risked an attack on Mr. S. above mentioned. By means of a registered letter; I was afraid unregistered letters would be ignored, but this one he will be obliged to read, and in it I have tried to draw his attention to some points which I fear he overlooked, or which he would take no notice of. It is a very 'undiplomatic' letter, very bold, but I am sure it will at least make an impression on him. But perhaps at first it will cause him to use a certain expletive which he certainly would not use in a sermon.

There really are no more unbelieving and hard-hearted and worldly people than clergymen and especially clergymen's wives (a rule with exceptions). But even clergymen have sometimes a human heart under an armour of triple steel.

But I am in a terrible suspense and am quite ready to go to Amsterdam, but as the journey is very expensive I may not waste my powder, and the trip to Amsterdam is my reserve if my letter has no effect . . .

I have sent Mauve a drawing of a man who digs potatoes in the field; I wanted to give him some sign of life from me. I wish he would come soon. As soon as he will have seen my studies I will send you some again. If you do not like my writing you so often and so long, then say stop, but perhaps there will soon come another reason for stopping, for instance when all the time that remains for correspondence will have to be devoted to *her*. These long letters will not continue for ever.

It is so curious that I am entirely in the dark about what happens at Amsterdam: I mean that I do not know anything, but only *feel*. How can one feel things at a distance? Aye, I can give you no explanation of that, but only fall in love yourself, and then you will perhaps also hear voices in the distance, and see little things which make you surmise larger ones, as one guesses there is a fire from seeing the smoke. Luckily the weather is warm and calm, that has a beneficial influence on people. If it were biting cold with a north wind my 'case in question' would be worse off.

Meanwhile the silver wedding of Uncle and Aunt S. is approaching, father and mother intend to go there. I am very glad you have written to them before that time, for I would rather not have them come out with their 'conscientious objections' about 'the untimeliness and indelicacy' of my love . . .

Vincent moved briefly to the Hague in the autumn of 1881 so that he could take lessons from Mauve.

✳ ✳ ✳

To Theo   (162)
The Hague, December 1881

. . . And Mauve gives me hope that perhaps I shall soon make something that is saleable. Mauve said: 'I always thought you a dullard, but now I see that it is not so,' and I can assure you that this simple word of Mauve pleased me more than a cartload full of Jesuitical compliments would have done . . .

'Meanwhile' I have been to Amsterdam. Uncle S. was rather angry though he gave vent to it in more polite words than 'damn you'. But notwithstanding this I am not sorry that I paid that visit. What must be done now, for you know I came back no less in love than I went, but not because she had encouraged me; on the contrary, she made me for a moment, or rather for twenty-four hours, profoundly miserable; but when I thought it over I seemed to see some light after all. When I thought it over I say, and that is more than romanticism or sentimentality does. But it looks less and less like gathering strawberries in spring, well the strawberries will no doubt come in due time . . .

I am afraid you sometimes cast aside a book because it is too realistic. Have pity and patience with this letter and read it through, though it may be rather crude.

As I wrote you from the Hague I have some things to talk over with you, now that I am back here. My trip to the Hague is something I cannot remember without emotion. When I came to Mauve my heart palpitated a little for I said to myself: Will he also try to put me off with fair promises, or shall I be treated differently here? And I found that he helped me in every way, practically and kindly, and encouraged me. Not however by approving of everything I did or said, on the contrary. But if he says to me: 'this or that is not right', he adds at the same time: 'but try it in this or that way', which is quite another thing than to criticize just for the sake of criticizing. If somebody says to you: 'you are ill', that does not help you much, but if he says, 'do this or that and you will recover', and his advice is no sham, that is the thing that will help you.

So when I left him I had a few painted studies and a few water-colours. Of course they are no masterpieces, but still I believe that there is something sound and true in them, at least more than in what I have made before. And so I think this is the beginning of my making serious things. And as I now have a few more technical resources at my disposal, namely, paint and brush, all things seem as it were new to me.

But – now we must put that in practice. And then the first thing is I must find a room large enough to be able to take sufficient distance.

When Mauve saw my studies he said at once: 'you are sitting too close to your model'. That makes it in many cases almost impossible to take the necessary measures for the proportion, so that it is certainly one of the first things I must attend to. So I must try to rent a large room somewhere, either a room or a barn.

Just think how I have been struggling along for years in a kind of false position. And now, now there comes a dawn of real light. I wish you could see the two water-colours which I brought with me, for you would see they are water-colours like any other water-colours. There may be many imperfections in them; I will be the first to admit that I am very much dissatisfied with them, but still they are quite different from what I made before, and look more bright and clear, but that does not exclude the fact that others in the future may become brighter and clearer still, but one cannot do right away what one wants. It will come gradually.

But though Mauve tells me that after having struggled on for a few more months and then coming back to him, say in March, I shall then make saleable drawings, still I am now in a very difficult period. The expenses for model, studio, drawing and painting materials increase and I do not earn anything as yet.

It is true father has said that I need not worry about the necessary expenses, and father is very happy with what Mauve told him, and also with the studies and drawings that I brought back. But I think it very miserable indeed that father will have to pay for it. We hope of course that it will turn out all right, but still it is a heavy load on my mind. For since I have been here father has not by any means profited by me, and more than once he has bought for instance a coat or a pair of trousers for me, which I would rather not have had, though I needed them, but I do not want father to spend money. The less so because the coat or trousers in question do not fit, and are only of little or no use at all. Well that is again one of the little miseries of human life. Besides, as I told you before, I hate not to be quite free . . . Father cannot sympathize with, or understand me and I cannot be reconciled to father's system – it oppresses me – it would choke me . . . all that rubbish about good and evil, morality and immortality, I care so very little for it. For indeed it is impossible always to know what is good and what is bad, what is moral and what is immoral. The morality or immorality brings me involuntarily back to K. . . .

And on a certain evening I strolled along the Keizersgracht looking for the house and I found it. I rang the bell and heard that the family were still at dinner. But then I was asked to come in. But they were all there except K. And each had a plate before them, but there was not one too many and this little detail struck me. They wanted to make me believe that K. was out, and had taken away her plate, but I knew that she was there, and I thought this rather like a comedy or a farce. After sometime I asked (after the usual greeting and small talk): 'But where is K.?' Then Uncle repeated my question, saying to his wife: 'Mother where is K.?' And mother answered 'K. is out'. And for the moment I did not inquire further . . . But after dinner the others disappeared and Uncle S. and his wife and the undersigned remained alone and settled down to discuss the case in question. Uncle S. opened the discussion as clergyman and father, and said that he was just about to send a letter to the undersigned, and that he would read that letter aloud. But I asked again: 'Where is K.?' (for I knew that she was in town). Then Uncle S. said 'K. left the house as soon as she heard that you were here.' Well I know her somewhat, but I declare that I did not know then nor do I know with certainty now, whether her coldness and rudeness was a good or a bad sign. This much I do know, that I never saw her so apparently or really cool, brusque and rude to anyone but me. So I did not say much and remained very calm.

Let me hear that letter, or not hear it, I said, I don't care much about it.

Then came the letter. The document was very reverend and very learned, there was really nothing in it, but that I was requested to stop my correspondence and the advice was given me to make very energetic efforts to put the thing out of my mind. At last the reading of the letter was finished. I just felt as if I had heard the clergyman in church after prancing up and down, with his voice say amen; it left me just as cool as an ordinary sermon.

And then I began, and said as calmly and politely as I could: yes I had heard those opinions before – but now – what further? But then Uncle S. looked up. He seemed full of consternation at my not being fully convinced that the utter limit of human capacity for feeling and thinking had been reached. According to him there was no 'further' possible. So we continued, and Aunt M. said a word now and then, and I got somewhat excited and lost my temper. And Uncle S. lost his temper too, as much as a clergyman can do so. And though he did not exactly say 'damn you', any other but a clergyman in Uncle S.'s mood would have said so.

. . . so I shifted my position a little and gave a little, so that at the end of the evening they told me I could stay for the night if I wished. Then I said: 'I am very much obliged, but if K. leaves the house when I come, I do not think it the time to stay here over night; I will go to my lodgings.' And then they asked: 'Where do you stay?' I said; 'I do not know where as yet'; and then uncle and aunt insisted they would take me to a good and cheap place. And dear me, those two old people went with me through the cold foggy, muddy streets, and they showed me indeed a very good and very cheap inn. I insisted on their not coming, and they insisted on showing me the way.

And you see there was something humane in that and it calmed me.

I stayed in Amsterdam for two days and I had another talk with Uncle S., but K. I did not see once, she kept out of my way whenever I came. And I said that they must well know, though they wished me to consider the question as settled and finished, I for my part could not do so. And then they firmly and steadily answered, 'I would learn to see that better afterwards' . . .

I felt quite lone and lorn during those three days in Amsterdam; I felt absolutely miserable . . . Till at last I began to feel quite depressed, and I said to myself: you are not becoming melancholy again, are you?

And then I said to myself: do not let yourself be stunned. And so, on a Sunday morning, I went for the last time to Uncle S. and said: 'Just listen, dear Uncle, if K. were an angel she would be too high for me, and I do not think I could remain in love with an angel. If she were a devil I would not want to have anything to do with her. In the present case I see in her a true woman with a woman's passions and moods, and I love her dearly, and that is the truth and I am glad of it. As long as she does not become an angel or a devil, the case in question is not finished.' And Uncle S. had not much to say in reply, and muttered something about a woman's passions. I do not remember well what he said about it, and then he went to church.

I still felt chilled through and through, to the depths of my soul . . . And I did not want to be stunned by that feeling. Then I thought: I should like to see a woman, I cannot live without love, without a woman. I would not give a farthing for life, if there were not something infinite, something deep, something real. But then I said to myself; you said 'she and no other', and you would go to another woman now, that is unreasonable, that is against all logic . . . I need a woman, I cannot, I may not, I will not live without love. I am but a man, and a man with passions, I must go to a woman, otherwise I freeze or turn to stone, or in short am stunned . . . One cannot with impunity live too long without a woman . . .

And dear me I had not far to seek. I found a woman, not young, not beautiful, nothing remarkable if you like, but perhaps you are somewhat curious. She was rather tall and strongly built, she did not have ladies' hands like K., but the hands of one who works much, but she was not coarse or common, and had something very womanly about her. She reminded me of some curious figure by Chardin or Frère, or perhaps Jan Steen. Well, what the French call 'une ouvrière'. She had had many cares, one could see that, and life had been hard for her, oh,

83

she was not distinguished, nothing extraordinary, nothing unusual. 'Toute femme à tout âge, si elle aime et si elle est bonne, peut donner à l'homme non l'infini du moment, mais le moment de l'infini.' Theo, to me there is such a wonderful charm in that slight fadedness, that something over which life has passed. Oh! she had a charm for me, I even saw in her something of Feyen Perrin or Perugino. You see I am not quite as innocent as a green-horn or as a baby in the cradle. It is not for the first time that I was unable to resist that feeling of affection, aye affection and love for those women, who are so damned and condemned and despised by the clergymen from the pulpit. I do not damn them or condemn them, neither do I despise them . . .

That woman has not cheated me – oh he who regards all those women as cheats, how wrong he is, and how little understanding does he show. That woman has been very good to me, very good, very kind, in what way I shall not tell my brother Theo, because I suspect my brother Theo of having some such same experience. So much the better for him.

And we talked about everything, about her life, about her cares, about her misery, about her health, and with her I had a more interesting conversation than for instance with my very learned, professor-like cousin . . .

It was a modest simple little room where she lived, the plain paper on the wall gave it a quiet grey tone yet warm like a picture by Chardin; a wooden floor with a mat and a piece of old crimson carpet, an ordinary kitchen stove, a chest of drawers and a large simple bed, in short the interior of a real working woman. She had to stand at the wash-tub the next day. Just so, quite right. In a black petticoat and dark blue camisole she would have been as charming to me as she was now in a brown or reddish grey dress. And she was no longer young, was perhaps as old as K. – and she had a child, yes she had had some experience of life, and her youth was gone, gone? – 'il n'y a point de vieille femme'. Oh, and she was strong and healthy – and yet not coarse or common . . .

And dear me, I love K. for a thousand reasons, but just because I believe in life and reality, I do not become abstract as I used to be, when I had the same thoughts as K. seems to have now, about God and religion. I do not give her up, but that crisis of soul anguish in which she perhaps is now, must have its time, and I can have patience with it, and nothing that she may do or say makes me angry. But while she clings and holds to the old things, I must work and keep my mind clear for painting and drawing and business . . .

After a violent row with his father, Vincent moved to The Hague where he would spend almost the next two years.

✳ ✳ ✳

To Theo   (166)
The Hague, Thursday evening [December 1881]

. . . On Christmas I had a violent scene with father and it went so far that father told me I had better leave the house. Well, he said it so decidedly that I actually left it the same day.

The real reason was that I did not go to church, and also said that if going to church was compulsory and if I was *forced* to go, I certainly should never go again out of consideration, as I had done rather regularly all the time I was in Etten.

I was in such a passion as I do not remember having ever been in my life, and I frankly said that I thought their whole system of religion horrible . . .

I went back to Mauve and said: 'listen Mauve, at Etten I cannot stay any longer and I must go and live somewhere else, by preference here.' Well, Mauve said: 'then stay'. And so I have rented a studio here, that is a room and an alcove that can be arranged for that purpose, cheap enough, on the outskirts of the town, on the Schenkweg, ten minutes from Mauve. Father said if I wanted money, he would lend it to me if necessary, but that is impossible now, I must be quite independent from father . . .

You can imagine I have a great many cares and worries. But still it gives me a feeling of satisfaction that I have gone *so* far that I cannot go back again, and though the path may be a difficult one, I now see it clearly before me.

Of course I must ask you Theo, if you will send me now and then, what you can spare, without inconveniencing yourself . . .

✳ ✳ ✳

To Theo   (167)
The Hague, January 1882

. . . De Bock does not improve on further acquaintance, he rather lacks
backbone, and he gets angry when one says some things which are only
the a.b.c. He has some feeling for landscape, he knows how to put some
charm in it . . . but one gets no hold on him. It is too vague, and
thin . . .

*However, Theo did not reply instantly to Vincent's letters. He was appalled by the
manner in which Vincent had quarrelled with their father, and finally wrote back:
'. . . When father wrote to me about it, I thought it might be a misunderstanding,
but you yourself say in your letter: it will not be so easily redressed. Don't you know
him then, and don't you feel that father cannot live as long as there is a quarrel
between you two? Coûte que coûte you must set the matter straight, and I am sure
that some day you will deeply repent having been so heartless in this matter.' . . .*
    Vincent wrote him a long, rambling reply followed by:

❋ ❋ ❋

To Theo   (170)
The Hague, undated [1882]

In my last letter I gave you, as I have done before, a short and concise
answer to some things, but for all that you must not think that I am
always in a freezing unfriendly mood, which Mauve would perhaps call
a green-soap or salt-water mood. Well, and even if I had written a
green-soap or salt-water letter, that would not be worse than if I had
taken it too sentimentally.
    You say: 'you will deeply repent it some day' – my dear boy, I think
I have done much of that repenting before this. I saw it coming and
tried to avoid it; well I did not succeed, and bygones are bygones. Shall
I repent still more, no, I really have no time for repenting. Drawing
becomes more and more a passion with me and it is a passion just like
that of a sailor for the sea.
    [I enclose] a little sketch of one of the smaller water-colours, it is a
little girl who is grinding coffee.
    You see I am seeking for tone, a head or a little hand that has light
and life in it, and that stands out against the drowsy dusk of the back-

ground, and then boldly against it that part of the chimney and stove – iron and stone – and a wooden floor. If I could get the drawing as I want it, I would make three-fourths of it in a green-soap style, and only the corner where the little girl sits I would treat tenderly, softly and with sentiment . . .

Many of the letters which followed were preoccupied with the worry of finding models and the wherewithal to pay for them and keep a roof over his head.

✳ ✳ ✳

To Theo   (171)
The Hague, undated [1882]

. . . So, I have work enough for the week that begins tomorrow, but I am afraid I have not money enough, for fr. 2.50 and a few cents is all I have left. What must I do now; if I go to Mauve or Mr Tersteeg and ask them, I do not think they would refuse me. But Mauve has already done so much, and to Mr Tersteeg I would rather sell a few small drawings than borrow money from him. So answer me soon, and if you can do something, send me some money so that I can work on. I feel, Theo, that there is a power within me, and I do what I can to bring it out and free it . . .

✳ ✳ ✳

To Theo   (172)
The Hague, Sunday evening [1882]

It is true I wrote you only yesterday, but I thought I would write you again. For though I still have a dose of courage left, it is sometimes very hard always to put on a good face before Mauve and Tersteeg and others . . . But it happens often enough that I am quite at a loss what to do. Now this morning I felt so miserable that I went to bed, I had a headache, and was feverish from worry, because I dread this week so much, and do not know how to get through it.

. . . I also have relatively still so few drawing materials or else defective ones. For the present it is sufficient, I have my painting box and easel and brushes, but, for instance, this week my drawing-board warped like a barrel, because it was too thin, and my easel also got damaged in a delivery, which is bad enough. Well, there are a lot of things which I still want or must improve, and of course all that need not be done at once, but it is the cause of daily small expenses which taken altogether worry me a great deal. Sometimes my clothes need repairing, and Mauve already has given me a few hints about that too, which I shall certainly carry out, but it cannot be done all at once. You know my clothes are chiefly old things of yours, that have been altered for me, or a few are bought ready-made and are of poor material. So they look shabby, and especially with all that dabbling in paint it is still more difficult to keep them decent; with boots it is the same. My underwear also begins to wear to shreds. You know that it is already a long time that I have been without means, and then many things get dilapidated. And then it sometimes happens that one becomes involuntarily terribly depressed, be it only for a moment, often just in the midst of feeling cheerful as I really am even now. So it was this morning; these are evil hours when one feels quite helpless and faint with over exertion . . .

✳ ✳ ✳

To Theo   (173)
The Hague, Thursday [1882]

. . . I am so angry with myself now because I cannot do what I should like to do, and at such a moment one feels as if one were lying bound hand and foot at the bottom of a deep dark well, utterly helpless. Now I am better, in so far that I got up again yesterday evening and rummaged around straightening things, and when this morning the model came of her own accord, though I only half expected her, I arranged how to pose her with Mauve and tried to draw a little, but I could not do it, and the whole evening I felt miserable and weak . . .

✳ ✳ ✳

To Theo   (178)
The Hague, 3 March 1882

Since I received your letter and the money, I have had a model every day, and I am head over ears in my work.

It is a new model I have now, though I had drawn her superficially once before. Or rather it is more than one model, for from the same family I have already had three persons, a woman of 45, like a figure by Eduard Frère, then her daughter of about 30 years, and a younger child of 10 or 12. They are poor people and I must say they are more than willing . . .

Tomorrow I have a children's party, two children that I must amuse and draw at the same time. I want some life in my studio, and have all kinds of acquaintances in the neighbourhood. Next Sunday I will have a boy from the Orphanage, a splendid type, but alas I can only have him a short time. It is perhaps true that I cannot get on very well with people who are very conventional, but, on the other hand, I can perhaps get on better with poor or so-called common people . . .

❊ ❊ ❊

To Theo (180)
The Hague, undated [1882]

. . . *Theo, it is almost miraculous!!!*

First comes your registered letter, secondly C. M. asks me to 'make for him twelve small pen drawings, views from the Hague, à propos of some that were ready. (The Paddemoes, de Geest, de Vleersteeg, were finished.) At fr. 2.50 a piece, price fixed by me, with the promise that if they suit him, he will take twelve more at his own price, which will be higher than mine. In the third place I just met Mauve, happily delivered of his large picture, and he promised to come and see me soon. So, 'ça va, ça marche, ça ira encore!'

And another thing struck me – very very deeply – I had told the model not to come today, I did not say why, but nevertheless the poor woman came and I protested. 'Yes, but I do not come to pose, I just came to see if you had something for dinner,' she had brought me a dish of beans and potatoes . . .

❊ ❊ ❊

To Theo (182)
The Hague, undated [1882]

. . . Theo I am decidedly not a landscape painter, when I shall make landscapes *there will always be something of the figure in them* . . .

If you became a painter, one of the things that would astonish you is that painting and everything connected with it, is really hard work from a physical point of view; besides the mental stress, the worry of mind, it requires a rather great exertion of strength, and that day by day.

✱ ✱ ✱

To Theo (184)
The Hague, undated [1882]

. . . C. M. has paid me, and given a new order, but a very difficult one, six special detailed views of the town. However, I will try to make them, for if I understand it right, I will get as much for these six as for the first twelve. And afterwards perhaps he will still want some sketches of Amsterdam . . .

My thanks for the package of splendid Ingres paper and for the studies. Some day when people begin to say that I can draw a little but not paint, I will perhaps suddenly come out with a picture at a moment when they least expect it . . .

There are two ways of considering painting: how not to do it, and how to do it, *how to do it* with much drawing and little colour.

How not to do it, with much colour and little drawing . . .

In the following letter Vincent encloses a drawing [Sorrow], *based on Christine, his new model.*

✱ ✱ ✱

To Theo (186)
The Hague, undated [1882]

The enclosed is in my opinion the best figure I have drawn as yet, therefore I thought I would send it to you.

This is not the study after the model, and yet it is directly after the model. You must know that I had two underlayers under my paper. I had been working hard to get the right contour and when I took the drawing from the board, it had been imprinted quite correctly on the two underlayers, and I finished them immediately from the first study . . .

✳ ✳ ✳

To Theo   (187)
The Hague, undated [1882]

. . . And now, yes I know that mother is ill, and I know many other sad things besides, either in our own family or in others.

And I am not insensible to it, and I think I should not be able to draw *Sorrow* if I did not feel it. But since this summer it has become so clear to me that the disharmony between father, mother and myself has become a chronic evil, because there has been misunderstanding and estrangement between us for too long a time. And now it has gone so far, that from both sides we must suffer for it.

I mean we might have helped each other more, if we had tried on both sides long ago to live in closer understanding and to share weal and woe, always remembering that parents and children must remain one . . .

I have just received a letter from Rappard; I have been for some time 'en froid' with him, but now we are again interested in each other's work. Probably he will soon come to see me . . .

News of the family row had filtered through to Mauve and Tersteeg and their attitude to Vincent changed.

✳ ✳ ✳

To Theo   (189)
The Hague, undated [1882]

. . . Towards the end of January, I think a fortnight after my arrival here, Mauve's attitude towards me changed suddenly – became as unfriendly as it had been friendly before.

I ascribed it to his not being satisfied with my work, and I was so anxious and worried over it, that it quite upset me and made me ill, as I wrote you at the time.

Mauve then came to see me, and gave me again the assurance that everything would come all right, and encouraged me. But then on a certain evening shortly after, he began to speak to me again in such a different way that it seemed as if there was quite a different man before me. I thought: my dear friend, it seems as if they have poisoned your ear with slander, but I was in the dark from which side the poisonous wind had blown. Mauve began among other things to imitate my speech and my manners, saying: 'your face looks like this', 'you speak like this', all in a spiteful way, but he is very clever at those things, and I must say it was like a well resembling caricature of me, but drawn with hatred. On that occasion he said a few things that only Tersteeg used to say about me. And I asked him: Mauve, have you seen Tersteeg lately? 'No', said Mauve, and we talked on, but about ten minutes later, he dropped the remark that Tersteeg had been to see him that same day. Then the thought of Tersteeg involuntarily stayed with me, and I thought: is it possible, my dear Tersteeg, that you are at the back of all this? And I wrote him a note, *not impolite*, deliberately not impolite, I only said to him: sir, I am so sorry when things are said about me, as for instance 'you do not earn your living', or 'you do not work': you must understand such things are too unreasonable to let them pass, and they grieve me to the heart. During the last years I have had too many of such things to grieve me, and I think there must come an end to it now.

And a few times I was told he [Mauve] was not at home, in short there were all the signs of a decided estrangement. I went to see him less and less, and Mauve never came to my house again, though it is not far away.

Mauve also became in his talk as narrow-minded, if I may call it so, as he used to be broad. I had to draw from casts, that was the principal thing, he said. I hate drawing from casts, but I had a few plaster hands and feet hanging in my studio, though not for the purpose of drawing. Once he spoke to me about drawing from casts in such a way as the worst teacher at the academy would not do, and I kept quiet, but when I got home I was so angry that I threw those poor plaster casts in the coal-bin, and they broke in pieces. And I thought: I will draw from casts only when they become whole and white again, and when there are no more hands and feet of living beings to draw from.

I then said to Mauve: man, do not speak to me again about plaster, for I cannot stand it. That was followed by a note from Mauve, that for two months he would not have anything to do with me. During those two months indeed we have not seen each other, but I have not been idle meanwhile, though I have not drawn from casts I can tell you, and I must say I worked with more animation and earnestness now that I was free. When the two months were almost past I just wrote to him to congratulate him on having finished his large picture, and once I spoke to him on the street for a moment.

Now the two months are long since past and he has not come to see me.

✳ ✳ ✳

To Theo (192)
The Hague, undated [1882]

Today I met Mauve and had a very painful conversation with him, which made it clear to me that Mauve and I are separated forever. Mauve has gone so far that he cannot retract, at least certainly would not want to do so. I had asked him to come and see my work and then to talk things over. Mauve refused point-blank: 'I will certainly not come to see you, that is all over.'

At last he said: 'you have a vicious character'. Then I turned around, it was in the dunes, and I walked home alone . . .

This winter I met a pregnant woman, deserted by the man whose child she bore.

A pregnant woman who in winter had to walk the streets, had to earn her bread, you understand how.

I took that woman for a model, and have worked with her all the winter. I could not pay her the full wages of a model, but that did not prevent my paying her rent, and, thank God, I have been able thus far to protect her and her child from hunger and cold, by sharing my own bread with her. When I met that woman she attracted my notice because she looked ill. I made her take baths, and as much nourishing food as I could, she has become much stronger. I went with her to Leyden, where there is a maternity hospital where she will be confined. (No wonder she was ill, the child was not in position, and she had to have an operation, the child had to be turned with forceps. However, there is a good chance of her getting through. She will be confined in June.)

It seems to me that every man worth his salt would have done the same in a similar case.

What I did was so simple and natural, that I thought I could keep it to myself. Posing was very difficult for her, but she has learned it, I have made progress in my drawing because I had a good model. The woman is now attached to me like a tame dove, I for my part can only marry once, and how can I do better than marry her, because that is the only way to help her, and otherwise misery would force her back in her old road, that ends in a precipice . . .

✳ ✳ ✳

To Theo   (193)
The Hague, undated [1882]

. . . I am between two fires – if to your letter I answer: yes, Theo you are right, I will give up Christine; then, in the first place I tell an untruth in agreeing with you, and in the second, I bind myself to commit a vile thing . . .

You see, Theo, I have had enough of it all, think it over and you will understand. Is my path less straight, because somebody says: 'you have gone astray'? . . .

I want to go through the joys and sorrows of domestic life, in order to paint it from my own experience. When I came back from Amsterdam I felt that my love, so true, so honest and strong, had literally been *killed*. But after death there is a resurrection. Resurgam.

Then I found Christine. There was no time to hesitate or to defer. I had to act. If I do not marry her it would have been kinder of me to have let her alone. But by this step a chasm will be made, I decidedly 'lower' myself, as they call it, but that is not forbidden, that is not wrong, though the world calls it so. I live as a labourer. That suits me, I wanted to do so before, but could not then carry it out. I hope that across the chasm you will continue to stretch out your hand to me. I mentioned fr. 150 a month, you said that I needed more.

Now I want to lay a straight path for my feet. If I postpone marriage there is something crooked in my position that is repulsive to me. She

94

and I will skimp and be as saving as possible, if we can only marry. I am thirty years old and she is thirty-two, so we are children no longer. As to her mother and her child, the latter takes away all stain from her, I respect a woman who is a mother and I do not ask after her past. I am glad that she has a child, that gives her exactly the experience she needs . . .

Acquainted with the prejudices of the world, I know that what I have to do is to retire from the sphere of my own class, which anyhow cast me out long ago. But that is all they can do, and they may go no further . . .

✳ ✳ ✳

To Theo   (194)
The Hague, undated [1882]

. . . Perhaps I can understand her better than anyone else, because she has a few peculiarities, that would have been repulsive to many others.

First her speech, which is very ugly and is a result of her illness, then her temper caused by a nervous disposition, so that she has fits of anger that would be unbearable to most people.

I understand those things, they do not bother me, and until now I have been able to manage them. She on her part understands my own temper, and it is like a tacit understanding between us not to find fault with each other . . .

Every day she learns better how to pose, and that is worth *so* much to me. She is no trouble, no hindrance, but she helps and she works with me. She has no pretensions, of wanting this or that, but when there is nothing but bread and coffee, she puts up with it and does not complain . . . As soon as she comes back from Leyden I will marry her, without telling anyone, quietly and without any fuss. Then we would be glad to have that house and we are prepared to live as simply as possible . . .

I wish her confinement were over, that is a heavy ordeal that still awaits her. But so far everything goes well, since that visit to Leyden . . .

Theo was clearly not happy with Vincent's ideas of marrying Christine.

✳ ✳ ✳

To Theo (197)
The Hague, undated [1882]

. . . after what happened with Mauve and Tersteeg, and after what I told you about Christine, I must ask you frankly: Theo, do these things make a change or separation between you and me? If it does not, I would be so happy, and will be twice as glad for your help and sympathy as before, if it does, it is better for me to know the worst than to be kept in suspense . . .

✳ ✳ ✳

To Theo (198)
The Hague, undated [May 1882]

. . . The person who is the father of Christine's first child argued exactly in the same way as your letter Theo, and in my opinion it is quite wrong. He was very kind to her, but did not marry her, even when she was with child by him, for the sake, as he said, of his rank and his family, etc. Christine was young then, and had met him after her father's death. She did not know what she knows now, and when he died, there she was all alone with her child, stranded without a penny. She had to walk the streets à contre cœur, fell ill, was brought to a hospital, all kinds of miseries . . .

✳ ✳ ✳

To Theo (199)
The Hague, undated [May 1882]

Because Christine suffered from cramps, etc., I thought it would be well for her to go once more to Leyden to find out exactly how things are. She has been there and has come back already, thank God she is all right, but as you know in March she had an operation, and has now again been examined. She needs care and must continue to have strengthening food and also some more baths if possible, but there are no complications, and there is every chance she will get through it.

In March the professor could not tell exactly when her confinement would be, but he thought it would be the end of May or the beginning of June. Now he says it will be late in June probably, and has changed her admission ticket to the hospital for the middle of June. This time he asked her many questions about whom she was living with and from what he said about it I know now for sure what I had guessed, that she would die if she had to walk the street again, and when I met her this winter it was but just in time to give her the needed help.

So, as I wrote you, I do not think of leaving her, for under that circumstances that would be a mean trick . . .

✳ ✳ ✳

To Anton van Rappard (9R)
The Hague, Sunday evening 1882

I have just put my drawings into the package for Amsterdam, as agreed. There are seven in all. The bigger of the two *Little Courts* is now quite flat after I mounted it on Bristol-board, and it now has more rapidity of line. Then there is the *Flower Nursery*, which I changed the way you suggested, that is, I studied the side of the ditch and the water in front of it and it really shows to advantage now, and expresses spring, I think, and a certain gentle calmness.

And the one of the *Carpenter's Shop* – from the window of my studio – I brought a new blackness into it, by working on it with the pen, and now 'the sun shines' because the lights are more expressive. Today I was at it quite early because I wanted to make another drawing and went among the dunes to draw a fish-drying barn seen from a height, like the *Carpenter's Shop*, and it is now nearly one o'clock in the morning, but thank the Lord everything is finished and I can look my dangerous landlord in the face. And so *ça ira encore*.

I was so glad to have seen you again, and what you told me about your work interested me very much, I assure you. I do so hope that we can arrange a few trips in this neighbourhood some time soon. I think you would find good material in these fish-drying barns. They really are marvellous – like Ruysdael (I mean it is something like his bleaching-fields of Overveen) . . .

Do you know the *Wayfarers* by Fred Walker? It is a large etching – an old blind man led by a boy along a frozen road on a winter evening, alongside is a ditch in which is frosted wood. It really is one of the most sublime creations in that genre – with quite a peculiarly modern sentiment to it. Perhaps less powerful than Dürer in *Ritter, Tod, und Teufel*, but maybe more intimate, and certainly as original and real.

It is a pity that the artists here know so little of the English. Take Mauve, for example; he was so enthusiastic when he saw a landscape by Millais, *Chill October*; but they have no faith in English art and their judgment is too superficial, I think. Mauve says all the time: 'That is literary art', but he does not stop to think that the English writers like Dickens and Ellis and Currer Bell [Emily and Charlotte Brontë] and, amongst the French, Balzac are so plastic, if I may express it thus, that they are as potent as Herkomer or Fildes or Israëls. And Dickens himself sometimes uses the expression '*I have sketched*'.

I myself hate scepticism and sentimentalism; I do not want to insinuate that the artists here are sceptical or sentimental, but sometimes they make it appear so – although in regard to nature they are serious and faithful, so I really have no right to criticize them, especially as I catch myself leaning towards sentimentality more than is my intention.

So much that is beautiful and picturesque is disappearing these days! I lately read something by the son of Charles Dickens; he said: 'If my father should return, he would find little of the London he described and called "Old London"; it is passing and is cleared away.' It is the same in our country – instead of the nice little courtyards, there appear rows of houses which are very unpicturesque, except when they are in the stage of construction. *Then* one has good things to look at: barns, scaffolding and workers. There is a street here behind the Bazar Street and de Laan van Meerdervoort, where I have seen beautiful things: spaces which were being dug out or filled in, barns, lumber, cabins, fences and many similar things.

What attracts me is the common people's kitchens and the third-class waiting-rooms. If I did not have to make my living by drawing views of the city, I would do nothing but figures of that type, but as I have not yet found customers for them and have the expense of the models, I cannot do it, but I must say that there are people who will gladly pose for me for nothing.

I am delighted with my present model, I mean that old woman; you saw her when you were here. Sometimes things don't go well and I get annoyed and swear; she learns better every day and understands me. For instance, when things go wrong, I fly into a temper, saying

'Goddamn!' etc. – as strong language as that – and I get up, etc. But she does not take it as a personal insult as so many naturally would; she lets me calm down and we start all over again. And she is patience itself in seeking the right pose. When I need to compare the height of a figure outside, as for instance on the beach with a fishing-boat as background, or when I have to catch the correct light, all I need to say is: 'Be there at such a time', and she is surely there.

Of course people gossip because I am always in her company, but why should that bother me? I have never had such good assistance as this ugly, haggard old woman's. In my eyes she is beautiful, and she is just what I want. She has lived, and sorrow and suffering have marked her – now I can find a use for her.

When the earth is not ploughed, you cannot plant anything in it; she has been ploughed and is useful, so she is worth more than many others, I mean 'unploughed' ones.

I hope you'll write me again soon, and if you agree, I would like to correspond regularly, if our work permits it, provided we warn each other should our 'practical' chats become 'unpractical' and we must not feel hurt at a warning such as was given in the case of Mr Tersteeg and myself, as I told you.

I am going again tomorrow to the drying-barns on the dunes.

A while ago I read the book on Millet written by his friend Sensier; it is very interesting and I can recommend it if you haven't yet read it. Much that can be known only to intimate friends is revealed in it, and there surely is a great deal that is new in it, at least I think so, and I had already read much about M. before I read this book. Well, adieu, with a handclasp.

❈ ❈ ❈

To Theo   (200)
The Hague, undated [May 1882]

. . . Yesterday I received a kind letter from father and mother which would please me very much if I could only believe that this feeling would continue . . .

❈ ❈ ❈

To Theo (202)
The Hague, 27 May 1882

Today, Saturday, I had a visit from Rappard, and I am glad he has been here. He asked after you many times. He saw among others the drawings which I am making for C. M. and they seemed to please him, especially a large one of that yard where Sien's [Christine's] mother lives.

. . . But, brother, it has been a hard fortnight for me. When I wrote to you about the middle of May I had only fr. 3 or fr. 3.50 left after I had paid the baker; and I have had hardly anything to eat but dried black bread with some coffee, and Sien also. Because we had bought some things for the baby and she had been to Leyden, etc.

Now the first of June I have to pay the house rent and I have nothing, literally nothing. I hope you will send something . . .

* * *

To Theo (204)
The Hague, 1 June 1882

. . . Now I am glad that you told me frankly what your thoughts were about Sien, viz. that she intrigues, and I let myself be fooled by her . . .

The case with Sien is that I am really attached to her, and she to me, she has become a faithful help who follows me everywhere, and becomes more indispensable every day.

My feeling for her is less passionate than what I felt for K. last year, but a love like that for Sien is the only thing I am still capable of, after having been disappointed in that first love. She and I are two unhappy ones who keep together and carry our burdens together, and in this way unhappiness is changed to joy, and the unbearable becomes bearable. Her mother is a little old woman exactly like Frère paints them. Now you understand quite well that I would not care much for the formality of marriage, if the family did not care for it, if I only remained faithful to her. But father I know for sure attaches great importance to this, and though he will not approve of my marrying her, he would think it still worse if I lived with her without being married . . .

* * *

To Theo (205)
The Hague, undated [June 1882]

. . . I have had news from C. M. in the form of a postal order for fr. 20, but without one written word. So I do not know as yet whether he will give me a new order or whether the drawings are to his liking. But in comparison with the price paid for the first one, fr. 30, and taking into consideration that this last package (the first contained twelve little ones, this one contained one small one; four like those I now send you; two large ones; so in all seven pieces) was more important than the first, it seems to me that C. M. was not in a good mood when he received them, or for some reason or other they did not please him . . .

✳ ✳ ✳

To Theo (206)
City Hospital, Brouwersgracht, undated [June 1882]

. . . When you come perhaps towards the end of June you will find me at work again I hope, but for the time being I am at the hospital, where I shall stay only a fortnight however. Already for three weeks I have suffered from insomnia and low fever, and bladder trouble.

So I have to stay quietly in bed here, must swallow many quinine pills, and also have injections now and then, either of pure water or with alum water; so it is as harmless as can be. Therefore you need not worry at all about it . . .

Sien comes to see me on visiting days and keeps an eye on the studio. Now you must know that the day before I came here I received a letter from C. M. in which he writes a whole lot about the 'interest' he feels for me, and which he says Mr Tersteeg has also shown me, but he did not approve of my having been so ungrateful to Tersteeg for his interest. It may be so. I am lying here calmly and quietly enough, but I can tell you, Theo, that I should certainly lose my temper if some person or other came to see me again with the kind of interest which Tersteeg showed me on certain occasions. And when I think how he pushed his interest so far as to dare to compare me with an opium smoker, then I am still astonished that I on my part did not show him my interest in the form of 'damn you' . . .

101

To Theo   (207)
City Hospital, undated [June 1882]

Few things have given me so much pleasure lately as hearing from home, things that set my mind at ease about their feelings towards me. Sien came to tell me that a parcel had been delivered at the studio, and I told her to go and open it and see what was in it, in case of a letter, to bring that with her; so I learned that they have sent a whole package of things, underwear and outer clothing, and cigars, and in the letter was also enclosed fr. 10. I cannot tell you how it touched me, it is much more than I expected, but they do not know everything as yet.

I am but weak and feeble, Theo, and I need absolute, absolute rest in order to recover, so everything that makes for peace is welcome . . .

Sien probably goes next Monday, for I think now she is better off in the hospital, and about the middle of June she will be admitted there. But she wanted to stay here for me, only I would not allow that . . .

✳ ✳ ✳

To Theo   (208)
City Hospital, 22 June 1882

. . . I have still to tell you that father came to visit me during the first days I was here, though it was but a short and very hurried visit, and I have not been able to speak seriously with him. I would have preferred his visiting me at another time when on both sides we could have enjoyed it more. Now it was very strange to me and seemed to me more or less like a dream, as does this whole affair of lying ill here . . .

✳ ✳ ✳

To Theo   (209)
The Hague, 1 July 1882

I have just got back to my studio and write to you at once. I cannot tell you how delightful it is to be better again, nor can I tell you how beautiful all things appeared to me on the way from the hospital; and how the light seemed clearer and the spaces more infinite and every object and figure more important . . .

To Theo   (210)
The Hague, undated [July1882]

. . . I have been to Leyden. Sien was confined last night, she has had a
very difficult time, but, thank God, her life has been saved and a very
nice little boy too . . .

∗ ∗ ∗

To Theo   (215)
The Hague, undated [July1882]

Friday I received the tidings from the hospital at Leyden that Sien
might come home Saturday, so I went there today and we came home
together, and now she is here on the Schenkweg and so far all is well,
both she and the baby. She can nurse it and the baby is quiet.

How I wish you could have seen her today. I assure you her appearance had quite changed since this winter, it has been a complete trans-
formation . . .

∗ ∗ ∗

To Theo   (216)
The Hague, Tuesday morning [July1882]

This time I have to tell you something about a visit from Mr Tersteeg.
This morning he came here and saw Sien and the children. I would
have wished that he showed a kind face to a young little mother just out
of child-bed. But that was asking too much.

Dear Theo, he spoke to me in a way that you can perhaps imagine.
'What was the meaning of that woman and that child?'
'How could I think of living with a woman, and children in the
bargain?' . . .

∗ ∗ ∗

To Theo (218)
The Hague, undated [July1882]

. . . Today I made a drawing of the baby's cradle with a few touches of colour in it.

I hope I shall able to draw that little cradle *persistently* a hundred times more, not counting what I did today.

✳ ✳ ✳

To Theo (219)
The Hague, Sunday morning [July1882]

. . . You must imagine me sitting before my attic window as early as four o'clock in the morning, studying, with my perspective instrument, the meadows and the Yard, when they are lighting the fires to make the coffee in the little cottages, and when the first workman comes loitering into the Yard. Over the red tile roofs a flock of white pigeons comes soaring between the black smoky chimneys. But behind it all, a wide stretch of soft tender green, miles and miles of flat meadow, and over it a grey sky, as calm, as peaceful, as Corot or van Goyen.

This view over the gabled roofs with the grass-grown gutters, at early day, and those first signs of life and awakening, the flying birds, the smoking chimneys, and that figure loitering far below in the Yard – this is the subject of my water-colour. I hope you will like it . . .

In answer to your letter I must say one thing, that your not knowing about Sien's child was not my fault, for when I told you about her I certainly mentioned it, but you probably thought of the child that was not then born . . .

✳ ✳ ✳

To Theo (220)
The Hague, Wednesday morning[July1882]

. . . When you come I know a few beautiful paths through the meadows, where it is so quiet and calm, that I am sure you will like it. I discovered there old and new labourers' cottages and other houses that are charac- teristic, with little gardens by the waterside, very pretty. I will go and draw there early tomorrow morning. It is a road that runs through the meadows of the Schenkweg to Enthoven's factory or the Zieke.

I saw there a dead willow trunk, just the thing for Barye for instance. It was hanging over a pool that was covered with reeds, quite alone and melancholy, and its bark was moss-grown and scaly, something like the skin of a serpent – greenish, yellowish, but for the greater part a dull black, with bare white spots and knotted branches. I am going to attack it tomorrow morning . . .

The less I get on with people the more I learn to have faith in nature and to concentrate on her.

All those things make me feel brighter and fresher – you will see that I am not afraid of a bright green or a soft blue, and the thousands of different greys, for there is scarcely any colour that is not grey – red-grey, yellow-grey, green-grey, blue-grey. This is the substance of the whole colour scheme . . .

❋ ❋ ❋

To Theo (221)
The Hague, 31 July 1882

. . . I have attacked that whopper of a pollard-willow, and I think it is the best of the water-colours – a gloomy landscape – that dead tree near a stagnant pool covered with reeds, in the distance a car shed of the Ryn railroad, where tracks cross each other, dingy black buildings, then green meadows, a cinder path, and a sky with drifting clouds, grey with a single bright white border, and the depths of blue where the clouds are parted.

. . . It is the painter's duty to be entirely absorbed by nature and to use all his intelligence to express sentiment in his work so that it becomes intelligible to other people. To work for the market is in my opinion not exactly the right way . . .

❋ ❋ ❋

To Theo (223)
The Hague, undated [August 1882]

In my last letter you will have found a little sketch of that perspective instrument I mentioned. I just came back from the black-smith, who made iron points to the sticks and iron corners on the frame.

It consists of two long poles; the frame is attached to them lengthwise or across with strong wooden pegs.

So on the shore or in the meadows or in the fields one can look through it *as through a window*. The vertical lines and the parallel line of the frame and the diagonal lines and the cross or else the division in squares, certainly give a few principal points, by the help of which one can make a firm drawing, which indicates the large lines and propor-tions – at least for those who have some instinct for perspective and some understanding of the reason why and the manner in which the perspective gives an apparent change of direction to the lines and a change of size to the planes and to the whole mass . . . I think you can imagine it is a delightful thing to point this instrument on the sea, on the green meadows, or in winter on the snowy fields, or in autumn on the fantastic network of thin and thick branches and trunks or on a stormy sky.

With long and continuous practice it enables one to draw quick as lightning, and once the drawing fixed, also to paint quick as lightning.

In fact, *for painting* it is absolutely the thing . . . sky-earth-sea – one needs the brush, or rather in order to express all that in drawing it is necessary to know and to understand the treatment of the brush. I certainly believe that if I paint for some time, it will have great influ-ence on my *drawing*. I already tried it in January, but then I had to stop, the reason decidedly being, except for a few other things, that I was too hesitating in my drawing. Now six months have passed that have been quite devoted to drawing. Well, it is with new courage that I start again to paint . . .

I bought a pair of strong and warm trousers, and as I had bought a pair of strong shoes just before you came, I am now prepared to weather the storm and rain. It is my decided aim to learn from this painting of landscape a few things about *technic* which I feel I need for *figure*, namely, to express different *materials*, and the *tone* and the *colour*. In one word, to express the bulk – the body – of things. Through your coming it became possible to me, but before you came there has not been a day that I did not think in this way about it . . .

Enclosed a small scratch of the Meerdervort Avenue. Those

vegetable gardens there have a kind of old Dutch character which always greatly appeal to me . . .

✳ ✳ ✳

To Theo   (225)
The Hague, 15 August 1882

. . . Now, since I have bought my paint and brushes, I have drudged and worked so hard on seven painted studies, that just now I am dead tired. There is among them one with a figure in it, a mother with her child, in the shadow of a large tree, in tone against the dune, on which the summer sun is shining – almost an Italian effect.

I simply could not restrain myself or keep my hands off it or allow myself any rest . . .

✳ ✳ ✳

To Theo   (226)
The Hague, Saturday evening [August 1882]

. . . It is the painting that makes me feel so happy these days. I restrained myself up to now, and stuck to drawing just because I know so many sad stories of people who threw themselves headlong into painting – who sought it in the technique and awoke disillusioned, without having made any progress but having become head-over-ears in debt from the expensive things they had spoiled . . .

There are in the colours hidden things of harmony or contrasts that involuntarily combine to work together and which could not be possibly used in another way . . .

✳ ✳ ✳

To Theo   (228)
The Hague, Sunday morning [August 1882]

. . . I am absorbed with all my strength in painting; I am absorbed in colour – until now I have restrained myself, and I am not sorry for it. If I had not drawn so much, I would not be able to catch and get hold of a figure that looks like an unfinished *terre cuite*. But now I feel myself on the high sea – the painting must be continued with all the strength I can give to it . . .

✻ ✻ ✻

To Theo (234)
The Hague, Monday morning [1882]

. . . Now I must still tell you that I had quite unexpectedly a very pleasant visit from father, at my house and at the studio, this I think infinitely better than that he should hear about me through others.

If people come to see me, well, then their impression is at least original, but I do not like opinions that are founded on what people say . . .

I was really very glad to see father and to talk to him. I heard again a great deal about Nuenen [his new parish], the churchyard with the old crosses. I cannot get it out of my head. I hope I shall be able to paint it some day . . .

✻ ✻ ✻

To Theo (236)
The Hague, Sunday [1882]

. . . Just fancy, I received this week to my great surprise a parcel from home, containing a winter coat, a pair of warm trousers and a warm woman's coat. It touched me very much . . .

✻ ✻ ✻

To Theo (242)
The Hague, undated [Autumn 1882]

. . . At times I feel a great longing to be in London again. I should so much love to know more about printing and woodcuts.

I feel a power in me which I must develop, a fire that I may not quench, but must keep ablaze, though I do not know to what result it will lead me, and shouldn't wonder if it were a gloomy one . . .

Today I have been working at old drawings from Etten, because I saw in the fields the pollard-willows again in the same leafless condition, and it reminded me of what I saw last year. Sometimes I have such a longing to make landscape, just as I crave a long walk to refresh myself, and in all nature, for instance in trees, I see expression and soul as it were . . .

✳ ✳ ✳

To Theo   (246)
The Hague, Wednesday morning [1882]

Together with this letter you will receive the first proofs of a lithograph, *A Digger*, and of a lithograph of a *Man who Drinks Coffee*. I should like to hear as soon as possible what you think of them. I intend still to re-touch them on the stone, and for that I want your opinion about them.

The drawings were better. I had worked hard on them, especially on the digger, now by transferring them on the stone and by printing, several things got lost.

But what I think of these prints is that there is something rough and unconventional in them that I wanted there, and this partly reconciles me to the loss of things that were in the drawing.

The drawing was not done only with lithographic chalk but was touched up with autographic ink. Now the stone has only partly caught that autographic ink, and we do not know to what reason it must be ascribed, probably to the water with which I diluted it.

At all events I have seen from it that where the ink caught, it gives strong black tones with which I hope to get better results afterwards. Then when the printer has more time, we will make experiments by bringing a kind of wash over it during the printing, and we will try different kinds of paper and different kinds of printing ink . . .

✳ ✳ ✳

To Theo   (251)
The Hague, undated [1882]

. . . The real thing is not an absolute copy of nature, but to know nature so well that what one makes is fresh and true, that is what is lacking in many.

Do you suppose, for instance, that de Bock knows what you know, no, very decidedly not. You will say that everybody has seen landscapes and figures from childhood on. The question is: has everybody also been reflective as a child, has everybody who has seen them loved also heath, fields, meadows, woods, and the snow and the rain and the storm? *Not* everybody has done that like you and I, it is a peculiar kind of surroundings and circumstances that must contribute to it, it is a peculiar kind of temperament and character too, which must help to make it take root . . .

✳ ✳ ✳

To Theo   (255)
The Hague, undated [December 1882

Before the year is gone, I feel I have to thank you again for all your help and friendship.

I haven't sent you anything for a long time, but I am saving for the time when you will come here.

I am sorry that I haven't succeeded this year in making a saleable drawing. I really do not know where the fault lies . . .

✳ ✳ ✳

To Theo   (256)
The Hague, undated [31 December 1882

. . . Please do not let it worry you that I have made nothing saleable this year, you once said the same thing to me, and if I say so now, it is because I see in the future a few things within my reach which I didn't see before. I sometimes think of a year ago when I came here to the Hague. I had imagined that the painters formed a kind of circle or society where warmth and cordiality and a certain kind of harmony reigned. This seemed to me quite natural and I didn't suppose it *could* be different.

Neither should I want to lose the ideas I had about it then, though I must modify them and distinguish between what is and what might be.

I cannot believe it a natural condition that there is so much cool-ness and disharmony. What's the reason, I do not know – and I am not called to investigate it, but I keep to the principle that I, for myself, must avoid two things, the first is that one must not quarrel, but instead of that, try to promote peace for others as well as for oneself. And the other is, in my opinion, that if one is a painter, one must not try to be something else than a painter in society; as a painter one must avoid other social ambitions and not try to be in the movement with the people who live in the Voorhout, Willemspark, etc. For in the old smoky dark studios there was a cosiness and originality that was infinitely better than what threatens to come in its stead . . .

✳ ✳ ✳

To Theo   (257)
The Hague, 3 January 1883

. . . When you come sooner or later, I can show you more and we can then speak about the future. You know well enough how little I am fit to cope either with dealers or with amateurs, and how contrary it is to my nature. I should like it so much if we could always continue as we do now, but it often makes me sad that I must always be a burden to you. But who knows if in time it will not come about so that you will be able to find someone who takes an interest in my work, who will take from your shoulders the burden which you took upon yourself at a most difficult time. This could only happen *then* when it has been quite proven that my work is serious, when it will speak for itself more clearly than it does now.

I am too fond of a very simple life for me to wish to change this but later on, in order to do greater things, I shall have greater expenses too. I think I shall always work with a model – always and always . . .

Theo had met a young woman, alone and sick, in Paris and had befriended her. He wrote to Vincent confiding in him. Vincent was very touched but in desperate straits himself, still had to ask for money.

✳ ✳ ✳

111

To Theo   (259)
The Hague, undated [1883]

... Well, it would certainly be a good thing if I could have extra, would
it be possible? I hesitate to ask it because you just wrote me that about
yourself, and I understand perfectly it brings you cares which I respect
and with which I sympathize. But the thing with me is that by working
so hard I got somewhat in arrears, and when I receive the money I
have to pay out at once more than half of it. I *cannot* live more econom-
ically than we do, I have economized wherever possible, but the work
develops, especially these last weeks, and I can hardly master it any
longer, that is to say the expenses it brings. Would it be possible for you
to send me a little more? I think you will understand it when you see
the studies. Well, forgive me for speaking about it, but I cannot do
otherwise, I am in arrears for the daily expenses, and that is the cause
of my being absolutely without a cent before the tenth day ...

✳ ✳ ✳

To Theo   (260)
The Hague, undated [1883]

... At this moment the woman with the children are sitting with me.
When I think of last year there is a great difference. The woman
[Sien] is stronger and stouter, has lost very very much of her agitated
air, the baby is the prettiest, healthiest, merriest little fellow you can
imagine, he crows like a cock, gets nothing but the breast, but is fat
and chubby ...

And the poor little girl, you see from the drawing that the former
deep misery has not been wiped out, and I often feel anxious about her,
but still she is quite different from last year, then it was very very bad,
now she is looking more childlike already.

Well, though not exactly quite normal, the situation is much better
than I dared to hope last year. And when I think it over, would it have
been better then, that the mother had had a miscarriage or that the
baby should have withered or pined away through want of milk, that
the little girl would have been more and more neglected and unclean,
and the woman herself would have got into an almost unutterably
miserable condition?

Well, when I see all this, I may not doubt any more, and I say: Forward, in good courage. In the woman, something simple, really motherly, shows itself – and as that gets stronger she is saved . . .

❋ ❋ ❋

To Theo (263)
The Hague, 3 February 1883

. . . I feel very weak of late. I am afraid I have been overworking myself, and how miserable are those 'dregs' of the work, that depression after over-exertion. Life has then the colour of dish-water; it becomes something like an ash-heap.

On such a day one would like to have the company of a friend . . .

On such days I am sometimes terribly worried about the future and am melancholy about my work, and feel quite helpless . . .

❋ ❋ ❋

To Theo (264)
The Hague, 5 February 1883

. . . Lad, I still feel but poorly, and I've had a very decided warning that I must be careful – my eyes felt so tired sometimes, but I wouldn't pay any attention to it. Now, last night, especially, there was a rather strong secretion of the tear glands, and the lashes stuck together, and my sight has been dim and troubled.

Ever since the middle of December I have been drudging incessantly, especially on those heads. This last week I have been out of doors a good deal to refresh myself. I have taken baths, washed my head often with cold water, etc., etc. But at such a time one feels so miserable, I have a large pile of studies – but they don't interest me then, and I find them all bad . . .

❋ ❋ ❋

To Theo   (265)
The Hague, 8 February 1883

. . . What a mystery life is, and love is a mystery within a mystery. It certainly never remains the same in a literal sense, but the changes are like the ebb and flow of the tide and leave the sea unchanged.

Since I wrote you last, I have given my eyes some rest and it has done me good, though they still ache now and then.

Do you know what I have been involuntarily thinking, that in the first period of a painter's life one unconsciously makes it very hard for oneself – by a feeling of not being able to master the work – by an uncertainty as to whether one will ever master it – by a great ambition to make progress, by a lack of self-confidence – one cannot banish a certain feeling of agitation, and one hurries oneself though one doesn't like to be hurried . . .

I sometimes think I will make an experiment, and try to work in quite a different way, that is, to dare more and to risk more, but I think that first I absolutely must study more the figure directly from the model . . .

Sometimes I cannot believe that I am only thirty years old, I feel so much older . . .

✳ ✳ ✳

To Theo   (266)
The Hague, undated [1883]

. . . I have often walked on the Geest of late, in those streets and alleys where I often walked with the woman last year, in the beginning. The weather was damp, everything was beautiful there then, and when I came home I said to the woman, 'It is still just the same as last year.' I tell you this because you spoke of disenchantment, no, no, it is true there is a withering and budding in love as in nature, but nothing dies entirely. It is true there is an ebb and flood, but the sea remains the sea. And in love, either for a woman, or for art, there are times of exhaustion and impotence, but there is no lasting disenchantment.

I consider love as well as friendship not only a feeling but an action, and as such, it demands exertion and activity, of which exhaustion and impatience are the consequence.

A sincere and true love is blessed, I think, though that doesn't prevent occasional hard times . . .

At times I regret that the woman with whom I live can understand neither books nor art. But (though she decidedly cannot do so) my being still so much attached to her, is that not a proof that there is something sincere between us? Perhaps she will learn it later on, and it may strengthen the bond between us, but now with the children you understand her hands are full already. And, through the children especially she comes in contact with reality and learns involuntarily. Books and reality and art are for me alike. Somebody who stood outside real life would bore me, but somebody who is right in it, knows and feels naturally.

If I did not look for art in reality, I should probably find her stupid, now I rather wish it were otherwise, but am after all contented with things as they are . . .

❋ ❋ ❋

To Theo   (269)
The Hague, undated [1883]

. . . Here follow a few curious sayings about water-colours: 'L'aquarelle est quelque chose de diabolique,' and the other is by Whistler, who said: 'Yes, I have done that in two hours, but I've studied for years in order to be able to accomplish this in two hours.'

Enough of this, I love water-colour too well ever to give it up entirely, I come back to it again and again. But the foundation of everything is the knowledge of the figure, so that one can draw readily men and women and children in every possible action . . .

❋ ❋ ❋

To Theo   (271)
The Hague, undated [1883]

. . . I have a burning desire in me to push on, and to make progress. There is another thing spurring me on, namely, that Rappard also works at full speed, more than he used to do, and I want to keep up with him, because then we'll get on better together and can profit more from each other . . .

To Theo (273)
The Hague, undated [1883]

I didn't intend to write so soon again – but as you know I am trying to make different kinds of drawings. And now today again, I made another sketch with the rest of that little piece of crayon – and afterwards washed in it with sepia. I think I find in crayon all kinds of qualities which make it an excellent means to express things from nature . . . Though this sketch is not sufficiently so, that little bit of sepia made so much difference in the general effect that I thought you could see in it, in connection with the one of yesterday, how that crayon can be used in different ways. I wrote yesterday to Rappard about the crayon, because I had to write him about different things of lithography, and as I wanted to send him a few sketches done with it, I used it for some drawings of our baby, in different positions, and I found it is very well fit for sketching too. One also can bring in demi-tones by means of bread-crumbs. Perhaps only the very deepest shadows cannot be very well done with it, but in many cases, one can use lithographic chalk then, which is also very rich in tone . . .

✳ ✳ ✳

To Theo (274)
The Hague, undated [1883]

. . . Now I have to tell you still about the surprise I have had. I received a letter from father, very cordial and cheerful, it seemed to me, with twenty-five guilders enclosed. Father wrote he had received some money, on which he had no longer counted, and he wanted me to share in it. Wasn't that nice of him, however, it quite embarrasses me.

But, involuntarily, a thought came into my mind. Can it be, perhaps, that father has heard, from someone or other, that I was very hard up? I hope that this was not his motive, for I think this idea of my circumstances would not be correct. And it might give father anxieties which would be quite out of place. You will understand my meaning better than father would if I should try to explain it to him.

In my opinion, I am often *rich as Croesus*, not in money, but (though it doesn't happen every day) rich, because I have found in my work something to which I can devote myself with heart and soul, and which gives inspiration and zest to life.

Of course my moods vary, but I have a certain average serenity. I have a certain *faith* in art, a certain confidence that it is a powerful stream, which drifts a man to the harbour . . .

❋ ❋ ❋

To Theo   (275)
The Hague, undated [1883]

. . . It was wonderfully beautiful with the snow and peculiar skies. But today the thawing of the snow was perhaps even more beautiful . . .

❋ ❋ ❋

To Theo   (277)
The Hague, undated [1883]

. . . I have a sower – a mower – a woman at the wash-tub – a woman miner – a seamstress – a digger – a woman with a spade – the almshouse men – a bénédicité – a fellow with a wheelbarrow full of manure. There are still more, if necessary, but I think you will under-stand that the very making of them, the looking at the models, the thinking it over, do not make one satisfied with one's work, but just the contrary, that is, one says – yes, that same thing, but better still and more serious . . .

❋ ❋ ❋

To Theo   (278)
The Hague, undated [1883]

. . . Lately I have been working with printer's ink, which is diluted with turpentine and applied with a brush. It gives very deep tones of black. Diluted with some Chinese white, it also gives good greys. By adding more or less turpentine, one can even wash it in very thinly . . .

❋ ❋ ❋

To Theo   (279)
The Hague, undated [1883]

. . . A woman, no matter how good and noble she may be by nature, if she has no means, and is not protected by her own family, in my opinion, in the present society, she runs a great immediate danger of being drowned in the pool of prostitution. What is more natural than to protect such a woman, and if it can be done in no other way, if circumstances lead to it, well, then, if *il faut y mettre sa peau*, and marry her.

At least I think one must, on principle, carry on that protection till she is definitely safe, to shield her with one's own breast, as it were. Even without real love?

Perhaps so – then it is a marriage of rationality maybe, but not in the sense of a marriage for selfish reasons. In what I have just said, you will find my thoughts about the question, 'How far one may go in helping an unfortunate woman?' The answer is: infinitely. However, in granting that in love, the first and principal thing is to be faithful, I remind you of your own saying, that 'Marriage (that is, the civil marriage) is such a queer thing.' This saying of yours expresses exactly how it is, and on that point I declare I do not know what is better or worse, to keep to it or not. It is what they call puzzling, it puzzles me, too, and I wish one could leave it out altogether. I think it well said 'If one marries, one doesn't marry only the woman herself, but the whole family into the bargain', which is sometimes awkward and miserable enough, when they are a bad set . . .

✻ ✻ ✻

To Theo   (280)
The Hague, undated [1883]

. . . I have full confidence that love, when true, cannot die, at least not where at the same time one acts with judgment. But I would like to scratch this out again, because it isn't correct, for love can certainly die – but there is a strength of revival in love . . .

✻ ✻ ✻

. . . As to what I wrote you about relations between women and their mothers, I can assure you, in my case, nine-tenths of the difficulties which I had with the woman originated directly or indirectly therein.

And yet those mothers are not exactly bad, though they act absolutely wrongly.

But they do not know what they are doing.

Women of about the age of fifty are often distrustful, and perhaps it is that very distrust and cunning that entangles them . . .

Do you know what I should prefer in the matter of relations between the woman and her mother – in my case where it has decidedly bad consequences – that the mother came to live with us entirely

I proposed it this winter, when the mother was very hard up . . . When your money arrived this morning, I had been without money – absolutely without a penny, for about a week. Besides, all my drawing material was exhausted. I was negotiating with Smulders about a lot of drawing-paper and took it, though the expense did not suit me at all now; but I wanted it absolutely, together with other materials, for instance, the printer's ink of the engravers, and lithographic chalk. And I had to pay for several things for the household and to lay up provisions. And had to pay models, which I had had meanwhile, in order to be able to work on. I am very, very sorry I have to ask for it, but if it is just possible, send me another ten francs. A week's work depends on it . . .

✳ ✳ ✳

. . . As the professor who confined her [Sien], told me, it will take years before the woman has completely recovered her health. That is to say, the nervous system remains very sensitive, and she possesses, in a high degree, the variableness of women.

The great danger is – as you will understand – her falling back in former errors. This danger, though of moral nature, is connected with the physical constitution. And what I should like to call oscillations between improvement and falling back to former bad habits, they worry me continually and seriously. Her temper is at times so, that it is almost unbearable even for me, violent, mischievous, bad. I can tell you I am sometimes in despair.

The little boy, however, does very well; the girl has formerly been very ill and neglected.

But the little chap is a miracle of vitality, seems to oppose himself already now against all social institutions and conventions. As far as I know, all babies are brought up on a kind of bread porridge. But this he has refused most energetically; though he has no teeth as yet, he bites resolutely at a piece of bread, and swallows all kinds of eatables with much laughing and cooing and all kinds of noises: but for porridge he absolutely keeps his mouth shut. He often sits with me in the studio on the floor in a corner, on a few sacks; he crows at the drawings and is always quiet in the studio, because he looks at the things on the wall. O, he is such a dear little fellow! . . .

❋ ❋ ❋

To Theo (285)
The Hague, undated [1883]

. . . Rappard has been here, and I borrowed 25 guilders from him, promising to pay them back in the autumn. I was very glad to see him – he came in the morning and stayed till the last train in the evening, and we spent the whole day looking at the studies and drawings, and he also made a sketch in printer's ink and turpentine, just to see what it was like. Now I go tomorrow to him, to see his work and his studio. It was a real pleasant day; he was rather changed both in appearance and in manners. I for my part, like him now much better than before.

He has become broader in his shoulders and I think broader in his views, on many things, too . . .

❋ ❋ ❋

To Theo (288)
The Hague, undated [1883]

. . . Theo, do you know what were the difficulties I had with the woman, when I wrote to you last – *her* family tried to draw her away from me; except with the mother I have not meddled with any of them, because I did not trust them. The more I tried to analyse the history of that family, the more I was strengthened in that opinion. Now, just because I kept out of their way, they plot against me and made a treacherous attack. I told the woman my opinion about their intentions, and said she had to choose between her family and me, but that I did not want any intercourse with any of them, in the very first place, because I thought that relations with her family would lead her back to her former bad life. The proposition of the family was that she, with her mother, should keep house for a brother of hers, who divorced his wife, and is rather an infamous scoundrel. The reason why the family advised her to leave me was, that I earned too little, and I was not good to her, and did it only for the posing, but would certainly leave her in the lurch . . .

✳ ✳ ✳

To Theo (295)
The Hague, undated [1883]

. . . Your letter came yesterday and was no little welcome. Many thanks. I was very hard up this time; I was absolutely penniless. The woman had no milk to nurse the baby those last days, and I too felt very faint. As a last effort I went in my desperation to Tersteeg. I thought I have nothing to lose by it, perhaps it is rather a way to bring about a better state of affairs; so I went there with a large sketch, about which I wrote to you in my last letter. I made of it a row of diggers, men and women, with a foreground of dumps of earth, and a glimpse of some roofs of a little village in the background. I said to Tersteeg that I understood perfectly well this sketch could not be anything for him, but that I came to show it him, because it was so long since he had seen anything of my work, and because I, for my part, wanted to give a proof that I did not feel any ill-will about what had happened last year. Well, he said that he did not carry any ill-will either; as to the drawing, he had told me last year that I ought to make water-colours, and he did not want to speak about it again, in order not to repeat himself. Then I told him that I had tried a water-colour now and then and had several of them in my studio, but that I myself had more heart for another kind of drawing, and felt more and more passion for strongly drawn figures . . .

He said he was glad to see from the drawing that I was at least working, and I asked him if there was any reason for him to doubt that I was working. Well, then a telegram came for him, and I went away . . .

✳ ✳ ✳

To Theo   (297)
The Hague, undated [1883]

. . . I have on hand a sower in a large field, with clumps of earth, which I think is better than the other sowers I tried before.

I have at least six more of them, as study for the figure alone, but now I have put him in a surrounding more especially as a real composition, and I have carefully studied earth and sky besides.

Then I have studies for the burning of weeds, and a man with a sack of potatoes on his back, and one with a wheelbarrow. When I think of Tersteeg's opinion, that I must make water-colours and, supposing I myself am wrong, try with all goodwill to change my mind, yet I cannot understand how these figures of the man with the sack, of the sower, of the old potato digger, of the wheelbarrow, of the man who burns weeds, would retain their personal character, if I made them in water-colour.

The result would be very mediocre . . .

✳ ✳ ✳

To Theo   (299)
The Hague, undated [1883]

. . . The thing which I should love immensely to make, which I feel I can make, provided certain circumstances of serious posing, is the figure of father on a path through the heath; the figure seriously drawn, with character, and I repeat a patch of brown heath through which a narrow white sand path leads, and a sky just delicately tinged, yet somewhat passionately brushed.

Then father and mother arm in arm – in an autumn landscape or against a hedge of beeches with withered leaves . . .

What I want to make is a drawing that will not exactly be understood by everyone: the figure essentially simplified with determinate neglect

122

of those details which do not belong to the real character, and are only accidental. For it must not be a portrait of father, but rather the type of a poor village clergyman who goes to visit the sick. In the same way, the couple arm in arm against the hedge of beeches, must be the type of a man and a woman who have grown old together in love and faith rather than the portraits of father and mother; though I hope they will pose for it . . .

✳ ✳ ✳

To Theo   (301)
The Hague, undated [1883]

. . . I am almost sorry to have started painting again, for if I cannot carry it through I wish I hadn't begun it. I can't do without colours, and colours are expensive, and because I owe still a little to Leurs and Stam I cannot get more on credit. And yet I love painting so . . .

✳ ✳ ✳

To Theo   (302)
The Hague, Sunday night [1883]

. . . I have in fact no other friend but you, and when I am in low spirits, I always think of you. I only wish you were here, that we might consult once more together about moving to the country.

Except what I told you, there is nothing particular the matter with me, and things are going well – but perhaps I am a little feverish or so, I feel miserable. I had to pay right and left, landlord, paint, baker, grocer, shoemaker, Heaven knows what, and but little is left. But the worst is, that after many such weeks, one feels one's power of resistance diminishing, and is overcome by a great feeling of weariness . . .

Things are looking dark just now. If it were only for me, but there is the thought of the woman and the children, poor creatures which one would keep safe, and feels responsible for . . .

✳ ✳ ✳

123

To Theo   (304)
The Hague, undated [1883]

. . . If I can get over my physical weakness, I will try and make progress.
I have put off again and again to take some nourishing food, because I
had to provide for others and for the work. But now I am at my wits'
end; no progress in my work can be expected before I am somewhat
stronger. I have seen but too clearly of late that my physical condition
influences it. I assure you that it is nothing but a prostration from over-
work and too little nourishment. Some people who have spoken about
me as if I had some kind of disease, would start it again, and that is a
slander of the worst kind, so keep it to yourself without speaking about
it when you come here. But the meagreness in my work is relatively a
thing apart, and will change when I can get well again. That what I
most long for is your coming, and that we may look over the work
together, and see each other again . . .

✳ ✳ ✳

To Theo   (307)
The Hague, undated [1883]

. . . [Enclosed] is a scratch of the path to the beach.
    During the walk, my thoughts were with you all the time . . .

✳ ✳ ✳

To Theo   (309)
The Hague, undated [1883]

. . . it is miserable enough that I still feel very faint, when I am not right
at my work, but I believe it is passing away. I will decidedly try hard to
lay up a provision of strength, for I shall need it to carry on the painting
of the figure with a firm hand.
    While painting, I feel of late a certain power of colour awakening in
me, stronger and different from what I felt till now . . .
    Those two studies, for instance, which I made while it was raining
– a muddy road with a little figure – they seem to me exactly the
opposite of some other studies. When I look at them I find coming

124

back the sentiment of that dreary rainy day, and in the figure, though it is nothing but a few patches of colour, is a kind of life, that is not called forth by correctness of drawing, for there is so to say no drawing. What I mean to suggest is that in these studies I believe there is something of that mysteriousness one gets by looking at nature through the eyelashes, so that the outlines are simplified to blots of colour . . .

❋ ❋ ❋

To Theo (313)
The Hague, undated [1883]

. . . There is no anguish greater than the soul's struggle between duty and love, both in their highest meaning. When I tell you I choose my duty, you understand everything.

I have never suspected her, nor do I now, nor shall I ever suspect her of having had financial reasons as her motives, more than is honest and just. She went as far as was reasonable, other people exaggerated. But for the rest, you understand I presume nothing about love for me, and what we talked on the road remains between us. Since then, things have happened that would not have been, if at a certain moment I had not stood in the first place before a decided 'no', and secondly before a promise that I would not stand in her way. In her I respected a sentiment of duty – her I have never suspected, shall never suspect her of anything mean.

Of myself know this one thing, that it is of the greatest importance not to deviate from one's duty, and that one may not compromise with duty. Duty is absolute . . .

❋ ❋ ❋

To Theo (314)
The Hague, 19 August 1883

. . . It is better that she were saved than that she were ruined.

This morning she says to me: 'As to what I did formerly, I do not even think of it, and have not spoken of it to mother either. I only know that if I have to go I shall not earn enough, especially as I shall have to

125

pay board for the children, and if in that case I walk the street, it will be because I must, not because I want to.' . . .

If you have said something to C. M. about my leaving the woman, perhaps, please take it back at once; I cannot do a thing which proves to be cruel or unmerciful. Whether I shall be happy with the woman in the future, I do not know, and it may be not – it will certainly not be perfect – but happiness is not the thing for which we are responsible, but what we are responsible for, is in how far we follow our conscience . . .

✳ ✳ ✳

To Theo (316)
The Hague, undated [1883]

. . . I for my part should love to go to Drenthe, especially after that visit from Rappard. So much so, that I have already gathered information if it would be easy or difficult to move the furniture thither . . .

✳ ✳ ✳

To Theo (317)
The Hague, undated [1883]

. . . You will get a small proof of how little firm the woman's character is, when I tell you that notwithstanding her recent firm promise not to go and see her mother again, she has been there after all. I told her that if she could not keep such a promise even for three days, how could she expect me to find her fit to keep a promise of faith for ever . . .

What you said – that you believe it would do her good if she left me – is a thing which I myself would think probable, if she did not go back to her people – in the first place, and secondly, if she had not to leave the only thing that keeps her relatively straight – her children . . .

✳ ✳ ✳

To Theo   (318)
The Hague, undated [1883]

. . . I often thought so myself, that if the woman would be obliged to leave me, to shift for herself, she would keep straight. But as she has two children, it is a very difficult case, but what shall I say – it is a thing which she brings about herself, but which the *circumstances bring about still more.* I underline the latter.

Do you know what I have done, I had today a quiet day with her, I talked it over with her seriously, explained to her fully how things stand with me, that I *must* go away for my work, and *must* have a year of few expenses and some earnings, in order to make up for a past that has been rather too much for me. That I foresaw, if I stayed with her, I should very soon not be able to help her any more, and would get into debt again here, where everything is so expensive, and there would be no way out. So that in short, she and I must be wise and separate as friends. That she must get her people to take the children, and that she must look for a place . . .

O brother, you see how it is, we would not part if we didn't have to. I repeat we would not part if we didn't have to. Have we not forgiven each other's faults each time, and made it up again? We know each other so well, that we can see no evil in each other. Is it love, I do not know, but there is something between us that cannot be undone . . .

✳ ✳ ✳

To Theo   (319)
The Hague, undated [1883]

. . . I must say that the woman bears up well. She is unhappy about it, so am I, but she is not disheartened and keeps busy. I had just bought a piece of stuff to make study linen of and have now given her this to make underwear for the kids, and some of my things can be altered for them too, so that she will not leave me empty-handed. So she is very busy sewing these things.

When I say we part as friends, it is true – but the parting is final, and after all I am more resigned than I thought, because her faults were such that for me, as for herself, it would have been a fatal thing to be bound together because one is, so to say, responsible for each other's faults . . .

I will certainly *never* take her in my house again, but I do not want to lose sight of her, for I am too fond of her and the children.

And for the very reason that it was and is a feeling different from passion, this is possible too.

I hope the plan of Drenthe may be carried out . . .

✳ ✳ ✳

To Theo (320)
The Hague, undated [1883]

. . . The plan is now, that she will live with her mother, they will go out as charwomen in turn, and try to get a living in an honest way . . .

PART FIVE

'I Feel a Power in Me'

Drenthe September–December 1883 – Nuenen December 1883–
November 1885 – Antwerp November 1885–February 1886

It was Vincent's artist friend Rappard who recommended the Drenthe, a wild and
unspoilt area in the extreme north of Holland close by the North Sea, where a number
of artists had settled. Vincent, who now finally decides to leave 'the woman', hopes
to meet some of them there but is disappointed. During this time he tries to persuade
his brother to give up his job at Goupil's in Paris, and become an artist too, although
still requiring his usual subventions, which irritates Theo, and the two brothers
briefly fall out in the spring of 1884. Although his drawing and painting skills are
progressing, he soon runs out of money and painting materials, and is obliged to
return to the family home at Nuenen (near Eindhoven), where his father's new parish
is. A laundry room is obligingly cleared for him as a studio, but relations with his
parents are tense, and Vincent finds larger premises for a studio with the Catholic
church.

In the summer of 1884 Vincent becomes involved with a neighbour, Margot
Begemann, and proposes, but her family object. The consequences are disastrous. In
the winter of 1884 he falls out with Rappard over the lithograph of his painting,
The Potato Eaters. *In March 1885 Vincent's father suddenly dies of a heart*
attack and Vincent moves out of the family house to live in his studio. In the autumn
Vincent is accused, wrongly, of fathering a child by one of his models; the Catholic
priest instructs his parishioners not to pose for him, and local feeling turns against
him. But by this time he has started painting landscapes and still-lifes.

Then in November 1885 he moves to Antwerp in the hope of finding dealers who
will handle his work. He has little success. He rents a studio and decorates its walls
with Japanese prints. He also attends the Academy to draw from nude models, but
his teacher advises him to spend at least a year drawing from plaster casts. It is

during this time that he first mentions the Impressionists (or rather his ignorance of them) in his letters.

After a few months in Antwerp, struggling to survive, undernourished and suffering from appalling toothache, he decides on an impulse to go to Paris, where his brother is now working, instead of going home to Nuenen to help his mother move to Breda.

. . . In order to give you an idea of one of the many things which gave me new sensations and feelings on my excursions, I will tell you, for instance, that one sees here peat barges in the *very middle of the heath*, drawn by men, women, children, white or black horses, just as in Holland, for instance, on the Ryswyk tow-path.

The heath is splendid. I saw sheepfolds and shepherds more beautiful than those in Brabant.

The kilns are more or less like that on Th. Rousseau's *Four Communa*. They stand in the gardens under old apple trees or between cabbages and celery. In many places there are beehives too. One can see on many faces that they are not in good health; it is not exactly healthy here, I believe; perhaps because of foul drinking water. I have seen a few girls of seventeen, or younger still, perhaps, who look very beautiful and youthful, but generally they are very soon faded. But that does not interfere with the great noble aspect of the figures of some, who, seen from near by, are already very faded.

In the village there are four or five canals to Meppel, to Dedemsvaart, to Coevorden, to Hollandsch Veld.

If one sails down them one sees here and there a curious old mill, farmyard, wharf, or lock, and always bustle of peat barges.

To give you an idea of the typicalness of these parts – while I was painting that cottage, two sheep and a goat came to browse *on the roof* of this house. The goat climbed on the top, and looked in at the chimney.

I often think with melancholy of the woman and the children, if they were only provided for; oh, it is the woman's own fault, one might say, and it would be true, but I am afraid her misfortunes will prove greater than her fault.

Theo, when I meet on the heath such a poor woman with a child on her arm, or at her breast, my eyes get moist. It reminds me of her, her weakness; her untidiness, too, contributes to make the likeness stronger.

I know that she is not good, that I have the fullest right to act as I do, that I *could not* stay with her yonder, that I really could not take her with me, that what I did was even sensible and wise, whatever you like, but, for all that, it pierces right through me when I see such a poor little figure feverish and miserable, and it makes my heart melt within me . . .

❋ ❋ ❋

To Theo (326)
Drenthe, undated [Autumn 1883]

. . . I had a letter from Rappard from West-Terschelling and he is very hard at work there, having been first here in Drenthe at Rolde in the neighbourhood of Assen. I hope to go and see him there this winter, and make a few studies . . .

❋ ❋ ❋

To Theo (327)
Hoogeveen (Drenthe), 24 September 1883

Today I send you by parcel post three studies which I hope are dry enough; however, if they stick to the sheet of paper which I put on them for precaution, sponge them off with tepid water. The smallest one especially is very much tarnished. In a week or so brush it over with the white of an egg, or in a month, with a little varnish, to restore the colour. I send them to you to give you an idea of the work, which will be better hereafter you know.

Last week I was deeper in the peat fields. I think it more and more beautiful here, and from the very beginning, I will contrive to stay in this neighbourhood. For it is so beautiful here that it will require still much more study to render it, and only very elaborate work can give an exact idea of the things as they are at bottom, in their serious, sober character. I have seen superb figures, but I repeat, a scenery that has so much nobility, so much dignity and gravity, must be treated with deep forethought and patience and steady work. Therefore, I must from the very beginning not consider it as if I came here just to have a glimpse of things, but if everything goes well, and if we may have some luck, it is a matter of course that I shall stay here for good . . .

❋ ❋ ❋

To Theo (328)
Drenthe, undated [1883]

As I feel a need to speak out frankly, I cannot hide from you that I am overcome by a feeling of great care, depression, a 'je ne sais quoi' of discouragement and despair more than I can tell. And if I cannot find comfort for it, it overwhelms me too strongly.

I take it so much to heart that I do not get on better with people in general; it quite worries me, because on it depends so much of my success in carrying out my work . . .

And if I look at my things, everything is too miserable, too insufficient, too dilapidated. We have gloomy rainy days here, and when I come to the corner of the garret where I have settled down, it is curiously melancholy there; through one single glass pane the light falls on an empty colour-box, on a bundle of brushes, the hair of which is quite worn down, in short, it is so curiously melancholy that luckily it has also a comical aspect, enough not to make one cry over it but to take it gaily. For all that, it is very disproportionate to my plans, is very disproportionate to the seriousness of my work – so here is an end to gaiety . . .

✳ ✳ ✳

To Theo (329)
Drenthe, undated [1883]

This morning the weather was better again, so I set out to paint. But it was impossible, four or five colours were lacking, and I came home so miserable . . .

You remember, perhaps, how it was with me in the Borinage. Well, I am rather afraid it would be the same thing here all over with me, and I must have some security before I risk myself further, otherwise I will go back . . .

Hoogeveen itself is classed as a town on the map, where it is marked with a red dot, but it is not so in reality (it has not even a tower). So I cannot get anything in the way of drawing materials. If I go deeper into the country, I shall be still more handicapped and must be prepared for everything, or, I repeat, it would be sheer madness. I would not hurry so if the far advanced season did not urge me to the greatest speed.

Remember that time is passing, and before I can have an answer from you perhaps again two weeks will have gone by. Before the real winter comes . . .

– today I saw a funeral in a barge, that was very curious – six women wrapped in coats in the boat that was pulled by the men along the canal through the heath, the clergyman in a three-cornered hat and breeches, exactly like a figure by Meissonier, followed on the other side; there are all kinds of curious things here. You must not be angry with me for writing like I do. I came here in too great a hurry, and only now I feel what I lack, and that I acted rather rashly – but what else could I do? . . .

❄ ❄ ❄

To Theo   (330)
New Amsterdam, undated [1883]

This once I write to you from the very remotest part of Drenthe, where I came after an endless long sail on the barge through the moors. I see no chance of describing the country as it ought to be done; words fail me for that, but imagine the banks of the canal as miles and miles of Michel's or Th. Rousseau's, van Goyen's or Ph. de Koninck's.

Level planes or strips of different colour, getting narrower and narrower as they approach the horizon. Accentuated here and there by a turf shed or small farm, or a couple of meagre birches, poplars, oaks – heaps of peat everywhere, and one constantly sails past barges with peat or bulrushes from the marshes. Here and there lean cows, delicate of colour, often sheep – pigs. The figures which now and then appear on the plain are generally of impressive character; sometimes they have an exquisite charm. I drew, for instance, a woman in the barge with crape on her cap, because she was in mourning, and afterwards a mother with a baby; the latter had a purple shawl over her head. There are a lot of Ostade types among them: physiognomies which remind one of pigs or crows, but now and then a little figure that is like the lily among thorns.

Well, I am very pleased with this excursion, for I am full of what I have seen. This evening the heath was inexpressibly beautiful. In one of the Boetzel Albums there is a Daubigny, which exactly gives that effect. The sky was of an indescribably delicate lilac white, no fleecy

Sketch of the view out of the window of Mr Stokes' school in Ramsgate. May 1876, Letter 67.

Churches of Petersham and Turnham Green. November 1876, Letter 82.

Au Charbonnage, Laeken. November 1878, Letter 126.

Two figure sketches, *En Route* and *Devant les Tisons*. Brussels, January 1881, Letter 140.

The parsonage at Etten, May 1881.

Sorrow, April 1882. Letter 186.

The port at Scheveningen.
July 1882.

Gordina de Groot, Head.
Nuenen, May 1885.

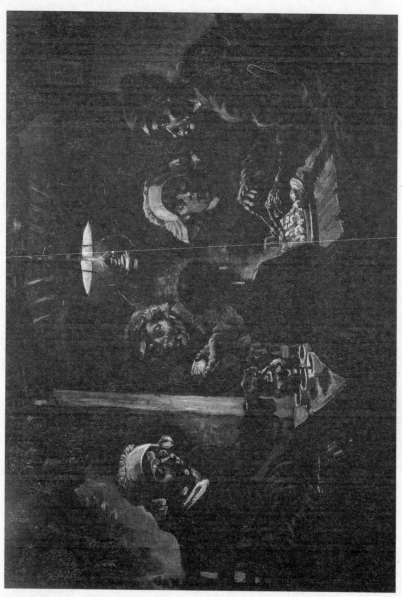

The Potato Eaters, Nuenen, April 1885, Letter 404.
Courtesy of Van Gogh Museum (Vincent van Gogh Foundation), Amsterdam.

Vincent's Bedroom in Arles, October 1888, Letter 554.
Courtesy of Van Gogh Museum (Vincent van Gogh Foundation), Amsterdam.

Portrait of Dr. Paul Gachet, June 1890, Letter 638.
© Francis G. Mayer/CORBIS.

clouds, for it was more compact and covered all the sky, but dashes of more or less tony lilac, grey, white, a single rent through which the blue gleamed. Then at the horizon, a glittering red streak, under which the very dark stretch of brown moor, and standing out against the red glimmering streak, a number of low-roofed little huts.

The place where I am now is New Amsterdam.

Father sent me a postal order of ten guilders, which, together with the money from you, makes me able to paint a little now . . .

❋ ❋ ❋

To Theo (331)
New Amsterdam, undated [1883]

. . . There are very often curious contrasts of black and white here. For instance a canal with white sandy banks, across a pitch-black plain. In the [enclosed] sketch you see it too, black figures against a white sky, and in the foreground again a variation of black and white in the sand . . .

❋ ❋ ❋

To Theo (333)
Drenthe, undated [1883]

. . . Today I have been walking behind the ploughers who were ploughing a potato field, with women trudging behind to pick up a few potatoes that were left.

This was quite a different field from the one I scratched yesterday for you, but it is a curious thing here, always exactly the same, and yet just enough variety, the same subjects like pictures of artists who work in the same genre and yet are different. Oh, it is so curious here, and *so* quiet, *so* peaceful. I can find no other word for it but peace. It is a question of wanting an entirely new thing, of undertaking a kind of renovation of yourself, in all simplicity with the fixed idea: *ça ira* . . .

Now art dealers have certain prejudices, which I think possible you have not shaken off yet, particularly the idea that painting is inborn – all right, inborn, but not so as is supposed; one must put out one's hands and *grasp* it – that grasping is a difficult thing – one must not wait

135

till it reveals itself. There is something, but not at all what people pretend. Practice makes perfect: by painting, one becomes a painter . . .

✳ ✳ ✳

To his parents (334)
Drenthe, 27 October 1883

I received your letter, many thanks.

The death of cousin A. touched me too. How suddenly things can happen.

I often thought she was not very happy, or rather, for my part, I do not doubt it for a single moment. I think one can hardly be happy as the wife of a banker, in the present time, least of all . . .

✳ ✳ ✳

To Theo (335)
Drenthe, undated [1883]

. . . Oh, I have had a letter from the poor woman [Sien]; she was glad that I wrote to her, but she worries about the children, and she goes out working as a charwoman. She is obliged to live with her mother. Poor things . . .

[Enclosed] are two evening effects; I am still working on that burner of weeds, which I have in a painted study better than before, so that it gives more the immensity of the plain, and the falling of twilight, the fire with a bit of smoke being the only spot of light. I went again and again in the evening to look at it, and on a muddy evening after the rain, I found this cottage . . .

✳ ✳ ✳

To Theo (339)
Drenthe, undated [1883]

. . . I will just make a scratch of the landscapes which I have on the easel. That is the kind of studies which I should like you to try at once:

To learn to look at the landscape at large, in its simple lines and contrasts of light and brown. The scratch at the top is what I saw today, it was absolutely Michel. That earth was superb in reality. I don't think my study ripe enough yet, but I was struck by the effect, and as to light and shade, it was, indeed, as I draw it for you here.

The one at the bottom is a tender green little cornfield in the foreground, and drooping grasses, behind the cottage, two piles of peat, again a glimpse of the heath, and a very light sky . . .

Think of Barbizon, that story is sublime. Those who originally started there, when they came there – they were by no means all outwardly what they were at bottom. The country formed them, they only knew: it is no good in town, I must go to the country. I suppose they thought, I must learn to work, become quite different, aye, the opposite to what I am now. They said I am no good now, I am going to renew myself in nature. As for me, I reason in the same way, and though I should go to Paris if I absolutely had to, and should find something to do there – I think my future here infinitely, infinitely better.

The greatest attraction for me in Paris, the thing which would help me most to make progress, is being with you, and the friction of ideas with somebody who knows what a picture is, and who understands the reason of my trials. Because you are in Paris, I approve of Paris, and as I should be less alone there, I would make better progress *even* there . . .

✳ ✳ ✳

To Theo   (340)
Drenthe, undated [1883]

I must just tell you about a trip to Zweeloo, the village where Liebermann stayed a long while, and where he made studies for his picture of the last Salon, that with the washerwomen. Where Termeulen and Jules Backhuyzen have also been a long time. Imagine a ride across the heath, at three o'clock in the morning in an open cart (I went with the landlord who had to go to the market at Assen), along a road or 'diek' as they call it here, which had been banked up with mud instead of sand. It was more curious still than going by barge. At the first glimpse of dawn, when the roosters everywhere began to crow near the sheds spread all over the heath, the few cottages we passed –

surrounded by thin poplars whose yellow leaves one could hear drop to earth – an old stumpy tower on a churchyard, with earthen wall and beech hedge – the level landscapes of heath or cornfields – it all, all, all became exactly like the most beautiful Corot's. A quietness, a mystery, a peace, as only he has painted it.

But when we arrived at Zweeloo at six o'clock in the morning it was still quite dark; the real Corot's I saw earlier still in the morning.

The entrance to the village was splendid: enormous mossy roofs of houses, stables, sheepfolds, barns.

The houses here lie amply between oak trees of a splendid bronze. In the moss are tones of gold green, in the ground, tones of reddish, or bluish or yellowish dark lilac-grey, in the green of the cornfields, tones of inexpressible purity, on the wet trunks, tones of black, contrasting with the golden rain of whirling, clustering autumn leaves hanging in loose tufts, as if they had been blown there, detached, and with the sky glimmering through them, from the poplars, the birches, the linden and the apple trees.

The sky smooth and clear, luminous, not white but a lilac which can hardly be deciphered, white scintillating with red, blue and yellow, in which everything is reflected, and which one feels everywhere above one, which is vaporous and melts together with thin mist beneath – harmonizing everything in a gamut of delicate grey. At Zweeloo, however, I didn't find a single painter, and people said *in winter, none* ever came.

I, on the contrary, hope to be there *just* this winter.

As there were no painters, I decided not to wait for the return of my landlord, but to walk back, and to make some drawings on the way. So I began a sketch of that little apple orchard, of which Liebermann made his large picture. And then I walked back the road along which we had driven early in the morning.

The whole country around Zweeloo is for the moment entirely covered – as far as the eye can reach – by young corn, that most, most tender green I know.

With a sky over it of a tender lilac-white, which gives an effect – I don't think it can be painted, but which is for me the keynote which one must know, in order to understand the keynotes of other effects.

A black patch of earth – infinite – a clear sky of tender lilac-white. From that earth sprouts the young corn, it is almost mouldy-looking with that corn. That's what the good fertile parts of Drenthe are at bottom; the whole, in a hazy atmosphere. Think of *le dernier jour de la création* by Brion; yesterday it seemed to me I understood the meaning of that picture.

The bad soil of Drenthe is just the same – but the black earth is blacker still – like soot – not lilac-black like the furrows, and drearily covered with ever-rotting heather and peat. I see that everywhere, the casualties on that infinite background, on the moors, the turf huts, in the fertile parts, very primitive buildings of farms and sheepfolds, with low, very low little walls and enormous mossy roofs. Oak trees all around.

When one has walked for hours and hours through that country, one feels that there is really nothing but that infinite earth – that mould of corn or heather, that infinite sky. Horses and men seem no larger than fleas. One is not aware of anything, be it ever so large in itself, one only knows that there is earth and sky. However, in one's quality of a little speck noticing other little specks – leaving the infinite apart – one finds every little speck to be a Millet.

I passed a little old church exactly, exactly *L'église de Greville*, from Millet's little picture at the Luxembourg; instead of the little peasant with his spade of that picture, there was here a shepherd with a flock of sheep walking along the hedge. In the background, there was not a glimpse of the sea, but only of the sea of young corn, the sea of the furrows instead of the sea of the waves.

The effect produced was the same. Then I saw ploughers very busy – a sandcart, a shepherd, menders of the road, dung carts. In a little inn on the road I drew an old woman at the spinning-wheel, a dark little silhouette as from a fairy-tale – a dark little silhouette against a light window, through which one saw the clear sky, and a small path through the delicate green, and a few geese picking grass.

And then when twilight fell – imagine the quiet, the peace of it all! Imagine then a little avenue of high poplars with autumn leaves, imagine a broad muddy road, all black mud, with an infinite heath to the right, and an endless heath to the left, a few black triangular silhouettes of turf huts, through the little windows of which shines the red light of the little fire, with a few pools of dirty yellowish water that reflect the sky, and in which trunks lie rotting; imagine that puddle in the evening twilight, with a white sky over it, everywhere the contrast of black and white. And in that puddle a rough figure – the shepherd – a heap of oval masses, half-wool, half-mud, that jostle against each other, push each other – the flock. You see them coming – you find yourself in the middle of them – you turn round and follow them. Slowly and reluctantly they trudge along the muddy road. However, there looms in the distance the farm – a few mossy roofs, and piles of straw and peat between the poplars.

The sheepfold is again like the silhouette of a triangle – dark. The door is wide open like the entrance to a dark cave. Through the chinks of the boards behind it gleams the light of the sky. The whole caravan of masses of wool and mud disappear in that cave – the shepherd and a woman with a lantern, shut the doors behind them.

That coming home of the flock in the twilight was the finale of the symphony I heard yesterday.

That day passed like a dream, I had been so absorbed the whole day in that pathetic music that I literally had forgotten even food and drink – I had taken a piece of brown bread and a cup of coffee in the little inn where I drew the spinning-wheel. The day was past, and from dawn till twilight, or rather from one night till the other, I had forgotten myself in that symphony.

I came home, and sitting near the fire, I felt I was hungry, yes, very hungry. But now you see how it is here. One feels exactly as if one had been at an exhibition of the *Cent chef-d'œuvres*, for instance; what does one bring home from such a day? Only a number of scratches. Yet there is another thing one brings home – a calm ardour to work . . .

✳ ✳ ✳

To Theo   (343)
Drenthe, 1 December 1883

Thanks for your letter and the enclosure. Your letter explains to me the reason of your silence. You thought that '*feeling myself well-off for the moment*,' I offered you an '*ultimatum*', like, for instance, the Nihilists perhaps send to the Czar.

Luckily, for you *and* for me, there is *no* question of such a thing here.

However, I understand your idea *now that I know it*, but that is the last straw indeed. In the first place, I meant something quite different – I simply meant 'I shouldn't want to thrive if you were the loser by it' – I should not want to develop the artist in me, if you had to suppress your artistry for my sake. I should never approve of your repressing the artist

140

in yourself, for the sake of whosoever it may be, for the sake of either father, mother, sister, brother or wife. That was my meaning – perhaps expressed nervously, and in wrong terms – but I most decidedly meant no more, or nothing else.

You understand it now, don't you?

But know this, Brother, that I am absolutely cut off from the outer world – except from you – so that it *made me crazy* when your letter did not come at the moment, when, far from 'being well-off', I was very hard pressed, *though I did not mention it,* because I feel myself rather above the cares that gnaw at my heart, which torture I perhaps can explain, but do *not* consider *merited* . . .

Because of your unaccountable silence, and because I connected it with perhaps new difficulties on the side of the directors, and because I myself was hopelessly hard pressed, through suspicion of the people at the inn, I wrote a note to father that as I had not heard from you, I did not know what to think of it, and that I begged father to lend me some money. I added that I was anxious both about you, and about myself, especially when thinking of the future, and that I wished that you and I, as boys, had become painters then, and that I didn't see why we two brothers could not be painters as yet.

So if father should write to you about it, you know how it is, but I myself (up till now, I have had no answer from father). I shall write father that your last letter has made it clear to me, that, for the moment G. & Co. remain G. & Co. To you, not to father, I add that Goupil & Co. has an influence on our family, curiously mixed of good and evil, but *at all events,* as it prevents much stagnation, the evil is for the moment not prevalent. That my heart knoweth its own bitterness, is a thing which I think you understand, and in consequence will pardon . . .

I shall be able to write to you more calmly from home.

There is certainly a field of action for me in Drenthe, but from the very beginning, I must be able to undertake it somewhat differently, and have more security about my finances . . .

I have still to pay Rappard, and I saved all I could . . .

As it is now, it *cannot* go on. I must try and find a way.

Of course, I do not say it is your fault, but even last year, I have not been able to save more than I did. And the harder I work, the harder I am pressed. We have now arrived at a point that I say, momentarily I cannot go on . . .

Vincent intended here to go back to his parents at Nuenen for just a short stay. As it turned out, he would stay at Nuenen for two years.

* * *

To Theo (344)
Nuenen, undated [December 1883]

Perhaps you were rather astonished when I told you briefly that I intended to go home for a while, and that now I write you from here. But first I have to thank you for your letter of the 1st December, which I just received here at Nuenen.

For the last three weeks already, I did not feel quite well – all kinds of little troubles from having caught cold, and also from nervousness.

One must try to break such a thing, and I felt it would get worse if I did not take a change.

So for several reasons I made up my mind to go home for a while. A thing which, however, I was very loath to do . . .

* * *

To Theo (345)
Nuenen, undated

I was lying awake half the night, Theo, after I wrote you last night . . .

I am sick at heart about the fact that, coming back after two years' absence, the welcome home was in every respect kind and cordial, but at bottom, there is not the least, least change whatever, in that what I must call blindness and ignorance, in the most extreme degree, as to the insight in our mutual position. And I feel again almost unbearably disturbed and perplexed.

You understand that I would not write as I do – having undertaken the journey hither of my own free will, having been the first to bend my pride – if I did not find real obstacles in my way.

If I now had noticed some eagerness to do as the Rappards have done, with the best results and as we began here also with good results, if I had noticed that father also had realized that he ought *not* to have shut his house to me, then I would have felt some confidence in the future.

Nothing, nothing, of all that.

Their cordial reception grieves me – their *yielding* without acknowledging their mistake, is, for me, perhaps worse than the mistake itself. Instead of a ready understanding, and contributing with a certain eagerness to my, and indirectly their own, well-being, I feel in everything a hesitation and delay, that lame my own ardour and energy, like a leaden atmosphere . . .

I have decided to go and see Rappard . . . Damn it, brother, the Rappards acted intelligently, but here!!!

✳ ✳ ✳

To Theo   (346)
Nuenen, undated

I feel how father and mother *instinctively* (I do not say *sensibly*) think about me.

They feel the same dread about taking me in the house, as they would about taking a big rough dog. He would run into the room with wet paws – and he is so rough. He will be in everybody's way. *And he barks so loud*. In short, he is a dirty beast.

All right – but the beast has a human history, and though but a dog, he has a human soul, and even a very sensitive one, that makes him feel how people think of him, what an ordinary dog cannot do.

And I, admitting that I am a kind of dog, rate them at their own value.

The dog feels that if they kept him, it would only be putting up with him, and tolerating him '*in this house*', so he will try to find another kennel. The dog is in fact father's son, and has been left rather too much in the street, where he could not but become more and more rough, but as father has forgotten that already years ago, one need not mention that.

And then – the dog might bite – he might go mad, and the constable would have to come to shoot him . . .

✳ ✳ ✳

Mauve once said to me: 'you will find yourself, if you go on painting, if
you penetrate deeper in art than you have done till now', he said so two
years ago.

Of late I often think about these words of his.

I have found myself – I am that dog . . .

[PS] Since writing this letter, I have again thought over your remarks,
and have again spoken with father. My decision not to stay here was
almost taken, no matter what they might think about it, or what might
be the consequences; but then the conversation took another turn, by
my saying: 'I am here now since two weeks, and do not feel a bit more
advanced than the first half-hour, now if we had understood each other
better, we would have things in order, and arranged by now – I have
no time to lose, and I must take a decision. A door must be either open
or closed. Anything between the two I do not understand, and does not
really exist in fact.'

So the result is, that the little room at home where the mangle stands,
will be at my disposal to put away my things, to use as studio too, in
case this might be necessary.

And they have now begun to clear out the room, which had been put
off while things were still undecided.

I can tell you one thing, which I see better now than when I wrote
you about father. I am softened in my opinion; I respect old age and its
weakness as you do, though it may not seem so to you, though you do
not believe this from me.

I also thought of the word of Michelet (who learned it from a scien-
tist) 'le mâle est très sauvage'. And as at this period of my life, I know
myself to have strong passions, which I think it is right to have – I look
upon myself as being indeed 'a savage'. And yet my passion abates,
when I stand before a weaker one, and I do not fight then . . .

❋ ❋ ❋

To Theo (355)
Nuenen, undated [1884]

. . . I am painting a loom of old, greenish, browned oak, in which the date 1730 is cut. Near that loom, before a little window which looks out on a green plot, stands a baby-chair, and a baby in it sits looking for hours at the flying to and fro of the shuttle.

I have painted that thing exactly as it was in nature, the loom with the little weaver, the little window, and the baby-chair, in the miserable little room, with clay floor.

Please write me some more details about the Manet exhibition; tell me which of his pictures are there. I have always found Manet's work very original. Do you know that article of Zola's on Manet? I am sorry to have seen but so very few of his pictures. I should like especially to see his nude women figures. I do not think it exaggerated that some people, for instance Zola, rave about him, although I, for my part, do not think he can be reckoned among the very first of this century. But his is a talent which *certainly* has its *raison d'être* and that is already a great thing . . .

✳ ✳ ✳

To Theo (358)
Nuenen, undated [1884]

. . . Just listen – after having read your letter about the drawings, I sent you at once a new water-colour of a weaver, and five pen drawings. For my part, I will tell you also frankly that I think it true what you say, that my work must become much better still, but at the same time, that your energy to sell them for me, may become somewhat firmer too.

You have *never sold a single one for me* – neither for much nor little – and in fact *you did not even try*.

You see, I am not *angry* about it, but – we must call things by their names. In the long run, I would certainly not put up with that.

You, for your part, can also continue to speak out frankly . . .

You do absolutely nothing to procure me some distraction, which I need so badly now and then – of meeting people, and seeing things.

Think it over lad, I do not hide my deepest thoughts from you. I weigh and balance one side as well as the other.

A *wife* you cannot give me, a *child* you cannot give me, work you cannot give me.

Money, yes.

But of what good is it to me, if I must do without the rest; your money remains sterile, because it is not used in the way I always wanted to – a labourer's home if needs be, but if one does not see that one gets a home of one's own, it fares badly with art.

And I for my part – I told you already plainly enough when I was younger, if I cannot get a good wife, I should take a bad one, better a bad one than none at all.

I know people enough, who assert flatly the contrary, and who are just as afraid to have 'children' as I am to have 'no children' . . .

✳ ✳ ✳

To Theo   (364)
Nuenen, undated [1884]

I just received your letter and enclosed fr. 250. If I may consider your letter as an answer to my proposal, I can indeed agree to what you say. In short, to avoid further discussion or quarrelling, in order to have some answer when in daily life, they accuse me of being without any 'source of income', I want to consider the money I may receive from you as money that I have earned!

Of course I will send you *my work every month*. As you say, that work is your property then, and I perfectly agree with you, that you have the full right to do anything with it, I even couldn't make any objection, if you liked to tear it in pieces . . .

✳ ✳ ✳

To Theo   (368)
Nuenen, undated [1884]

I have waited too long to answer your last letter, and I will tell you the reason. Let me begin by thanking you for your letter and enclosed fr. 200. And then I will tell you, that today I just finished arranging a spacious new studio, which I have rented.

Two rooms, a big one, and a smaller one adjoining . . .

I think I shall be able to work there much better than in the little room at home . . .

❋ ❋ ❋

To Theo (370)
Nuenen, undated [1884]

. . . to revert to that question of painting an evening sky, or a blonde woman with a drab-colour like the grey of the pavement, if one considers this well, that question has a *double* meaning.

In the first place:

A dark colour may seem *light*, this is in fact more a question of *tone*. But then, as regards the real *colour*, a reddish grey, relatively little red, will appear more or less red, according to the adjoining colours.

And with blue and yellow it is the same.

One has to put but a very little yellow in a colour to make it seem very yellow, if one puts that colour in, or next a violet, or lilac tone.

I remember how somebody tried to paint a red roof, on which the light was falling, by means of vermilion and chrome, etc.! That did not do.

Jaap Maris did it in many a water-colour, by putting a very little bit of glacis of red-ochre on a colour that was reddish. And it perfectly expressed the sunlight on the red roofs.

As soon as I have time, I will copy from that article on Delacroix another part about the laws that always remain true for colours. I sometimes think that people, when they speak about *colour*, really mean *tone*.

And perhaps there are at present more *ton*ists than *colour*ists . . .

❋ ❋ ❋

To Theo (371)
Nuenen, undated [1884]

. . . The *laws* of the colours are unutterably beautiful, just because they are *not accidental* . . .

With regard to black – *by chance* I did not use it in these studies [the spinning woman and the old man winding thread] as I needed, among others, some stronger effects than black, and indigo with terra sienna, prussian blue with burnt sienna, really give much deeper tones than pure black itself. When I hear people say 'in nature there is no black' I sometimes think, in colours there is, in fact, no black either.

You must, however, beware of falling into the error, that the colourists do not use black, for, of course, as soon as an element of blue, red, or yellow is mixed with black, it becomes a grey, namely, a dark, reddish, yellowish or bluish grey. In Ch. Blanc *Les Artistes de mon Temps*, I found very interesting, for instance, what he says about the technique of Velasquez, whose shadows and half-tones, consist mostly of *colourless, cool greys*, the chief elements of which are black and a little white. In which neutral, colourless milieux, the least cloud or shade of red, already takes effect . . .

✳ ✳ ✳

To Theo (372)
Nuenen, undated [1884]

. . . But that what struck me most in the nature of late I have not started yet, for want of a good model. The half-ripe cornfields are at present of a dark golden tone, ruddy or gold bronze. This is raised to a maximum of effect by opposition to the broken cobalt tone of the sky.

Imagine in such a background, women's figures, very rough, very energetic, with sun-bronzed faces and arms and feet, with dusty, coarse indigo clothes and a black bonnet in the form of a baret on the short-cut hair, while on the way to their work they pass between the corn along a dusty path of ruddy violet, with some green weeds, carrying rakes on their shoulders, or a loaf of black bread under the arm – a pitcher or brass coffee kettle. I saw that same subject repeatedly of late, and in all kinds of variations.

Very rich, and at the same time very sober, very refined, artistical. And I am quite absorbed in it.

But my colour bill has run up so high that I must be wary of starting new things in a big size, the more so, because it will cost me much in models; if I could only get fit models, just of the type I want (rough, flat faces with low foreheads and thick lips, not sharp, but full and Millet-like) and with those very same clothes.

For it demands great exactness, and one is not at liberty to deviate from the colours of the costume, as the effect lies in the analogy of the broken indigo tone, with the broken cobalt tone, intensified by the secret elements of orange, in the ruddy bronze of the corn . . .

❋ ❋ ❋

To Theo   (374)
Nuenen, August 1884

I just want to drop you a line while you are in London . . .

How I should love to walk with you in London, particularly in real London weather, when the City, especially in certain old parts near the river, has aspects that are very melancholy, but, at the same time have a remarkably striking character, which some English artists of these days have begun to make, after they had learnt from the French to observe and to paint. But unluckily, it is very difficult to get a view of that English art which for you and for me is really the most interesting. In exhibitions, the *greater part* of the pictures generally is *not* sympathetic.

I hope however, that you will meet here and there with things which will make you understand. Now I, for my part, always remember some English pictures, for instance *Chill October* by Millais, for instance the drawings of Fred. Walker and Pinwell. Just notice the Hobbema in the National Gallery; you will not forget a few very beautiful Constables there, among others *Cornfield*, nor that other one in South Kensington, called *Valley Farm* . . .

Last week, I was every day in the fields during the harvest, of which I made a composition . . .

❋ ❋ ❋

To Anton van Rappard   (42R)
Nuenen, 1884

It is a long time since I wrote you. First I waited for an answer to my last letter and I suppose the reason it wasn't forthcoming was that you had gone to Drenthe. Then I was very busy myself and could not get round to writing. Do try and find a moment to let us know how things are with you: what you have been doing, and especially tell me how your picture of *The Fish-Auction* is progressing.

I'll continue now about myself. Last summer I saw a house in Eindhoven belonging to a rich retired goldsmith. He collected a number of beautiful antiques, which he sold again. He is an amateur painter and his house is again filled with ugly as well as beautiful pieces of antique furniture, and now he wants to paint the walls of one of his rooms. He wants murals. He has a plan for it, and I went over to see the panels on the walls. There are six, about 1½ metres long and about 60 centimetres high, which he wants to cover with scenes. He intended to paint the Last Supper, and he showed me the plan of the drawing, which was half Gothic and half modern in style. I said to him that, in my opinion, it would be better for the appetites of the diners, since it was a dining-room, if they could look at country scenes of the neighbourhood instead of at the Last Supper; and the good old fellow did not contradict me. Well, after a visit to my studio, I made him some rough drafts of six *motifs* from peasant life: a *Sower*, a *Ploughman*, *Harvesters*, *Potato-Diggers*, a frosty *Winter Scene with an Ox-Cart* and a *Shepherd*. I am still working on them. I made arrangements with him that the six canvases are to be for myself, but that I am to make them the size of his panels so that he can use them to make his copies from, and he pays me for the materials, the models I am using, paint and so forth. But the canvases remain my property and will be returned to me after he is through with them. This arrangement enables me to paint them, which I would not have been able to do had I to pay for all materials and other things. And it is work that I enjoy, and I am working hard at it.

It is giving me a good deal of trouble, however, to tell him the things he needs to know while he is copying them. The sketches of the *Ploughman*, the *Sower* and the *Shepherd* are already finished and of the right dimensions, 1½ metres by 60 centimetres, and smaller ones of the *Harvesters* and the *Winter Scene with an Ox-Cart*. So you can imagine I am not exactly sitting idle.

✻ ✻ ✻

To Anton van Rappard   (43R)
Nuenen, September 1884

. . . I have so much enjoyed working on the six canvases about which I wrote you; they are all painted sketches so far, and are already at the house of the person interested. When he has finished copying them, they will be my property and I'll finish them. The subjects are: *Potato-Diggers, Ox-Plough, Harvesters, Sower, Shepherd* (storm effect), *Wood-Choppers* (snow effect) . . .

✳ ✳ ✳

To Anton van Rappard   (45R)
Nuenen, September 1884

A single word, hastily: my parents have asked me whether I had heard from you with regard to your visit. I said that I knew the time would be around October, but I had not yet the right date. Between ourselves, let me tell you that, although *you are welcome at all times and we expect you at any time*, I believe it would be more convenient at home if you came in *October* rather than in November, because I heard them say they would have other visitors *later* . . .

Something else – if you come, you must come by way of *Eindhoven* and let me know by what train, so I can be at the station to meet you. Then we can go together to see the man for whom I am making those decorations – the six canvases about which I wrote you. The amateur is copying them now, and they are all there. He is quite a nice old fellow; he is a goldsmith and also deals in brass and metal church ornaments. I think, if you leave Utrecht in the morning, you'll be in Eindhoven a little after noon. This will be just the right time for us to go there together, and toward evening we can either take the train or walk to Nuenen.

✳ ✳ ✳

To Theo   (375)
Nuenen, undated [1884]

. . . Something terrible has happened, Theo, which hardly anybody here knows, or suspects, or may ever know, so for Heaven's sake keep it to yourself. To tell you everything, I would have to fill a volume – I can't do it. Miss X. [Margot Begemann, Vincent's neighbour, to whom he had formed an 'attachment'] has taken poison, in a moment of despair, when she had had an explanation with her family, and they

151

slandered her and me, she became so upset that she did it (in a moment of decided *mania*, I think). Theo, I had already consulted the doctor about certain symptoms of hers, three days before, I had secretly warned her brother that I was afraid she would get brain fever, and that I was sorry to state that, in my eyes, the family X. acted extremely imprudently in speaking to her as they did. This had no effect, at least, no other than that they told me to wait two years, which I decidedly refused to do, saying that *if* there was a question of marriage it had to be very soon or not at all.

Well, Theo, you have read *Mm. Bovary*, do you remember the *first* Mm. Bovary who died in a nervous attack, here it was something like that, but complicated by having taken poison.

She had often said when we were quietly walking together, 'I wish I could die now' – I had never paid any attention to it.

One morning, however, she slipped to the ground. At first I only thought it was weakness. But it became worse and worse. Well, now you understand the rest. It was strychnine she took, but the dose has been too small, or perhaps she took chloroform or laudanum with it as anodyne which would be the very counter-poison against strychnine. However, she has taken in time the counter-poison, which the doctor prescribed. She has been sent off immediately to a doctor in Utrecht, and is said to have gone abroad. I think it *probable* that she will get quite well again, but I am afraid there will follow a long time of nervous suffering for her – in what form, more or less serious, that is the question. But she is well taken care of now. You will understand how much I am cast down by this accident. It was such a terrible fright, boy, we were alone in the fields when I heard it. But luckily, the poison has at least lost its effect by now [words missing] . . . But for Heaven's sake, what is the meaning of that standing, and of that religion which the respectable people keep up, oh, they are perfectly *absurd* things, which make of society a kind of lunatic asylum, a perfectly topsy-turvy world – oh, that mysticism. You will understand how these last few days, everything, everything passed through my mind, and how absorbed I was in this sad story. Now that she has tried this and failed, I think it has given her such a fright, that she will not easily try it a second time, the failure of a suicide is the best remedy against a future suicide . . .

✻ ✻ ✻

Just a word to tell you that I have been to Utrecht to visit her [Margot].

I also had an interview with the physician with whom she is staying, because I wanted to hear his advice, what I must or must not do, for the sake of the health and future of the patient, either continue our relation or break it off.

I want in this matter no other advice than that of a physician. And I have heard that her health is greatly shaken – though she is recovering – that in fact, according to the doctor, who has known her from childhood, and who also was her mother's physician – she has *always* had a very frail constitution, and will always have, that for the moment there are *two* dangerous things, that she is too weak to marry at least now, but at the same time, a separation would be dangerous too.

So some time will have to pass over it, and then I shall receive a decided hint what will be the best for her, separation or not.

Of course, I shall always remain her friend, *mutually* we are perhaps *too much* attached to each other . . .

I think it deeply pathetic that this woman (while yet so *weak* and defeated by five or six other women that *she took poison*) says in a kind of triumph, as if she had gained a victory, and as if she had found *rest*: 'I too have loved at last.'

She had never really loved before.

As for me, these days are sometimes full of anguish that makes me *sick*, that can neither be diverted nor stilled, but, in short, with forethought, *I have always respected her*, concerning a certain point that socially would have dishonoured her (though if I had wanted it, I had her in my power), so that socially she can perfectly maintain her position, and *if* she *understood it well*, she would have a splendid chance to take her revenge and get satisfaction from those very women who defeated her. And I will lend her a helping hand in this, but she does not always understand, or understands *too late*. Well.

It is a pity that I did not meet her *before*, for instance, ten years ago. Now she gives me the impression of a Cremona violin, which has been spoilt by bad, bungling repairers . . .

The only thing I ever saw again of K. was a picture taken a year later; was she changed for the worse? On the contrary, *more interesting*.

That disturbing the tranquillity of a woman, as theological people call it (sometimes theologians *sans le savoir*), is sometimes *the breaking of stagnation or melancholy*, which steals upon many people, and is *worse* than *death itself*. To hurl them back to life, to love, some people think it terrible, and one must thoroughly weigh and balance how far one may go. But if one does it from other motives than egotism, well, then the women themselves will sometimes become *angry* and may even hate, instead of love, *que soit*.

But they will *not easily despise* the man who has done it. While they do despise the men who have extinguished the manliness in themselves. Well, those are the deep things of life . . .

❋ ❋ ❋

To Theo   (378)
Nuenen, undated [1884]

. . . As to *this* woman in question, it remains a mystery to me how it must end, but neither she nor I will do *foolish* things.

I am afraid that the old bigotry will *again* benumb and freeze her, with that damned icy coldness, which *already once*, in the distant past, almost *killed* her, long years ago. Oh, I am no friend of the present Christianity, though its *Founder* was sublime, the present Christianity I know but too well. That icy coldness bewitched even me in my youth, but I take my revenge since, how? by worshipping the love which they, the theologians, call *sin*, by respecting a whore, etc., and *not* respecting many would-be respectable, pious ladies . . .

You do not know how paralysing it is, that staring of a blank canvas, which says to the painter: *you don't know anything*; the canvas stares at you like an idiot, and it hypnotizes some painters, so that they themselves become idiots. Many painters are afraid of the blank canvas, but the blank canvas is afraid of the real passionate painter, who dares – and who has once for all broken that spell of 'you cannot' . . .

❋ ❋ ❋

To Theo   (383)
Nuenen, October 1884

. . . Rappard is still here, and will stay another week, as he is head over ears in his work.

154

We have been talking a good deal about Impressionism. I think that you would range his work under that head. But here in Holland it is rather difficult to find out what Impressionism really means.

But both he and I are very interested in the tendencies of the present day. And it is a fact that unexpected, new conceptions begin to arise. That pictures are being painted in quite a different tone than some years ago. The last thing I made is rather a large study of an avenue of poplars, with yellow autumn leaves, the sun casting, here and there, sparkling spots on the fallen leaves on the ground, alternated by the long-cast shadows of the stems. At the end of the road is a small cottage, and over it all the blue sky through the autumn leaves.

I think that in a year, if I spend that year again painting much and constantly, I shall change much in method of painting and in colour, and that I shall become rather darker than lighter . . .

* * *

To Theo (386)
Nuenen, undated

. . . I don't think I am mistaken in regard to Tersteeg and Mauve, when I venture to say there is certainly a chance of getting at them, and winning them over. They may be won over by colour, and by working hard. I see a chance of giving them a convincing proof that I have a notion of, and sentiment for colour. And then portraits are more and more in demand, and there are not so very many who can make them, and I want to try to learn to paint a head with character, I have just got enthusiastic about it of late, because my notion of colour has become more firm . . .

* * *

To Theo (392)
Nuenen, [January 1885]

. . . Hardly ever did I begin a year of gloomier aspect, in a gloomier mood, nor do I expect any future of success, but a future of strife.

It is dreary outside, the fields a mass of lumps of black earth, and some snow, with mostly days of mist and mire in between, the red sun in the evening and in the morning, crows, withered grass, and faded, rotting green, black shrubs, and the branches of the poplars and willows rigid, like wire against the dismal sky. This is what I see in passing, and it is quite in harmony with the interiors, very gloomy, these dark winter days . . .

Vincent had conceived the idea of painting fifty peasant heads.

❊ ❊ ❊

To Theo   (394)
Nuenen, undated [1885]

. . . I am very busy painting those heads. I paint in the daytime and draw in the evening. In this way I have painted at least some thirty already and drawn as many.

With this result, that I see a chance of doing it better still ere long I hope.

I think that *for figure in general it will help me.* Today I had one white and black against the flesh-colour.

And I am also seeking for blue all the time. The peasants' figures are as a rule blue here. That blue in the ripe corn or against the withered leaves of a beech hedge, so that the faded shades of darker and lighter blue are vivified and drawn out by contrast with the golden tones of reddish brown, is very beautiful and has struck me here from the very first. The people here instinctively wear the most beautiful blue that I have ever seen.

It is coarse linen which they weave themselves, warp black, wool blue, the result of which is a black and blue striped pattern. When this fades and becomes somewhat discoloured by wind and weather it is an infinitely quiet, delicate tone, which just brings out the flesh colours . . .

But this is a question of colour and what matters more to me at the point where I am now is the question of form . . .

On 26 March 1885, Vincent's father, Pastor Theodorus van Gogh, died suddenly of a heart attack after walking home across the fields.

❊ ❊ ❊

I felt the same as you did, when you wrote that you could not work as usual the first days, with me it was the same.

Indeed, those were days we shall not easily forget. And yet the total impression was not terrible, only solemn. Life is not long for anybody, and the question is only to make something of it.

Today I painted better again, the first two heads turned out badly, that of today is a young girl's almost a child's head. As to colour it is a contrast of bright red with pale green against the flesh colour of the little face, there is already such a head among those you took with you.

Of course I intend go on working hard, but it is absolutely necessary for me to settle my bill for colours as soon as possible. Every year about this time I have been able to pay off and buy some new painting materials. And this year I have painted so much the last months that I really need them more than ever.

When you were here I did not want to talk much about it or contradict you much, but when you said that I should change some day and that I should not always stay here, any more than Mauve had always stayed at Bloemendaal, it may be true, but I for myself see no good in moving, because I have a good studio here, and the scenery is very beautiful.

Don't forget I am positively convinced that a painter of rural life can do no better than take Barbizon for an example.

To dwell and to live in the very midst of what one paints, for in the country nature has every day a new and different aspect . . .

✻ ✻ ✻

I am still greatly under the impression of what has just happened – so I have worked on quietly these two Sundays.

Mother is looking well, and the many letters she has to write give her some distraction for the present. But, of course, she feels her loss heavily.

I do not know whether you remember how in January, when the

fields were covered with snow, and the sun rose fiery red out of the mist, I wrote to you that I scarcely ever had begun a new year in a more despondent mood.

It is a fact that there will be much trouble in store for us all. Of course you will understand that it is not for my own pleasure that I shall go and live in the studio. It makes things again more complicated for me, but I am quite sure that it is better for the others if I leave. So I am fully decided. Probably mother will go next year to Leyden. Then I shall be the only one of us who stays in Brabant.

And it does not seem at all improbable but that I shall stay there for the rest of my days. In fact I have no other wish than to live deep, deep in the heart of the country, and to paint rural life. I feel that my work lies there, so I shall keep my hand to the plough, and cut my furrow steadily . . .

✳ ✳ ✳

To Theo (399)
Nuenen, undated [1885]

. . . It is late in the evening, but I want to tell you once more how heartily I hope that our correspondence will become in the future somewhat more animated than it was of late.

Enclosed you will find two scratches from a few studies I made, while at the same time I am working again at those peasants around the dish of potatoes. I just came home from this cottage and have been working at it by lamplight, though I began it by daylight this time.

I painted it on a rather large canvas, and as the sketch is now I think there is some life in it.

But yet I am sure C. M., for instance, would find fault with the drawing, etc. Do you know what is a positive argument against that? That the beautiful effects of light in nature demand a very quick hand in drawing . . .

Now I know quite well that the great masters, especially in the period of their ripest experience, knew both how to be elaborate in this finishing, and at the same time to keep a thing full of life. But that certainly will be for the present beyond my power. As far as I have got now, however, I see a chance of giving a true impression of what I see.

Not always literally exact, rather never exact, for one sees nature through one's own temperament.

The advice I want to give, you know, is the following: Do not let the time pass by, help me to work as much as ever possible, and from now keep all the studies together.

I do not like to sign any of them yet, for I do not want them to circulate as pictures, which one would have to buy up again afterwards, when one had got some reputation. But it is a good thing if you show them, for you will see that some day we shall find somebody who wants to do the same thing I propose to you now, viz. to make a collection of studies . . .

Try to speak to somebody of *Le Chat Noir* and ask them if they want a sketch of those potato-eaters, if so, of what size, for that is all the same to me.

✳ ✳ ✳

To Theo (400)
Nuenen, undated [Spring 1885]

. . . I think I shall move about the first of May; though, of course, I am on good terms with mother and the sisters – yet I see and feel it is better so, for in the long run it would hardly be possible to live together. For which I can neither blame them, nor myself personally, but rather the incongruity of ideas between persons who want to keep a certain rank and a peasant-painter who does not think of such things.

When I call myself a peasant-painter, that is a real fact, and it will become more and more clear to you in the future, I feel at home there. And it has not been in vain that I spent so many evenings with the miners, and peat-diggers, and weavers, and peasants, musing by the fire, unless I was too hard at work for musing.

By witnessing peasant life continually, at all hours of the day, I have become so absorbed in it that I hardly ever think of anything else . . .

✳ ✳ ✳

. . . With the same mail you will receive a number of copies of the lithograph. Please give Mr Portier as many as he wants. And I enclose a letter for him, which I am afraid you will think rather long, and, in consequence, unpractical. But I thought that what I had to say, couldn't be expressed in more concise terms, and that the chief point is to give him arguments for his own instinctive feelings. And in fact, what I write to him, I say it also to you.

There is a school – I believe – of Impressionists. But I know very little about it. But I do know who are the original and most important masters, around whom, like round an axis – the landscape and peasant painters will turn. Delacroix, Corot, Millet and the rest. That is my own opinion, not correctly formulated.

I mean there are (rather than persons) rules or principles or fundamental truths for *drawing*, as well as for *colour*, upon which *one proves to fall back*, when one finds out an actual truth.

In drawing, for instance – that question of drawing figure beginning with the circle – that is to say taking for basis the elliptic planes. A thing which the ancient Greeks knew already, and which will remain till the end of the world. As to colour, those everlasting problems, for instance, that first question Corot addressed to Français, when Français (who had already a reputation) asked Corot (who then had nothing but a negative or rather bad reputation) when he (F.) came to Corot, to get some information: 'Qu'est-ce que c'est un ton rompu? Qu'est-ce que c'est un ton neutre?'

Which can better be shown on the palette than expressed in words.

So what I want to tell Portier in this letter, is my decided belief in Eugène Delacroix and the people of that time.

And at the same time, as the picture which I have on hand is different from lamplights by Dou or van Schendel, it is perhaps not superfluous to point out how one of the most beautiful things of the painters of this country has been the painting of *black*, which yet has *light* in it. Well, just read my letter and you will see that it is not unintelligible, and that it treats a subject that just occurred to me while painting.

I hope to have some chance with that picture of the potato-eaters.

I have also on hand a red sunset.

In order to paint rural life one must be master of so many things. But, on the other hand, I don't know anything at which one works with so much calm, in the sense of serenity, however much struggle one may have in material things . . .

To change the subject. How typical is that saying about the figures of Millet: *'Son paysan semble peint avec la terre qu'il ensemence!'* How exact and how true. And how important it is to know how to mix on the palette those colours which have no name, and yet are the real foundation of everything . . .

❋ ❋ ❋

To Theo   (403)
Nuenen, undated [1885]

. . . I want to tell you that I am working at the potato-eaters, and I have painted new studies of the heads, especially the hands are greatly altered.

What I try most is to bring *life* into it.

I wonder what Portier will say about it when it is finished?

. . . in the picture I give free scope to my own head in the sense of *thought* or imagination, which is not so much the case in *studies* where no creative process is allowed, but where one finds food for one's imagination in reality, in order to make it exact . . .

❋ ❋ ❋

To Anton van Rappard   (51R)
Nuenen, undated [1885]

Today I sent you a basket containing birds' nests. I have some others in my own studio. They are thrush, blackbird, yellow oriole, wren and finch nests. I hope they arrive in good condition.

Do you know much about Eugène Delacroix? I have read a splendid article about him by Silvestre. I will write down a few words that impressed me. The article ended thus: 'Ainsi mourut presqu'en souriant Eugène Delacroix – peintre de grande race – qui avait un soleil dans la tête et un orage dans le cœur – qui des guerriers passa aux saints – des amants aux tigres – et des tigres aux fleurs.' These words struck me. The article as a whole pointed out how in his pictures the mood of colour and tone was one with the meaning.

In colour, juxtaposition gives us complementary relationships: from black to white, from yellow to violet, from orange to blue, from red to green. And see this: Delacroix writes to a friend: 'La chapelle où j'ai peint ma Piéta était tellement obscure que je n'ai pas su d'abord comment peindre pour faire parler mon tableau – j'ai été obligé alors de peindre dans le cadavre du Christ les ombres avec du bleu de prusse – les lumières avec du jaune de chrome pur.'

To this the writer adds: 'Il faut être Delacroix pour oser cela.' Then somewhere else I read: 'Lorsque Delacroix peint – c'est comme le lion qui dévore le morceau.' The article of Silvestre is all about this point.

What tremendous fellows these French painters are: Millet, Delacroix, Corot, Troyon, Daubigny, Rousseau, Daumier and Jacque – not to forget Jules Dupré! A new one of the same type is Lhermitte.

I want to tell you something else about Delacroix: he had a discussion with a friend as to working absolutely from Nature, and he said on that occasion that we have to get our *studies* from Nature, but that the real picture should be done *from memory*. That friend was walking with him on the boulevard when they had that argument, which ran rather high, and when they separated, the other was not quite convinced. Delacroix allowed him to walk a bit ahead of him; then, making a speaking-trumpet of his hands, he called out quite loudly in the middle of the street, to the consternation of the respectable citizens passing by: '*Par cœur! Par cœur!*' . . .

✳ ✳ ✳

To Theo   (404)
Nuenen, 30 April 1885

On your birthday I send you best wishes for good health and serenity. I should have liked to send you the picture of the potato-eaters on that day, but though it is getting on well, it is not quite finished yet.

Though the definite picture will have been painted in a relatively short time, and for the greater part from memory, yet it has taken a whole winter of painting study-heads and hands.

And as to those few days in which I have painted it now, it has been a regular battle, but one for which I feel great animation.

Though every moment I was afraid I should never get out of it. But painting is also 'agir-créer'.

When the weavers weave that cloth, which I think is called cheviot, or also the peculiar Scottish plaids, then you know their aim is, for the cheviot, to get special broken colours and greys, and for the many-coloured checkered cloth, to make the most vivid colours balance each other, so that, instead of the tissue being crude, the *effet produit* of the pattern is harmonious at a distance.

A grey, woven from red, blue, yellow, dirty white and black threads, a blue that is *broken* by a green, and orange-red, or yellow thread, are quite different from *plain colours*, that is to say they are more iridescent, and primary colours become *hard*, cold and *dead* next to them. But for the weaver or rather the designer of the pattern or the combination of colours it is not always easy to fix his estimation of the number of threads and their direction, as little as it is easy to blend the strokes of the brush into an harmonious whole.

If you could compare the first painted studies I made on my arrival here at Nuenen and the picture now on hand, I think you would see that as to colour some ground has been gained . . .

As to the potato-eaters, it is a picture that shows well in gold, I am sure of that, but it would show as well on a wall, papered in the deep colour of ripe corn.

Without such a setting *it simply cannot be seen.*

Against a dark background it does not show off well, and not at all against a dull background. That is because it gives a glance in a very grey interior . . .

I have tried to make it clear how those people, eating their potatoes under the lamplight, have dug the earth with those very hands they put in the dish, and so it speaks of *manual labour*, and how they have honestly earned their food.

I have wanted to give the impression of quite a different way of living than that of us civilized people. Therefore I am not at all anxious for everyone to like it or to admire it at once.

All winter long I have had in hand the threads of this tissue, and have searched for the definite pattern, and though it has become a tissue of a rough and coarse aspect, nevertheless the threads have been selected carefully and according to certain rules. And it might prove to be a real *peasant picture. I know it is* . . .

. . . it would be wrong, I think, to give a peasant picture a certain conventional smoothness. If a peasant picture smells of bacon, smoke, potato-steam, all right, that's not unhealthy, if a stable smells of dung, all right, that belongs to a stable; if the field has an odour of ripe corn or potatoes or of guano or manure, that's healthy, especially for people from the city.

Such pictures may *teach* them something. But to be perfumed is not what a peasant picture needs . . .

I think the potato-eaters will get finished after all; the last days are almost dangerous for a picture, as you know, because when it is not quite dry, one cannot work in it with a large brush without the great chance of spoiling it. And the alterations must be made quietly and calmly with a small brush. Therefore I have simply taken it to my friend and told him to take care that I should not spoil it in that way and that I should come to his house to give those finishing touches. You will see, it has originality . . .

✳ ✳ ✳

To Anton van Rappard (52R)
Nuenen, 1885

I have just received your letter (to my surprise). I hereby return it – with greetings,

Vincent

Vincent attached Rappard's letter about his lithograph The Potato Eaters; *which is given below:*

Utrecht, May 24, 1885

AMICE!

I was pleased indeed to receive a sign of life from you, even if the sign was not entirely what I could have wished it to be.

The news of your father's death came so unexpectedly that I was eager for further information, which, however, has not come.

If I remember correctly, it was through my superficial way of reading newspapers – skipping the small announcements – that I did not learn of it in the first place from Het Nieuws van den Dag. *Anyhow, what I do know is that very, very shortly after the receipt of the formal announcement I called on a friend, who had already read about it in the newspaper.*

164

Did you think that I cared so little about your father and that I took so little interest in the happenings of your family that the usual formal notice of so sad a loss was sufficient for my interest?

Then you are very much mistaken.

In connexion with what you have just sent me, I want to go back for a moment to your last letter, in which you speak about the art of expressing oneself clearly in words.

I want to point out to you that even though I express myself badly when speaking, I can do it well in writing, if I take sufficient care.

What I wrote you about your manner of working expresses precisely what I meant to express – although I did not take great pains in the matter – with the result that the style was perhaps none too agreeable. I hoped and still hope that I was mistaken about the manner in which you do your work, but that is just why I am so sorry to see, from what you send me, a complete confirmation of my opinion about your way of working; it gave me quite a shock.

You'll agree with me that such work cannot be taken seriously. You can do better than that, fortunately, but why then should you be so superficial in your way of viewing and treating everything? Why not study the action of the models? In your work they are just posing. That coquettish little hand of the woman in the background, how unreal! And what connexion is there between the coffee-pot, the table and the hand that rests on the handle? What is the kettle doing there? It does not stand on anything; it is not held – so what then? And why is the man to the right not allowed to have a knee, an abdomen and lungs? Or perhaps they are in his back? And why should his arm be a yard too short, and why does he lack half of his nose? And why must the woman at the left have a little pipe-stem with a die at the end, instead of a nose?

And you dare, while working in such a manner, to invoke the names of Millet and Breton? Go on, now!

Art is too great a thing to be treated so carelessly!

Adieu, believe me,

    Always your friend,

      A. G. A. v. Rappard

✳ ✳ ✳

To Anton van Rappard   (53R)
Nuenen, undated [1885]

Because of what has happened, I have decided to write to you, not because I like to, but because I want to make myself clear.

There are two reasons for my return of your last letter. Each one in itself, in my opinion, would be a sufficient cause. The first reason is this: I did not like your remarks about my lithograph, even if they were justified. Suppose I could not even contradict them – even then you had no right to ignore all my work in such an insulting manner as you have.

And, secondly, as you have received, not only from me, but also from my family, more friendship than you ever gave, *you can not claim* that at the occasion of my father's death it was *our duty* to send you anything more than the announcement. *Why should I* have written you concerning my father's death when you had not even answered my last letter? Why should I, especially when you wrote to my mother, and not to me, on the occasion of my father's death? It made such a peculiar impression on the family that they were still talking about it when I arrived, and were wondering why you did not write to me. Not that I really care whether you wrote then, or now, or at any other time.

You know that for many years I have not been on such good terms with the family at home. At the death of my father, *I had to do* the correspondence with the near relatives. As soon as the family arrived, however, I withdrew entirely from this duty, and possible negligence reflects on my family and not on me. And as a matter of fact, I want to tell you that an exception was made with you, for I asked at home if they had sent you a notice, and it seemed they had forgotten to. Well, more than enough has been said about this. The reason that I am writing is not to answer your remarks about those things, also not to repeat the remarks I made concerning what you said about painting. You may reread your own letter and see if you still think you were right. If you really mean that, if you make up your mind to, you can express yourself very well, then the best thing is simply to let you think that.

But to come to the point, the reason I am writing you is simply because (though it was not *I*, but *you* who were insulting in the first place) I have known you so long that it seems a pity to break off our acquaintance for such a reason. What I have to say to you is as a painter to a painter, and as you and I paint, things will remain as they are, whether we know each other or not.

The question was of Millet – all right – I'll answer you, *Amice*. You wrote me: 'And you dare to invoke to the names of Millet and Breton?' . . .

In reply I say simply this for your serious consideration: do not fight with me. You see, I am going my own way, and I do not seek a quarrel with anyone, not even with you. I would let you say whatever you wanted, even if you used some more of those expressions. I wouldn't care a button! Let that be enough for the present. You have often said that I do not pay attention to the form of the figure. It is beneath me to pay attention to it, my dear fellow, and it is beneath you to say such an unwarranted thing. You have now known me for years. Have you ever seen me working in any other way than with a model, and have I ever spared the often heavy expense, although you know how poor I am? What you wrote to me over and over again, not only in the last letter, but in former ones as well, until I got sick of reading it, was about *technique*, which is the reason that you did not answer my last letter. What I answered, and what I answer again, is: the conventional meaning, which is more and more being given to the word, is different from the true meaning, which is *science*. Well, Meissonier himself says: 'La Science, nul ne l'a.' *La Science*, however, is not the same as *de la science*. That, in the first place, you will not contradict. But even that is not right, yet. Look at Haverman, for example; people say of him (as you do) that he has so much *technique*. Or let's go beyond Haverman, to many others; they have something that is equal to that kind of knowledge of art which Haverman has. There is Jacquet, of the French artists, who is really better. My reasoning is simply this – that to draw a figure with academic correctness and an even, convincing brushstroke has little to do with the needs, the compelling needs, in the field of present-day painting. Anyway, less than we think, generally speaking.

If you should say of Haverman that he has much *métier* instead of *technique*, for once I would agree with you. Perhaps you will understand what I mean if I say that, when Haverman sits before a pretty lady's or girl's head, he'll make it prettier than nearly anyone else, I know, but put him before a *peasant*, and he will not even make a beginning. His art, so far as I can see, seems to apply especially to subjects that are not so much needed; it is suitable to subjects that are entirely contrary to Millet or Lhermitte, and it is mostly parallel to that of Cabanel, who, with what I call *métier*, told us little that lasted or helped art forward. And I beg of you, do not *confuse* this with the manner of painting of a Millet or a Lhermitte.

What I said and still say is that the word 'technique' is used too freely in a conventional way, and it is not always being used in good faith. The *technique* of all those Italians and Spaniards is being praised, and they are more conventional, they have more routine, than most people. With men like Haverman, I am afraid that *métier* becomes so quickly routine, and then what is it worth?

What I want to ask you now is – what is really the reason that you have broken with me?

The reason I am writing you again is precisely because of my love for Millet and for Breton, and for everyone who paints *the peasants and the common people,* and I count you among them. I do not say this because you meant much to me as a friend, *Amice,* because, as a friend, you meant very little, and excuse me if, for the first and last time, I say this squarely to your face – I do not know of a drier friendship than yours. And so, in the first place, I am not speaking as I do for such a reason; in the second place, our friendship might have become *greater.*

I do not let any opportunity slip to find models, etc., and I have not been small about the matter, either, keeping my resources a secret; on the contrary, when any painter comes to this neighbourhood, I am always glad to show him around.

You know that it is not always easy to find models who will pose, and I do not mind letting the artists have a *pied-à-terre* here, which, after all, is not such an indifferent thing for artists. And I tell you this because if you wish to paint here you need not feel embarrassed because of this little spat. I live now by myself, but just the same you can stay with me in my studio. Perhaps this sounds a little condescending, coming from me to you, and does not mean a thing to you. Well, that is all right, really. I am so used to insults that they do not even hurt me. A person like you might not understand how cold a letter like yours leaves me . . . and being as insensible about it as a lamp-post, I have no grudge even against you. What I do have is enough clearness and serenity to answer as I do now.

Do you want to break with me? All right.

Do you want to keep on painting here? Then don't be upset about this little bickering in our correspondence . . .

The things you painted here the last time you were here had, and still have, my full sympathy, and, *Amice* Rappard, I am writing because you worked so damned well that last time, and because I have said to myself: 'Perhaps he prefers everything to be as it was.'

You must make up your mind. I say this squarely. Besides having all respect for your painting, I have a little fear about you for the *future* somehow, and I wonder whether or not you will keep it up. Sometimes I think, given the social position and standing you have, it cannot be otherwise; you are exposed to many things, and perhaps you cannot in the long run keep up the standard you have at this moment. I mean, as an artist. I do not concern myself with the rest.

I am speaking to you as painter to painter. If you want to look for pictures here, *everything will be as before.* You can come here and stay with me just the same, even if I do live alone, just as formerly. You see, I thought it had meant something to you perhaps, and still might mean something. And I will add this: If you can find something elsewhere that suits you just as well – all right. I have no reason to grieve about it, and then, adieu.

You did not write anything about *your* work, and I did not write about *mine.*

Believe me, do not quarrel with me about Millet. Millet is someone about whom I will not quarrel, although I will not refuse to discuss him.

✳ ✳ ✳

To Anton van Rappard (54R)
Nuenen, 1885

I have received your letter; it is more tedious and drier than ever.

However, as you say in it: 'I want to answer your letter at once so as not to strengthen you in your idea that, as far as I am concerned, there exists any idea of breaking,' I want to repeat to you again, once and for all, that there is in my house a spare room which is at your disposal as well as at that of other artists who want to come to make studies here.

I want to advise you and Wenkebach, whom I shall see tomorrow, to come occasionally, as there are very many beautiful things to see here. If that means anything to you, all right; if not, it is the same with me, but if you do come, each of us must go his own way.

As regards the lithograph, here is my explanation – I did it altogether from memory on a day that I was working at an entirely new method of procedure, and was looking for new ideas as to how to put it up. It is nothing but a proof, which will later have to be engraved on the stone; originally it was much better, and in the later composition it is painted much better, even if there are mistakes in the arms and nose,

169

about which you flew into a rage. As to the picture, the one I painted, I am not sorry I did it, even if there are mistakes in it. I can't say that your letter of today is of any use or at all necessary. Be assured that when you say that your confidence in me is gone, as well as those other things, I remain quite undisturbed; in saying this of me, you are no different from other people. I leave those people alone. They may say, think, behave toward me, precisely as they like; that's their responsibility. I am not obliged to listen to that continual nagging at me. My parents, my teachers, the Messrs Goupil, and all sorts of friends and acquaintances besides have told me so many things for 'my own good' (disagreeable things), that in the end the load has become a little too heavy, so now I let them say whatever they like. I take no more notice of it, my friend, and since I started on this policy, I have not gone backwards. I know it, for sure.

In answer I say this: It is true that your work is good, but that does not mean that you are always in the right, my friend, that there are no other roads and ways than yours to attain something worthwhile. I would, as a matter of fact, like very much to talk to you, but do not conclude from this that I mean to consult you; but it seems we are not getting anywhere, it becomes worse and worse.

As to 'self-knowledge', who has it? Here also *'la science, nul ne l'a'*; *'de la science'*, as to oneself, one's good or bad tendencies, everyone has them, and I started with saying I had mine. We all need self-knowledge. But do not think, through your lack of it, that you never err, and that you do not often hurt others terribly with your superficial judgments.

I know we all do that, and still we have to try to get on with each other, but since we are speaking of 'self-knowledge' – no, my friend, it is of deep regret to me that you started that subject, because I am afraid that is your weakest point, at all events as a man. But, *enfin*, I am going to tell you what I think when I think of you:

As for your work, I think what you are doing at present is splendid; but here is a thought which I have in me – I do not want to hide one thing, as I have known you for a rather long time. There was a time – a little while before and a short time after your illness – when as a man you were much less matter-of-fact than at other times; you were broader, softer, more liberal and sincere. Now you are again talking to me just as in former days, the terribly pedantic Rappard of a certain Academy. I am sorry to find that this friend has returned, and I am even more sorry that I have lost the friend of the exceptional period

170

when he had changed and improved. Where and how I observed that? I just try to think. And about his work? Is his work going to be broader, fuller, nobler only for a short time? Do you know the answer to that? This idea of mine is written on only a half-sheet of paper, but it shows that I am sometimes afraid that your work will lose the nobler element. I am telling you this very simply and plainly, I think.

Whatever my mistakes may be, I have a sincere desire to be kind to other people. I put too much heart in my work to be insincere, as you are always accusing me of being. I do not need to take to heart what you say, and I don't, and as to your remarks that I need someone to tell me these things – it may be. But it may be that I myself am the person to do so, and there are many other people who are nagging me just like you; I can do without them.

Greetings, but your letter was not just, on the whole, even if there were details in it that were right to a certain extent.

You did not write anything about your work, neither did I about mine.

✳ ✳ ✳

To Theo   (415)
Nuenen, undated [1885]

I had a visit today of Wenkebach, a painter from Utrecht, who is a friend of Rappard's. He is a landscape painter and I often saw his name mentioned and he received a medal in London at the same time with Rappard. He has seen my work, those cottages which I am going to send you and also the drawings of figures.

I told him I was sorry to say there had been misunderstandings between Rappard and me, which I could hardly explain otherwise, than that he had been chaffing at my work with other people from the Hague, and as he had not seen anything of it for a long time he had involuntarily been turned against me. I showed Wenkebach figures which Rappard used to like, and at the same time the new ones, and showed him that indeed I had changed in some respects and would change still more, but that what I made now was certainly not inferior.

Then he said that he did not doubt but Rappard would take back what he had written.

Then I showed him that, as to colour, I certainly do not want to paint *always* dark. Some of the cottages are even quite clear.

But that my aim is to proceed from the primary colours: red, blue, yellow and not from grey.

We had a long discussion about colour, and among other things he said, he had noticed how Jaap Maris in old water-colours also frequently used ruddy, brownish grey, red colours. So that if one puts them beside one of his present drawings, they become quite red.

It is the same with Israëls.

Perhaps I do more harm than good now by telling you this, because it is but part of a conversation, and I ought to tell the whole of it. But we have spoken about it before, so you will perhaps understand it in its real connection. In order to get an *honest, sound* palette, *to stick to it*, it is necessary to practise also the stronger gamuts, and to continue to use them, especially in these days, when imitators (not the masters themselves) of the great painters in *grey* want to paint more and more, always and everything *clear*.

So Wenkebach said, for instance, that he liked the picture of the old tower also for its technique, I painted it last year, with a lot of bitumen in it. He said he found it quite original.

The same with other old things. That water-mill, the plough with oxen, the avenue with autumn effect.

But what pleased me most of all, was that he liked the figures. He called them Millet-like. But I know for sure that I will get them better still, if only I have some chance with the money, and can continue to work on them full speed, but that is what rather worries me and, for this month I am *absolutely* pinched. I am literally without a penny.

We shall have hard times, it is not all my fault, but only by perseverance we still have a chance of reaping, after some time, what we are sowing.

And it worries me enough that you have all that money trouble, I wish I could lighten it somewhat for you . . .

❊ ❊ ❊

To Anton van Rappard   (55R)
Nuenen, 1885

To my great regret I have not yet had an answer from you. The more

I think about it, the nearer I come to the conclusion that I am willing to compromise. So if you care to retract a correspond ence which in my opinion is not worthy of you, I once more repeat, I am willing to look upon the whole matter as a misunderstanding and our friendship need not change, but on one positive condition, you must yourself realize that you have made a mistake. As I do not wish, under any condition, to let this thing drag along any longer, I beg of you to answer me within a week. Your letter will tell me your attitude and then I can decide.

If it happens that you do not write this week, then I am not *interested in your answer any more.* Then time will show whether your criticisms of my work and of myself were justified or not, whether they were or were not in good faith.

* * *

To Anton van Rappard (56R)
Eindhoven, 21 July 1885

We must stop our bickering and bothering, in the first place because it begins to look like the dispute between a couple of obstinate clergymen who had different opinions about the geographical position of the road that leads to Holiness. They grew so ardent in their dispute that, at the same moment, each threw his wig into the other's face. The wigs are part of the picture, and how can we, with the best intentions in the world, go on, since we have arrived at the psychological moment and neither of us possesses the indispensable implement in question.

Therefore I am at the end of my wits and I am sorry we started something which we seem to be unable to carry to the bitter end – in the way mentioned above, which would have been the only worthy one.

I really think that the dispute has a ridiculous side, and it might become more and more so, which is one of the reasons I can't continue it any longer. It is too absurd. On your part you have to stop it, too, be sensible. Remember what gets into a man's mind does not always come straight from his conscience. Whether *your conscience* dictated those letters to you, whether it was your *duty* to write them, what does it matter! Laugh about it. As you were sincere in your thought that it was your duty and your conscience which dictated what you wrote, I'll wipe the slate clean from my side as well as yours; so now then – *be done with it* . . .

✳ ✳ ✳

To Theo (421)
Nuenen, undated [1885]

To my letter of the day before yesterday I want to add, that yesterday I received a letter from Rappard, and that our quarrel has been quite made up, that he has sent me a sketch of a large picture of a brickyard which he is painting. It looks very original, if you wanted to name other pictures in the same style, it would be, for instance, Meunier whose miners you saw in Antwerp.

He has taken a small house outside Utrecht, close to the brickyard, nothing but a studio (with a skylight) he also intends to go back to Terschelling, so he is again quite absorbed in nature and in my opinion, that is better than to work in the city. But I want to tell you that I hope we two shall also come to a better understanding. Just as little as I could accept his criticism can I be satisfied with the present condition in which I am too much hampered in my work by my financial difficulties,

I don't want you alone to put this right, but I simply want that we together (and not I alone) do our best to improve the situation. I know that for you too, it costs trouble and is not easy and as such I readily appreciate it, but to take trouble for a certain aim is no misfortune, and to have to fight is the condition of every honest victory.

And as things are getting worse and worse for me, instead of better, they finally get so bad that I really must complain.

And I repeat let us keep that little painting business of mine in good order, for sooner or later we may need it badly. If storm is threatening, one must keep the boats in good order.

That man in the Hague is Leurs, he does not live any longer in the Practizijnshoek, but in the Molenstraat.

He begs me to send him more than one picture in order to have more than one chance and he offers me his two show-windows. And as he himself is very much in need of money, he will not spare trouble.

I sent him a few cottages, the old churchtower and some smaller studies with figures.

174

And while these are on show, I shall make some new ones to keep things going.

There is some chance of also getting a second man at the Hague. But the principal thing for me is to be able *to go on with my work* . . .

❊ ❊ ❊

To Theo (423)
Nuenen, undated [1885]

. . . These last two weeks I had a lot of worry from the priests, who told me, evidently with the best intentions, and feeling themselves obliged like other people to meddle with it, that I ought not to get too familiar with people below my rank; expressing themselves to *me* in these terms but using towards 'the people of lower rank' quite a different tone, namely, forbidding them to have themselves painted. I simply told it at once to the Burgomaster and pointed out to him that it was a thing that did not concern the priests at all, who have to keep to their own territory of more abstract things.

At all events, they stopped their opposition for the moment and I hope it will remain so. A girl I had often painted was with child, and they suspected me, though it was not so . . .

❊ ❊ ❊

To Theo (425)
Nuenen, undated [1885]

. . . That affair with the priest did not worry me any further. But of course there will always remain God-fearing natives in the village, who will persist in suspecting me, for one thing is sure, that the priest would only too gladly throw the whole blame of that affair on me. However as I am quite innocent, the gossip from that side leaves me perfectly indifferent; as long as they don't hinder me in my painting, I don't take any notice of it whatever. With the peasants where the accident happened, where I often used to paint, I remained on good terms, and I am as welcome in their home as I used to be. I am now busy painting still-lifes of my birds' nests, four of which are finished; I think some people, who are good observers of nature, might like

175

them, because of the colours of the moss, the dry leaves and the grasses . . .

Vincent had a wonderful collection of birds' nests (legal at that time!) and had been painting a series of still-lifes from them, arguing that in still-life, they required a different treatment from in their natural settings. He had also become intensely interested in colour.

✳ ✳ ✳

To Theo   (428)
Nuenen, undated [1885]

. . . Well, the birds' nests have also been painted on purpose against a black background, because I openly want to express in these studies, that the objects do not appear in their natural surroundings, but against a conventional background. A *living* nest in nature is quite different, one hardly sees the nest itself, one sees the birds . . .

But tell me, *black* and *white*, may they be used or not, are they forbidden fruit?

I don't think so, Frans Hals even has twenty-seven blacks. White, but you know yourself, what characteristic pictures some modern colourists make of white on white. What is the meaning of that word: *one may not?* Delacroix called them *rests*, used them as such. You must not have a prejudice against them, for if only used in their place, and in harmony with the rest, one may of course use every tone . . .

✳ ✳ ✳

To Theo   (430)
Nuenen, 4 November 1885

. . . Don't let it trouble you when I just leave the brush strokes in my studies, as I put them on, with smaller or larger clods of paint. That does not matter at all, if one leaves them for a year (or half a year is enough), and then scrapes them off quickly with a razor, one gets a much more solid colour than would be the case after painting flimsily. For the sake of the conservation and preserving the colours of a picture, it is necessary that especially the light parts are painted solidly. And this scraping off has been done by the old masters as well as by the French painters of today. I believe that glacis of a transparent colour often get quite dark and disappear in time, if they are applied before the picture in its preparation is thoroughly dry, but applied *later*, they certainly will keep. You yourself made the observation that my studies in the studio became rather better than worse in colour by time. I think this comes from putting the paint on solidly, and not using oil. When it is a year old, the little oil which the paint always contains has evaporated, and there remains the healthy solid part . . .

✳ ✳ ✳

To Theo   (431)
Nuenen, undated [1885]

. . . I think that I am making progress with my work. Last night something happened to me which I will tell you as minutely as I can. You know those three pollard oaks at the bottom of the garden at home; I have plodded on them for the fourth time. I had been at them three days . . .

The difficulty was the tufts of havana leaves, to model them and give them the form, the colour, the tone. Then in the evening I took it to that acquaintance of mine in Eindhoven [the goldsmith], who has rather a stylish drawing-room, where we put it on the wall (grey paper, furniture black with gold). Well, never before was I so convinced that I shall make things that do well, that I shall succeed in calculating my colours, so that I have it in my power to make effect. This was havana, soft green and white (grey), even *pure* white, direct from the tube (you see that I, for my part, though I speak about black, have no prejudice against the other extreme, the utmost extreme even).

Now, though that man has money, though he took a fancy to it, I felt such a glow of courage, when I saw that it was good, that as it hung there, it raised an atmosphere, by the soft melancholy harmony of that combination of colours *that I could not sell it.*

But as he had a fancy for it, I gave it him . . .

At the end of November 1885 Vincent headed for Antwerp, where he hoped to contact some dealers who would take on his work. Once there he rented a studio over a paint dealer's.

Antwerp, Saturday evening [November 1885]

. . . I have walked along the docks and the quays several times
already, in all directions. Especially when one comes from the sand
and the heath and the quiet of a peasant village, and has for a
long time been in none but quiet surroundings, the contrast is
curious . . .

A white horse in the mud, in a corner where heaps of merchandise
are lying covered by oilcloth – against old black smoky walls of the
warehouse. Quite simple, but an effect of Black and White.

Through the window of a very elegant English bar, one will look out
on the dirtiest mire, and on a ship, where, for instance, dainty
merchandise like hides and buffalo horns, is being unloaded by huge
dock hands or exotic sailors; a very dainty fair young English girl is
standing at the window looking at it, or at something else. The interior
with the figure altogether in tone, and for light – the silvery sky above
that mud, and the buffalo horns, again a series of rather sharp
contrasts. There will be Flemish sailors, with almost too healthy faces,
with broad shoulders, strong and full, and thoroughly Antwerp folk,
eating mussels, or drinking beer, and that will happen with a lot of
noise and movement – as opposition – a tiny figure in black with her
little hands against the body, comes stealing noiselessly along the grey
walls. Framed by raven-black hair – a small oval face, brown? orange-
yellow? I don't know. For a moment she lifts her eyelids, and looks with
an askant glance from a pair of jet black eyes.

It is a Chinese girl, mysterious, quiet like a mouse – small, bug-like
in character. What a contrast to that group of Flemish mussel eaters.
Another contrast – one passes through a very narrow street, between
tremendously high houses, warehouses and sheds.

But down below in the street pubs of all nationalities with attending
masculine and feminine individuals, shops with eatables, seamen's
clothes, motley and crowded.

That street is long, every minute one sees something typical. Now
and again there is a row, when a quarrel is going on, intenser than elsewhere, for instance there you are walking, looking about, and suddenly
there arises a hurrah, and all kinds of shouting. In broad daylight a
sailor is being thrown out of a public-house by the girls, and followed
by a furious fellow and a bunch of women, of whom he seems rather

afraid – at least I saw him scramble over a heap of sacks and disappear through a warehouse window.

Now, when one has enough of all this tumult – at the end of the piers where the Harwich and Havre steamers lie at anchor, having the city behind, one sees in front nothing, absolutely nothing but an infinite expanse of flat, half-inundated fields, awfully dreary and wet, waving dry rushes, mud, the river with a single little black boat, the water in the foreground grey, the sky, foggy and cold, grey – quiet like a desert.

Now one sees a girl who is splendid of health, and who looks at least loyal, simple and jolly, then again a face so sly and false, that it makes one afraid, as of a hyena. Not to forget the faces damaged by smallpox, which have the colour of boiled shrimps, with pale grey eyes, without eyebrows, and little sleek thin hair, the colour of real pigs' bristles or somewhat more yellow; Swedish or Danish types. It would be fine to work there, but how and where?

For one would very soon get into a scrape.

However I have crossed quite a number of streets and back streets without meeting with adventures, and I have sat and talked quite jovially to various girls that seemed to take me for a skipper.

My studio is not bad, especially as I have pinned a lot of little Japanese pictures on the wall, which amuse me very much. You know those little women's figures in gardens, or on the beach, horsemen, flowers, knotty thorn branches . . .

✳ ✳ ✳

To Theo (438)
Antwerp, December [1885]

Thanks for your letter and enclosed fr. 150. I want to tell you that I am glad I came here. Last week I painted three more studies, one with backs of old houses, seen from my window, two in the park. One of those I have exhibited at a dealer's. Further, I have given the ones I brought along from the country, in commission, to two others. At a fourth, I can exhibit a view on the quay as soon as the weather permits me to make it, because he had a Mols together with which he could exhibit another one. Then I have got an address from this dealer, where he assured me I should be well received . . .

It is hard, terribly hard, to keep on working, when one does not sell, and when one literally has to pay for one's colours from what would not be too much for eating, drinking and lodgings, calculated ever so strictly. And then besides the models. But all the same there is a chance, and even a good one, because, comparatively speaking, there are but few painters at work nowadays . . .

I feel a power in me to do something, I see that my work holds out against other work, and that gives me a great love to work, and of late when I was in the country, I commenced to doubt, because I noticed that Portier does not seem to care for my things any more . . .

❉ ❉ ❉

To Theo (439)
Antwerp, undated [1885]

. . . Rubens certainly makes a strong impression on me, I think his drawing tremendously good, I mean the drawing of heads and hands in themselves. I am fairly carried away by his way of drawing the lines in a face with dashes of pure red, or of modelling the fingers in the hands by the same kind of dashes. I go to the Museum fairly often and then I look at little else but a few heads and hands of his and of Jordaens. I know he is not as intimate as Hals and Rembrandt, but they are so alive, those heads themselves . . .

I made the acquaintance of Tyck, the best paint manufacturer here, and he was very kind in giving me information about some colours. The green colours, for instance, they are solid. I also asked him things about the technic of Rubens, which he answered in a way that proved to me how well he analyses how things are done, what everybody does not do, and yet it is a very useful thing . . .

I like Rubens just for his open-hearted way of painting, his working with the most simple means . . .

❉ ❉ ❉

To Theo (440)
Antwerp, undated [1885]

Today for the first time I feel rather faint – I had painted a picture of *Het Steen* and went to show it to some dealers. Two were not at home, and one did not like it, and one complained bitterly that, in a fortnight, literally not a single person had shown his face in the store. This is not very encouraging, especially when the weather is chilly and gloomy, and when one has changed one's last five franc piece and doesn't know how to get through the next two weeks.

As long as I am painting I do not feel faint, but in the long run those times between are sometimes rather too melancholy, and it grieves me when I don't get on, and am always in a bad fix. Do you know, for instance, that as long as I have been here, I have had but three warm meals, and for the rest nothing but bread. In this way one becomes vegetarian more than is good for one. Especially as it was the same thing in Nuenen for half a year, and even then I could not pay my colours bill . . .

❋ ❋ ❋

To Theo   (441)
Antwerp, 19 December 1885

. . . I am at the end of my tether, with my last remaining fr. 5 I had to buy two canvases for those two portraits, and the laundry woman has just brought my washing, so that for the moment I have only a few centimes left.

So I must ask you most urgently, for Heaven's sake don't put off writing, and send me much or little, according to what you can spare, but know that I am literally starving . . .

❋ ❋ ❋

To Theo   (442)
Antwerp, 28 December 1885

. . . My thoughts are all the time full of Rembrandt and Hals these days, not because I see so many of their pictures, but because I see among the people here so many types that remind me of that time.

I still go often to those popular balls, to see the heads of the women, and the heads of the sailors and soldiers. One pays the entrance fee of 20 or 30 centimes, and drinks a glass of beer, for they drink very little spirits, and one can amuse oneself a whole evening, at least I do, by looking how these people enjoy themselves . . .

I notice that I have been underfed too long, and when I received your money my stomach could not digest the food; but I will try to remedy that . . .

Cobalt is a divine colour, and there is nothing so beautiful to bring atmosphere around things. Carmine is the red of wine, and it is warm and witty like wine.

The same for emerald-green. It is bad economy not to use these colours, the same for cadmium. [All these are very expensive colours.]

✳ ✳ ✳

To Theo   (443)
Antwerp, January 1886

. . . As to the end of the month – I beg you most kindly but absolutely – let one of your creditors wait, i.e. at least for fr. 50 (they can stand it, do not be afraid), but please do not let it be me, for *even then* it will still be tough for me . . .

In January Vincent began to think of joining Theo in Paris, and once the idea had got into his head, he wanted to go immediately. Theo, however, wanted him to wait until he had found a bigger apartment. In the meantime Theo also wanted Vincent to help their mother move from Nuenen to Breda, but Vincent still wanted to come to Paris. He was suffering from bad toothache and undernourishment.

✳ ✳ ✳

To Theo   (448)
Antwerp, February [1886]

. . . I thought my teeth were bad because of another reason, and I did not know that my stomach had deteriorated to such a degree. It is stupid if you will, but one has sometimes to choose between two evils, and is bound either on one side or the other.

During the last month it began to trouble me a great deal; I began also to cough continually too, and expectorate a greyish phlegm, etc., so that I began to feel anxious. But we will try to redress it.

You see I am not stronger than other people in so far that if I neglected myself too much, it would be the same with me as with so *many* painters (so very many if one thinks about it), I should catch my death, or worse still – become crazy or an idiot.

✳ ✳ ✳

To Theo (449)
Antwerp, undated [February 1886]

. . . What the doctor tells me is that I absolutely must take better care of myself, and until I feel stronger I must take more rest.

It is an *absolute* breakdown . . .

✳ ✳ ✳

To Theo (452)
Antwerp, undated [February 1886]

. . . My being in Nuenen at least for the month of March would only be for the sake of the moving, and I have to be there still for the sake of my change of domicile. But as to myself, I am quite willing not to go back there at all . . .

✳ ✳ ✳

To Theo (456)
Antwerp, 18 February 1886

At the moment that all my money is gone, absolutely gone, I write to you once again.

If you can send anything, be it only fr. 5, do so. There are still ten days in the month left, and how am I to get through them? For I have absolutely *nothing* left. Even at the baker's, *nothing*.

I know but one thing, that all those things prove decidedly that I cannot act otherwise than I wrote you – namely – by not postponing going to Paris . . .

Vincent left Antwerp in March and went straight to Paris.

PART SIX

'Extraordinary Exaltation'

Paris March 1886–February 1888 – Arles February
1888–May 1889 – St Rémy May 1889–May 1890
– Auvers-sur-Oise May–July 1890

Vincent will remain in Paris with his brother Theo for two years, first at his flat near the Boulevard de Clichy and then moving to a larger one in Rue Lépic, Montmartre. Since the brothers are living together, few letters exist from this period, but we do know that Vincent joined Félix Cormon's Atelier, where he met other students who would go on to be Impressionists: Louis Anquetin, Emile Bernard, John Russell and Henri de Toulouse-Lautrec. Vincent worked from plaster casts and painted flower studies, very much in the style of the Barbizon painter, Adolphe Monticelli, whom he greatly admired. He remade contact with Alexander Reid, a Scottish painter-dealer whom he had known in London, and through Theo, who now managed a gallery for Boussod-Valadon (who had taken over from Goupil's), he met Degas and Monet. At Tanguy's, a paint supplier, who would take artists' paintings in exchange for materials, he met Paul Signac, Camille Pissarro and his son Lucien, Cézanne and Gauguin, and he also visited Seurat's studio.

What we do know from the letters is that in March 1887 he mounts an exhibition of Japanese prints at the Café Tambourin, owned by his mistress, Agostina Segatori, an artist's model. (Of this he wrote to his sister Wil: 'I still continue to have the most impossible and highly unsuitable love affairs, from which as a rule I come away in shame and disgrace'.)

And in December 1887 he organized an exhibition of Impressionists of the Petit Boulevard at the Grand Bouillon, Restaurant du Chalet on Avenue de Clichy. He did not sell any of his own paintings, but managed an exchange with Gauguin. Vincent also exhibited at the Théâtre Libre with Seurat and Signac. Theo could not exhibit Vincent's work in his own gallery, but did interest smaller dealers such as Tanguy, Portier, Thomas and Martin in Vincent's work.

Despite this, Vincent finds Paris an impossible place to work in and in March 1888, again on a sudden impulse, he moves to Arles, where the light, sun and intense colours give him 'extraordinary exultation'. Here he works in a fever at his painting. His long-term ambition was always to start an artists' cooperative along the lines of Barbizon and Pont-Aven. With Theo's help, they arrange for Gauguin to be the first and hope that others will join them later. When after long prevarication, Gauguin finally arrives, their conversations are, Vincent reports, 'terribly electric' – all too electric, and cutting off part of his ear after a quarrel, Vincent begins his agonising descent into mental illness.

Only too aware that he is slipping into madness, he admits himself voluntarily first to the asylum of Saint Paul de Mausole at St Rémy, not far from Arles, where he continues to paint prolifically. His periods of clarity produce some of his best work, but his surroundings depress him utterly. Finally he moves to Auvers-sur-Oise, on the outskirts of Paris, into the care of Dr Gachet.

Vincent arrived unexpectedly in Paris, from Antwerp, scribbled this note with a piece of black chalk at the station and sent it to Theo by a porter. Theo had wished him to wait till June, when he would have rented a larger flat. He stayed with Theo in the Rue de Laval, and moved with him in June to the Rue Lepic, in Montmartre.

✳ ✳ ✳

To Theo (459)
Paris, March 1886

Do not be cross with me for having come all at once like this, I have thought about it so much, and I believe that in this way we shall save time. Shall be at the Louvre from midday or sooner if you like.

Let me know please at what time you could come to the Salle Carrée. As for expense, I tell you again, this comes to the same thing. I have some money left, of course, and before I spend any of it I want to speak to you. We shall fix things up, you will see.

So, come as soon as possible.

I shake your hand.

The next letter dates from the summer of that year. Theo was on his yearly holiday trip to Holland, and wanted to interest his uncles as to his plan for starting in business on his own account, but was unsuccessful.

✳ ✳ ✳

To Theo (460)
Paris, Summer 1886

. . . it is already all to the good that you have broached the subject and broken the ice in so far that you have spoken of it to the uncles in Holland. And I do not think I was wrong in my 'it must be full speed ahead', because I see 'full steam ahead' in the future, and in the present too, as far as our energy is concerned . . .

As for my work, I painted the sequel to those flowers which you have. A branch of white lilies – white, pink, green – against black, something like black Japanese lacquer inlaid with mother-of-pearl, which you know – then a bunch of orange tiger lilies against a blue background, then a bunch of dahlias, violet against a yellow background, and red gladioli in a blue vase against light yellow . . .

I am quite willing to exchange for two water-colours by Isabey [Eugène-Gabriel 1803–86, French painter much influenced by Delacroix and Bonington], especially if there are figures. Try to make an exchange for the sequel that I have here, and to get something else with it . . .

Over a year elapses between this last letter and the next, when Theo is again on holiday in Holland.

Vincent, along with Emile Bernard, Anquetin and Toulouse-Lautrec, had exhibited some Japanese prints and paintings at the Café Tambourin, owned by Segatori. Vincent had also painted decorations for the walls. When the café goes bankrupt, his mistress refuses to give them back.

✳ ✳ ✳

To Theo   (461)
Paris, Summer 1887

. . . I have been to the Tambourin, because if I did not go they would think that I dared not.

And I said to the Segatori, that I did not judge her in this business, but that it was for her to judge herself.

That I had torn up the receipt for the pictures, but that she ought to return *everything*.

That if she had not been somehow mixed up with what happened to me she would have come to see me the next day.

That since she had not come to see me, I took it that she knew they were trying to pick a quarrel with me, but that she had tried to warn me when she said 'Go away', which I did not understand at the time and perhaps didn't want to understand either. To this she answered that the pictures and all the rest were at my disposal.

She maintained that it was I who had tried to pick a quarrel – which doesn't surprise me – knowing that if she took my part they would treat her abominably.

I saw the waiter also when I went in, but he made himself scarce.

Now, I did not want to take the pictures straight off, but I said that when you came back we could talk about it, because the pictures

188

belonged to you as much as to me, and that in the meanwhile I urged her to think once more over what had happened. She did not look well, and was as white as wax, which is not a good sign.

She did not know that the waiter had gone up to your place. If that is true I should be all the more inclined to believe that she tried to warn me that they were trying to pick a quarrel with me, rather than that she put up the job herself. She cannot do as she likes. So now I will wait for your return to do anything.

I have done two pictures since you left.

I have still two louis left, and I am afraid I shall not be able manage from now till your return.

You see, when I began to work at Asnières I had plenty of canvases, and Tanguy was very good to me. To do him justice he is just as good still, but his old witch of a wife got wind of what was going on and opposed it. So I let loose about her to Tanguy and said it was her own fault if I did not get anything more from them. Old Tanguy is sensible enough to hold his tongue, and all the same he will do whatever I want of him.

But with all this, work isn't too easy. I saw de Lautrec today; he has sold a picture, I think through Portier. They brought a water-colour of Mme Mesdag, which I think very beautiful . . .

✳ ✳ ✳

To Theo   (462)
Paris, Summer 1887

. . . I was touched by what you wrote about home – 'They are fairly well but still it is sad to see them.' A dozen years ago you would have sworn that at any rate the family would always prosper and get on. It would be a great satisfaction to mother if your marriage came off, and for the sake of your health and your work you ought not to remain single.

As for me – I feel I am losing the desire for marriage and children, and now and then it saddens me that I should be feeling like that at thirty-five just when it should be the opposite. And sometimes I have a grudge at this rotten painting. It was Richepin who said somewhere:

'The love of art means loss of real love'
(L'amour de l'art fait perdre l'amour vrai)

I think that is terribly true, but on the other hand real love makes you disgusted with art.

And at times already I feel old and broken, and yet still enough of a lover not to be a real enthusiast for painting. To succeed one must have ambition, and ambition seems to me absurd. What will come of it I don't know; I would like above all things to be less of a burden to you – and that is not impossible in the future – for I hope to make such progress that you will be able to show my stuff boldly without compromising yourself.

And then I will take myself off somewhere down south, to get away from the sight of so many painters that disgust me as men.

You can be sure of one thing, that I will not try to do any more work for the Tambourin. I think besides that it is going into other hands, and I certainly shall not try to stop it.

As for the Segatori, that's very different. I have still some affection for her and I hope she still has some for me.

But just now she is in a bad way; she is neither a free agent nor mistress in her own house, and worst of all she is ill and in pain.

Although I would not say this openly, my own opinion is that she has procured an abortion (unless indeed she has had miscarriage), but any way in her position I do not blame her. In two months' time she will be better, I hope, and then perhaps she will be grateful that I did not bother her. But bear in mind that once she is well, if she refuses in cold blood to give me what belongs to me, or does me any wrong I shall not spare her – but that will not be necessary. I know her well enough to trust her still. And mind you, if she manages to keep her place going, from the point of view of business I should not blame her for choosing to be top dog, and not under dog. If in order to get on she tramples on my toes a bit, well, she has my leave. When I saw her again she did not trample on my heart, which she would have done if she had been as bad as people said.

I saw Tanguy yesterday, and he has put a canvas I've just done in his window. I have done four since you left, and I have a big one on hand.

I know that these big long canvases are difficult to sell, but later on people will see that there is open air in them and that they are in a good vein . . .

When Vincent moved to Arles in February 1888, he arrived in snow.

✳ ✳ ✳

During the journey I thought of you at least as much as I did of the new country I was seeing . . .

It seems to me almost impossible to work in Paris unless one has some place of retreat where one can revive oneself and get back one's tranquillity and poise. Without that one would get hopelessly brutalised.

And now I'll begin by telling you that there's about two feet of snow everywhere, and more still falling. Arles doesn't seem to me any bigger than Breda or Mons.

Before getting to Tarascon I noticed a magnificent country of huge yellow rocks, piled up in the strangest and stateliest forms. In the little village between these rocks were rows of small round trees with olive green or grey-green leaves, which might quite likely be lemon trees.

But here at Arles the country seems flat. I have seen some splendid red stretches of soil planted with vines, with a background of mountains of the most delicate lilac. And the landscapes in the snow, with the summits white against a sky as luminous as the snow, were just like the winter landscapes that the Japanese have painted . . .

During his stay in Paris, it seems that Vincent had learned much from Theo about the art-dealing world, and had become intensely interested in it. Many of his letters from Arles (only a few mentions of which are quoted here, for reasons of space) are concerned with offering Theo advice in that field. Theo was already dealing in pictures from the Impressionists.

✳ ✳ ✳

. . . It seems to me that if we are to keep the right to be masters of our own ground where the Impressionists are concerned, so that there can be no doubt as to our good faith towards Reid, we might let him do as he likes, without interference from us, about the Monticellis at Marseilles. Insisting on this, that our interest in the dead painter is only indirectly from the money standpoint.

If you agree to this, you can actually also tell him from me that if he intends to come to Marseilles to buy Monticellis he has nothing to fear from us, but that we have the right to ask what he intends to do, seeing that we have got the start of him on this ground.

As for the Impressionists, it seems to me fair that it should be by your agency, if not directly by you, that they should be introduced into England. And if Reid should get in first, we should be justified in maintaining that he had acted towards us in bad faith, more especially since we gave him a free hand about the Marseilles Monticellis . . .

I have thought now and then that my blood is actually beginning to think of circulating, which is more than it ever did that last while in Paris. I could not have stood it much longer . . .

✳ ✳ ✳

To Theo (466)
Arles, undated [1888]

. . . I have had a letter from Gauguin telling me that he had been ill in bed a fortnight. That he is on the rocks, as he has had to pay some crying debts. He wants to know if you have sold anything for him, but he can't write to you for fear of bothering you. He is so pressed for a little money that he would be ready to reduce the price of his pictures still further.

The only thing I can do in this business is to write to Russell [an American artist who had painted Vincent's portrait], and this I am doing today.

And after all we have already tried to make Tersteeg buy one. But what is to be done? He must be hard pressed.

Would you risk taking the seascape from him for the firm? If that were possible he would be safe for the moment.

Do as you think best about the exhibition of the Independents. What do you say to showing the two big landscapes of the Butte Montmartre? It is more or less all one to me. I am counting rather more on this year's work.

Down here it is freezing hard and in the country the snow is still lying. I have a study of a landscape in white with the town in the background. Then two little studies of a branch of almond already in flower in spite of it. So much for today. I am also writing a note to Koning [Arnold Koning, a Dutch painter who was now sharing Theo's flat].

Vincent had formed an idealistic notion of developing an artists' cooperative whereby they might get a better deal for their pictures and share proceeds between them, so that, in theory, they would all benefit, when some artists' work sold better than others.

Vincent calls Monet, Sisley, Renoir, Degas, etc., whose work was shown by Theo on the Boulevard Montmartre, 'The Painters of the Grand Boulevard', whilst he calls himself, Bernard, Anquetin, Gauguin and Lautrec, who used to exhibit in the restaurant on the Boulevard Clichy, 'The Painters of the Petit Boulevard'.

✳ ✳ ✳

To Theo   (468)
Arles, 10 March 1888

. . . Perhaps it would be easier to get a few dealers and collectors to agree to buy the Impressionist pictures, than to get the artists to agree to go equal shares in the price of the pictures sold. All the same the artists couldn't do better than to combine, hand over their pictures to the Association, and share the proceeds of the sales, so that the Society could at least guarantee its members a chance to live and to work.

If Degas, Claude Monet, Renoir, Sisley and C. Pissarro would take the initiative and say – 'Look here, we five give each ten pictures (or rather we each give to the value of 10,000 frs to be estimated by expert members such as Tersteeg and yourself, co-opted by the Society, said experts likewise to put in capital in the form of pictures) and we further undertake to give each year the value of . . .

'And we invite you, Guillaumin, Seurat, Gauguin, etc. etc., to combine with us (your pictures to undergo the same expert valuation).'

Thus the great Impressionists of the Grand Boulevard, while giving pictures which would become general property, would keep their prestige, and the others could no longer reproach them for keeping to themselves the advantages of a reputation acquired in the first place no doubt by their personal efforts and individual genius, but all the same a reputation that is growing, buttressed and actually maintained by the pictures of a whole battalion of artists, who up to now have been working in continual beggary.

Anyway it is to be hoped that it will come off, and that Tersteeg and you will become expert members (perhaps along with Portier?) . . . I congratulate you on the purchase of the Seurat; with what I shall send you you must try to arrange another exchange with Seurat as well . . .

❊ ❊ ❊

To Theo (469)
Arles, undated [1888]

. . . As for the work, I brought back a canvas of 15 [cm in width] today. It is a drawbridge with a little cart going over it, outlined against a blue sky – the river blue as well, the banks orange coloured with green grass and a group of washerwomen in smocks and many coloured caps. And another landscape with a little country bridge and more washer-women.

Also an avenue of plane trees near the station. Altogether twelve studies, since I have been here.

The weather here is changeable, often windy, and murky skies, but the almond trees are beginning to flower everywhere. I am very glad that the pictures should go to the Independents. You are right to go and see Signac at his house. I was very glad to see from your letter of today that he has made a better impression on you than he did the first time. In any case I am glad to know that after today you will not be alone in the flat.

Remember me kindly to Koning. Are you well? I am better myself, except that it is real forced labour to eat, as I have a touch of fever and no appetite, but it's only a matter for time and patience . . .

Here I am seeing new things, I am learning, and if I go rather softly, my body doesn't refuse to keep me going . . .

I was present at the inquiry into a crime committed at the door of a brothel here; two Italians killed two Zouaves. I took the opportunity to go into one of the brothels in a small street call 'des ricolettes'.

That is the extent of my amorous adventures among the Arlesiens. The mob *all but* (the Southerner like Tartarin being heartier in good intention than in action) the mob, I say, all but lynched the murderers confined in the Hotel de Ville, but in reprisal all Italians – men and women, the Savoyard monkeys included – have been forced to leave the town.

I should not have told you of this, except that it means I've seen the streets of this town full of excited crowds. And indeed it was a fine sight.

I made my last three studies with the perspective frame I told you of. I attach some importance to the use of the frame because it seems to me not unlikely that in the near future many artists will make use of it, just as the old German and Italian painters certainly did, and, as I am inclined to think, the Flemish too. The modern use of it may differ from the ancient practice, but in the same way isn't it true that in the process of painting in oils one gets very different effects today from those of the men who invented the process, Jan and Hubert Van Eyck? And the moral of that is that it's my constant hope that I am not working for myself alone. I believe in the absolute necessity for a new art of colour, of design, and – of the artistic life. And if we work in that faith, it seems to me there is a chance that our hope is not in vain. You must know that I am actually ready to send you off some studies, only I can't yet roll them. My love to you. I shall write on Sunday to Bernard and to De Lautrec, because I solemnly promised to, and shall send you those letters as well. I am heartily sorry for Gauguin's plight, especially that now his health is shaken he hasn't the kind of temperament that profits by hardships, on the contrary, this will only knock him up, and that will spoil him for his work . . .

✳ ✳ ✳

To Theo (471)
Arles, undated [1888]

. . . I have just finished a group of apricot trees in blossom in a little orchard of fresh green. I've been worried by the sunset with figures and a bridge that I spoke of to Bernard. The bad weather prevented me working on the spot and I've completely ruined it trying to finish it at home. However I began again at once, the same subject on another canvas, but as the weather was quite different, in grey tones and without figures.

It would not be a bad idea for you to send Tersteeg one of my studies: would you say the bridge at Clichy with the yellow sky and two houses reflected in the water – or the butterflies or the field of poppies could go for that matter, though I hope to do better here . . .

Thank you very much also for all the steps you have taken towards the exhibition of the Independents. I am very glad in the end that they have been put with the other Impressionists.

But though it doesn't in the least matter this time, in future my name ought to be put in the catalogue as I sign it on the canvas, viz. Vincent and not van Gogh, for the simple reason that they do not know how to pronounce the latter name here . . .

It would not come amiss if you add to your consignment the little head of the Breton woman by friend Bernard. He must be shown that all the Impressionists are good, and their work very varied.

I think our friend Reid regrets falling out with us, but unfortunately it's quite impossible to offer him the same advantages again, or to try to let him have the pictures on commission. It is not enough to be fond of the pictures, and he seems to me to have no feeling for the artists . . .

Paris doesn't pay: I should be sorry to see the Seurats in a provincial musée or in a cellar, those pictures ought to stay in living hands – if Tersteeg would . . . If three permanent exhibitions are started, there must be one great Seurat in Paris, one in London, and one in Marseilles . . .

✳ ✳ ✳

To Theo (472)
Arles, undated [1888]

. . . I have been working on a canvas of 20 in the open air in an orchard, lilac ploughland, a reed fence, two rose-coloured peach trees, against a sky of glorious blue and white. Probably the best landscape I have done. I had just brought it home when I received from our sister a Dutch notice in memory of Mauve, with his portrait (very good the portrait), the text, poor and nothing in it, a pretty water-colour. Something – I don't know what – took hold of me and brought a lump to my throat, and I wrote on my picture

Souvenir of Mauve
Vincent and Theo.

and if you agree we two will send it, such as it is, to Mme Mauve. I chose the best study I've painted here on purpose . . .

I have great difficulty in painting because of the wind, but I fasten my easel to pegs driven into the ground and work in spite of it, it is too lovely . . .

✳ ✳ ✳

To Theo   (473)
Arles, undated [1888]

. . . Here is a plan of attack which will cost us several of the best pictures you and I have concocted between us, and worth certainly, shall we say, several 1000 franc notes. Anyhow they cost us money and a shred of our lives.

But it would be an open reply to certain tacit insinuations, treating us as though we were dead, and it would likewise be a revenge for your last year's visit when there was so little warmth and such in the welcome you got. But enough of that.

Suppose that we first of all give the *Souvenir of Mauve* to Jet Mauve, suppose that I dedicate a study to Breibner (I have one exactly like the study which I exchanged with L. Pissarro and the one Reid has, of oranges, foreground white, background blue), suppose that we also give a study to our sister Wil. Suppose that we give to the Musée Moderne at the Hague, since we have so many memories of the Hague, the two views of Montmartre exhibited at the Independents.

Remains one thing not so easily settled, since Tersteeg has written you 'Send me some Impressionists, but only those pictures that you yourself think the best', and since you for your part sent a picture of mine in that consignment, I find myself in the not very easy position of having to *convince* Tersteeg that I am actually a genuine Impressionist of the Petit Boulevard, and that I intend to remain so.

Well, he shall have a picture of mine in his own collection. I have been turning it over these days and I have thought of an odd thing, not like what I generally do. It is the drawbridge with the little yellow cart and the group of women washing, a study in which the ground is bright orange, the grass bright green and the sky and water blue.

It only needs a frame specially designed for it in royal blue and gold, the mount blue, the outside moulding gold, if necessary the frame could be in blue plush, but it would be better painted. I think I can assure you that the work I'm doing here is better than in the Asnières country last spring.

In the whole plan there is nothing absolutely fixed except the dedication: *Souvenir de Mauve,* and the dedication to Tersteeg . . .

Believe me, Tersteeg will not refuse the picture . . .

✻ ✻ ✻

To Theo   (474)
Arles, undated [1888]

. . . The air here certainly does me good. I wish you could fill your lungs with it; one effect it has on me is comical enough, one small glass of brandy makes me tipsy here, so that as I don't have to fall back on stimulants to make my blood circulate, there is less strain on my constitution. The only thing is that my stomach has been terribly weak since I came here. I hope to make great progress this year, and indeed I need to.

I have a fresh orchard, as good as the rose-coloured peach trees, apricot trees of a very pale rose. At the moment I am working on some plum trees, yellowish white, with thousands of black branches. I am using a tremendous lot of colours and canvases . . .

This month will come hard on both you and me, but if you can manage. it will be to our advantage to make the most we can of the orchards in bloom. I am well started now, and I think I must have ten more, the same subject. You know, I am changeable in my work, and this craze for painting orchards will not last for ever. After this it may be the arenas. Then I must do a *tremendous* lot of drawing, because I want to make some drawings in the manner of Japanese prints.

You will see that the rose-coloured peach trees were painted with a sort of passion.

I must also have a starry night with cypresses, or perhaps above all, a field of ripe corn; there are some wonderful nights here. I am in a continual fever of work . . .

✻ ✻ ✻

. . . You will please ask old Tasset or old l'Hôte his absolutely lowest price for 10 yards of his canvas with plaster or absorbent, and let me know the result of the discussion which you will probably have with the good man, about the delivery of the above-mentioned goods. Here is the list:

20 Flake white, big tubes.
10 ditto zinc white.
15 Malachite green, double tubes.
10 Chrome yellow, *lemon* ditto.
10 Chrome yellow (No. two) double tubes.
 3 Vermilion ditto.
 3 Chrome yellow No. three ditto.
 6 Geranium lake, small tubes ⎱ Newly pounded,
12 Crimson lake, small tubes ⎰ if they are greasy
 2 Carmine, small tubes   ⎰ I shall send them back.
 4 Prussian blue, small tubes.
 4 Cinnabar green, very light, small tubes.
 2 Orange lead, small tubes.
 6 Emerald green, small tubes.

. . . So far I have spent more on my paints, canvas, etc., than on myself. I have still another orchard for you but for heaven's sake send me the paints without delay. The season for the blossom is so soon over . . .

❉ ❉ ❉

. . . You were right to tell Tasset that he must put in the geranium lake all the same; he has sent it, I have just checked it. *All the colours that the Impressionists have brought into fashion are unstable,* so there is all the more reason to use them boldly too crude, time will tone them down only too well.

So, of all the colours I ordered, the three chromes (orange, yellow, lemon-yellow), the Prussian blue, the emerald, the crimson lakes, the Malachite green, or the orange lead, hardly one of them is to be found on the Dutch palette, in Maris, Mauve or Israëls. It is only to be found in Delacroix, who had a passion for the two colours which are most condemned, and with most reason, lemon-yellow and Prussian blue . . .

❉ ❉ ❉

To Theo   (478)
Arles, 20 April 1888

. . . Here is a sketch of an orchard that I planned more particularly for you to celebrate the 1st of May. It's absolutely clear, and done in a flash. A frenzied daubing of the faintest yellow and lilac on the first massy white . . .

❉ ❉ ❉

To Theo   (480)
Arles, May 1888

. . . I don't see the whole future before me black, but I do see it bristling with difficulties and sometimes I ask myself if they won't be too much for me. But this is mostly in moments of physical weakness, and last week I had such fierce toothache that much against my will I had to waste time.

However, I have just sent you a roll of small pen and ink drawings, a dozen I think. By which you will see that if I have stopped painting I haven't stopped working. You will find among them a hasty sketch on yellow paper, a lawn in the square as you come into the town, and a building at the back, rather like this [the sketch below in the original letter].

Well, today I've taken the right wing of this concern, which contains four rooms, or rather two with two closets. It is painted yellow outside, whitewashed inside, gets all the sun. I have taken it for 15 fr. a month.

Now my idea would be to furnish one room, that on the first floor, so as to be able to sleep there. That will leave the studio, the shop, for the whole campaign as long as it lasts in the south, and now I am independent of all the tricks of innkeepers . . .

I could quite well share with someone in the new studio, and I should like it. Perhaps Gauguin will come to the south. Perhaps I could come to some arrangement with MacKnight [Dodge McKnight, an American artist]. Then the cooking could be done in one's own place.

In any case the studio is too public for me to think it might tempt any little woman, and a petticoat crisis couldn't easily end in a liaison. Besides, morals here seem to be less inhuman, and less contrary to nature than in Paris. But with my disposition, to go on the spree and to work are in no way compatible, and in the present circumstances, one must content one's self with painting pictures. It is not really living at all, but what is one to do? And indeed this artistic life, which we know is not *the* real life, seems to me so vital, and one would be ungrateful not to be content with it.

I have one great worry the less, now that I have found the little white studio. I looked in vain at heaps of rooms. It will sound funny to you that the lavatory is next door, in a fairly big hotel which belongs to the same proprietor . . .

✳ ✳ ✳

To Theo   (481)
Arles, 4 May 1888

. . . I was at Fontvieilles yesterday at MacKnight's; he had a good pastel – a tree in rose-colour – and two water-colours begun, and I found him working at the head of an old woman in charcoal. He is at the stage when new theories of colour plague him, and while they prevent him working on the old system, he is not sufficiently master of his new palette to succeed in this one. He seemed very shy about showing me the things, I had to go there for that express purpose, and tell him that I was *absolutely* set on seeing his work.

It is not impossible that he may come to stay with me for some time here. I think we should both benefit by it.

I think very often here of Renoir and that pure clean line of his. That is just how things and people look in this clear air . . .

I was certainly going the right way for a stroke when I left Paris. I paid for it nicely afterwards! When I stopped drinking, when I stopped smoking so much, when I began again to think instead of trying not to think – Good Lord, the depression and the prostration of it! Work in these magnificent natural surroundings has helped my morale, but even now there are some efforts too much for me: my strength fails me . . .

✴ ✴ ✴

To Theo (482)
Arles, 5 May 1888

. . . It is a filthy town this, in the old streets. As for the women of Arles that there's so much talk about – there is, isn't there? – do you want to know my real opinion of them? They are, no question about it, really charming, but no longer what they must have been. As things are now, they are more often like a Mignard than a Mantegna, for they are in their decadence. That doesn't prevent them being beautiful – very beautiful . . .

There are women like a Fragonard and like a Renoir. And some that can't be labelled by anything that's been done yet in painting. The best thing to do would be to make portraits, all kinds of portraits of women and children. But I don't think that I am the man to do it.

But I should be heartily glad if this Bel Ami of the Midi, which Monticelli – was not – but was by way of being – whom I feel to be coming, though I know it isn't myself – I should be heartily glad, I say, if a kind of Guy de Maupassant in painting came along to paint light-heartedly the beautiful people and things that there are here. As for me, I shall go on working and here and there among my work there will be things which will last, but who will be in figure painting what Claude Monet is in landscape? However, you must feel with me that such a one will come. Rodin? He does not work in colour, it is not he. But the painter of the future will be *such a colourist as has never yet been*. Manet was working towards it, but as you know the Impressionists have already got stronger colour than Manet. But this painter who is to come – I can't imagine him living in little cafés, working away with false teeth, and going to the Zouaves' brothels, as I do . . .

✴ ✴ ✴

202

To Theo (483)
Arles, undated [May 1888]

. . . You will see some lovely things at Claude Monet's. And you will think what I send very poor stuff in comparison. I am just now dissatisfied with myself and dissatisfied with what I do, but I have just a glimmer of hope that I'm going to do better in the end.

And then I hope that later on other artists will rise up in this lovely country and do for it what the Japanese have done for theirs. And to work towards that is not so bad . . .

✻ ✻ ✻

To Theo (484)
Arles, undated [May 1888]

I am sending you in the case all the studies I have except a few that I have destroyed, but I am not signing all of them; there are a dozen that I have taken off the stretchers and fourteen on stretchers.

There is a little landscape with a hovel, white, red and green, and a cypress beside it; you have the drawing of it, and I did the whole painting of it in the house. This will show you that, if you like, I can make little pictures like the Japanese prints, of all these drawings. But we can talk about that when you have seen them . . .

✻ ✻ ✻

To Theo (487)
Arles, undated [May 1888]

I am writing again a line to tell you that I have been to see the gentleman that the Arab Jew in *Tartarin* calls 'le Zouge de paix'.

Anyway I have got back 12 francs, and the innkeeper was reprimanded for keeping back my luggage seeing that he had no right to keep it when I did not refuse to pay. If he had won his case it would have injured me, for he would not have failed to say everywhere that I could not, or would not pay, and that he had been obliged to keep my luggage. Whereas now – for I left at the same time as he did – he said as we were going along that he had lost his temper, but that he had not meant to insult me.

I think myself that is likely just what he was trying to do, and seeing that I had had enough of his shanty and that he could not manage to keep me, he would have tried to blacken me in this place where I am now. So that's that. If I had wanted to get what is probably the fair reduction I ought to have claimed more for instance for damages. If I let myself be had by the first comer here, you can imagine that soon I should not know where to turn. I have found a better restaurant where I can get a meal for 1 franc . . .

✳ ✳ ✳

To Theo (488)
Arles, undated [May 1888]

. . . I have done two new studies, a bridge and the side of a high road. In character many subjects here are exactly like Holland, the difference is in the colour. There is that sulphur yellow everywhere the sun lights on.

You know that we saw a magnificent Renoir of a garden of roses. I was expecting to find subjects like that here, and indeed while the orchards were in bloom it was so. Now the appearance of things has changed and become much harsher. But the green, and the blue! I must say several landscapes of Cézanne which I know give this very well, and I am sorry not to have seen more. The other day I saw a subject exactly like the lovely Monticelli landscape with the poplars which we saw at Reid's.

To find Renoir's gardens again you would probably have to go to Nice. I have seen very few roses here . . .

✳ ✳ ✳

To Theo (489)
Arles, undated [May 1888]

. . . I have done two still-lifes this week.

A coffee pot in blue enamel, a cup (on the left), royal blue and gold, a milk jug in squares of pale blue and white, a cup – on the right – of white with a blue and orange pattern, on an earthen plate of greyish yellow, a jug in earthenware or majolica, blue with a pattern in reds, greens and browns, and lastly two oranges and three lemons; the table is covered with a blue cloth, the background is greenish yellow, so that there are six different blues, and four or five yellows and oranges.

The other still-life is the majolica pot with wild flowers.

. . . And so, if we believe in the new art, and in the artists of the future, our faith does not cheat us. When good old Corot said a few days before his death – 'I last night saw in a dream landscapes with skies all rose,' well, haven't they come, those skies of rose and yellow and green into the bargain, in the Impressionist landscapes? All which means that there are things one feels are to come, and they come in very truth.

And as for us who are not, I incline to think, nearly so close to death, we feel nevertheless that this thing is greater than we are, and its life of longer span than ours . . .

✳ ✳ ✳

To Theo (490)
Arles, undated [May 1888]

I read a notice in *l'Intransigeant* that there is to be an exhibition of Impressionists at Durand Ruel's – there will be some of Caillebotte's [Gustave Caillebotte (1848–94), a follower of Impressionism] – I have never seen any of his stuff, and I want to ask you to write me what it is like, there will be sure to be other remarkable things. Today I sent you some more drawings, and I am putting in still another two. These are views taken from a rocky hill-slope, from which you see the country towards Crau (very good wine comes from there), the town of Arles, and the country towards Fontvieilles. The contrast between the wild and romantic foreground, and the distant perspective, wide and still, with horizontal lines shading off into the chain of the Alps, so famous for the great climbing feats of Tartarin P.C.A., and of the Alpine Club – this contrast is very striking . . .

✳ ✳ ✳

To Theo (491)
Arles, undated [1888]

. . . I am working happily.

I have asked for some water-colours, because I would like to make

205

some pen drawings, to be coloured afterwards with a flat wash like the Japanese prints.

I hope that you will have as fine a Sunday in Paris as here; there is a glorious sun, and no wind . . .

✳ ✳ ✳

To Theo (492)
Arles, 29 May 1888

. . . If you think that the *Souvenir of Mauve* is tolerable, you should put it in the next lot for the Hague, in a plain white frame.

If you find among them a study that seems to you more suitable for Tersteeg, you can put it in without dedication and keep the one with his dedication, which you can then scrape off. Because it is better to give him one without any dedication. Then he can pretend that he hadn't realized it was a present and can send it back without saying anything, if he would rather not have anything from me . . .

Would you like me to go to America with you? It would only be fair that these people should pay for my passage.

I am indifferent about most things, but not about this – that you should not first of all really regain your health.

But I think that you must steep yourself once again more and more in nature and in the world of artists.

And I would rather see you independent of the Goupils, and dealing with the Impressionists on your own account, than this other life of travelling about with expensive pictures belonging to these people. When our uncle was a partner with them, he got plenty out of it for some years – but look what it cost him . . .

Odd, but one evening lately at Mont Majour I saw a red sunset, its rays falling on the trunks and foliage of pines growing among a tumble of rocks, colouring the trunks and foliage with orange fire, while the other pines in the distance stood out in Prussian blue against a sky of tender blue green, cerulean. It was just the effect of that Claude Monet; it was superb. The white sand and the layers of white rocks under the trees took on tints of blue . . .

As for me I am decidedly better, and my digestion has improved tremendously during the month past. I still have bursts of senseless involuntary excitement or else utter sluggishness some days, but that will pass as I become steadier. I expect to make an excursion to Saintes Maries, and see the Mediterranean at last . . .

❋ ❋ ❋

To Theo   (493)
Arles, undated [1888]

I have been thinking about Gauguin, and here it is. If Gauguin was to come here, there is Gauguin's journey, and there are two beds or two mattresses, which in that case we absolutely must buy. But afterwards, as Gauguin is a sailor, we shall probably manage to grub at home.

And the two of us will live on the same money that I spend by myself.

You know that I have always thought it idiotic the way that painters live alone, etc. You always lose when you are isolated.

But you may think it a good idea for us to share, and fix a sum – say 250 per month, if every month besides and in addition to my work, you get a Gauguin.

Provided that we did not exceed this sum, would it not even be a gain?

Besides it has always been my idea to join with other people. So here is a rough draft of a letter to Gauguin, which I will write, if you approve, with whatever changes will doubtless have to be made in the phrasing. But this is how I wrote it first.

Take the thing as a plain matter of business, that is the best way for everyone, and let's treat it squarely as such. Only, seeing that you are not in business on your own account, you may perhaps see fit to let me take it on myself and Gauguin join in with me as a chum.

I judged that you wanted to help him, just as I myself am distressed at his taking ill, and it's a thing that doesn't mend from one day to the next. We cannot suggest anything better than this, and others would not do so much.

As for me, it worries me to spend so much money on myself alone, but to remedy it the only thing is for me to find a woman with money, or some fellows who will join with me to paint.

I don't see the woman, but I do see the fellows . . .

❋ ❋ ❋

. . . I have had a letter from Gauguin who says he has got from you a letter enclosing 50 fr., which touched him greatly, and in which you said something of the plan. As I had sent my letter to him to you, he had not yet received the more definite proposal when he wrote.

But he says that he knows by experience when he was with his friend Laval at Martinique they managed much better together than when they were alone, so that he quite agreed as to the advantages there would be in living together.

He says that the pains in his bowels still continue, and he seems to me to be very depressed.

He speaks of some hope he has of finding a capital of 600,000 francs, to set up a dealer for Impressionist pictures, and that he will explain his plan, and would like you to be at the head of the undertaking. I should not be surprised if this hope is a Fata Morgana, a mirage of destitution, the more destitute you are, especially if you are ill – the more you think of such possibilities. This scheme looks to me simply another proof that he is foundering, and that it would be better to get him going as quickly as possible . . .

I have a new subject in hand, fields green and yellow as far as the eye can reach. I have already drawn it twice and I am beginning it again as a painting; it is exactly like a Solomon Konink, you know – the pupil of Rembrandt, who painted vast level plains. Or it is like Michel, or like Jules Dupré, but anyway it is very different from the gardens of roses. It is true that I have only been through one part of Provence, and that in the other there is the kind of scenery that you get for instance in Claude Monet . . .

It is quite certain that if in exchange for the money given to Gauguin one could buy his pictures at their present price, there would be no risk of losing money. I would very much like you to have all his pictures of Martinique. Well, let us do what we can . . .

✳ ✳ ✳

To Theo (497)
Arles, undated [1888]

. . . Instinctively these days I keep remembering what I have seen of Cézanne, because he has just got – as in the *Harvest* we saw at Portier's – the harsh side of Provence. It has become very different from what it was in Spring, and yet I have certainly no less love for this countryside, burnt up as it begins to be from now on. Everywhere now here is old gold, bronze, copper one might say, and this with the green azure of the sky blanched with heat: a delicious colour, extraordinarily harmonious, with the blended tones of Delacroix.

If Gauguin were willing to join in, I think it would be a step forward for us. It would establish us squarely as the exploiters of the South, and nobody could complain of that. I must manage to get the firmness of colouring that I got in that picture that kills the rest. I'm thinking of what Portier used to say, that seen by themselves the Cézannes he had looked nothing, but bring them near other pictures and they washed the colour out of everything else. He used to say too that the Cézannes did well in gold, which means the gamut of colour was pitched very high. So perhaps, perhaps I am on the track, and I am getting my eye in for this kind of country . . .

✳ ✳ ✳

To Theo (498)
Arles, undated [1888]

. . . I must talk about what you wrote in your letter. I congratulate you on having the Monet exhibition in your place, and I am very sorry not to see it. Certainly it will not do Tersteeg any harm to see this exhibition; he will come round to it yet, but, as you thought too, it will be late. Certainly it is odd that he has changed his mind about Zola. I know from experience that he once couldn't bear to hear a word about him. What a queer character Tersteeg is; he has that excellent quality that however hard and fixed his opinions may be, once he has realized that a thing is actually different from what he thought it, as with Zola for instance, he changes round and becomes enthusiastic for it. Lord, what a pity that you and he don't see eye to eye in business now. But that's that; it is what I think is called fatality.

You have been lucky to meet Guy de Maupassant. I have read his first book, *Des Vers*, poems dedicated to his master Flaubert; there is one 'Au bord de l'eau', which is already *himself*. What Van der Meer of Delft is to Rembrandt among the painters, he is to Zola among the French novelists.

Altogether Tersteeg's visit was not all that I had dared to hope, and I do not disguise from myself that I made a false calculation based on the likelihood of his cooperation.

And in the business with Gauguin too, perhaps. Let's think about it. I thought that he was on the rocks, and there was I with money, and this lad who does better work than I do with none; so I say, he ought to have half, and let him, if he likes.

But if Gauguin isn't on the rocks, then I am in no great hurry. And I withdraw categorically, and the only question left for me is simply this; if I looked about for someone to chum with, would it be a good thing, would it be to my brother's advantage and mine, and would the other fellow lose by it, or would he gain . . .

I think a society of Impressionists would be a thing of the same nature as the Society of the Twelve English Pre-Raphaelites, and I think that it could come into existence. Then I incline to think that the artists would guarantee mutually among themselves a livelihood, each consenting to give a considerable number of pictures to the Society, and that the gains as well as the losses should be taken in common.

I do not think that this Society would last indefinitely, but I think that while it lasted we would live courageously, and produce . . .

❋ ❋ ❋

To Theo (499)
Les Saintes Maries de la Mer, undated [1888]

I am writing to you from Stes Maries on the shore of the Mediterranean at last. The Mediterranean has the colours of mackerel, changeable I mean. You don't always know if it is green or violet, you can't even say it's blue, because the next moment the changing light has taken on a tinge of rose colour or grey.

A family is a queer thing – quite involuntarily and in spite of myself I have been thinking here between whiles of our sailor uncle, who must many a time have seen the shores of this sea.

I brought three canvases and have covered them – two seascapes, a view of the village, and then some drawings which I will send you by post, when I return tomorrow to Arles . . .

Next month it will be the season for open air bathing here. The number of bathers varies from twenty to fifty . . .

One night I went for a walk by the sea along the empty shore. It was not gay, but neither was it sad – it was – beautiful. The deep blue sky was flecked with clouds of a blue deeper than the fundamental blue of intense cobalt, and others of a clearer blue, like the blue whiteness of the Milky Way. On the blue depth the stars were sparkling, greenish, yellow, white, rose, brighter, flashing more like jewels, than they do at home – even in Paris: opals you might call them, emeralds, lapis, sapphires.

The sea was very deep ultramarine – the shore a sort of violet and faint russet as I saw it, and on the dunes (about seventeen feet high they are) some bushes Prussian blue. . .

❋ ❋ ❋

To Theo   (500)
Arles, undated [1888]

. . . Now that I have seen the sea here, I am absolutely convinced of the importance of staying in the Midi, and of absolutely piling on, exaggerating the colour – Africa not so far away . . .

About this staying on in the South, even if it is dearer, consider: we like Japanese painting, we have felt its influence, all the Impressionists have that in common; then why not go to Japan, that is to say to the equivalent of Japan, the South?

Only it is bad policy to stay here alone, when two or three could help each other to live cheaply.

I wish you could spend some time here, you would feel it after a while, one's sight changes, you see things with an eye more Japanese, you feel colour differently. The Japanese draw quickly, very quickly, like a lightning flash, because their nerves are finer, their feeling simpler . . .

I have only been here a few months, but tell me this – could I, in Paris, have done the drawing of the boats *in an hour?* Even without the frame, I do it now without measuring, just by letting my pen go . . .

❋ ❋ ❋

. . . I have had a week's hard, close work among the cornfields in full sun. The result is some studies of cornfields, landscapes, and – a sketch of a sower.

A ploughed field, a big field with clods of violet earth – climbing towards the horizon, a sower in blue and white. On the horizon a field of short ripe corn.

Over all a yellow sky with a yellow sun.

You can tell from this simple naming of the tones that it's a composition where colour plays a very important part.

And the sketch, such as it is – a canvas of 25 – torments me, making me wonder if I should not take it up seriously and make a tremendous picture of it. My word, I do want to . . .

I have had a longing on me for such a long time to do a sower, but the things I've wanted for a long time never come off. And so I am almost afraid of it. And yet, after Millet and Lhermitte what still remains to be done is – a sower in colour and on a big scale.

Let us talk of something else – I have a model at last – a Zouave – a lad with a small face, with the neck of a bull, and the eye of a tiger, and I began with one portrait, and began again with another; the half-length I did of him was fearfully hard, in a blue uniform, the blue of enamelled saucepans, with braid of a faded reddish orange, and two pale lemon stars on his breast, an ordinary blue, and very hard to do. That bronzed, feline head of his with the reddish cap, against a green door and the orange bricks of a wall. So it's a savage combination of incongruous tones, not easy to manage . . .

❋ ❋ ❋

. . . I worked yesterday and today at the sower, which is completely rehandled. The sky is yellow and green, the ground violet and orange. There is certainly a picture of this kind to be painted of this splendid subject, and I hope it will get done some day, by me or by another . . .

I have a view of the Rhone – the iron bridge at Trinquetaille, in which the sky and the river are the colour of absinthe, the quays a shade of lilac, the figures leaning on their elbows on the parapet blackish, the iron bridge an intense blue, with a note of vivid orange in the blue background, and a note of intense malachite green. Another very rough effort, and yet I am trying to get at something utterly heart-broken and therefore utterly heart-breaking . . .

❋ ❋ ❋

To Theo (504)
Arles, undated [1888]

. . . Do you remember among the little drawings a wooden bridge with a washing place, and a view of the town in the distance? I have just painted that subject in a large size.

I must warn you that everyone will think that I work too fast.

Don't you believe a word of it.

Is it not emotion, the sincerity of one's feeling for nature, that draws us, and if the emotions are sometimes so strong that one works without knowing one works, when sometimes the strokes come with a sequence and a coherence like words in a speech or a letter, then one must remember that it has not always been so, and that in the time to come there will again be heavy days, empty of inspiration.

So one must strike while the iron is hot . . .

❋ ❋ ❋

To Theo (506)
Arles, undated [1888]

I have come back from a day at Mont Majour, and my friend the second lieutenant [the Zouave] was with me. We explored the old garden together, and stole some excellent figs. If it had been bigger it would have made me think of Zola's Paradou, great reeds, vines, ivy, fig trees, olives, pomegranates with lusty flowers of the brightest orange, hundred-year-old cypresses, ash trees, and willows, rock oaks, half-broken flights of steps, ogive windows in ruins, blocks of white rock covered with lichen, and scattered fragments of crumbling walls here and there among the green. I brought back another big drawing, but not of the garden. That makes three drawings. When I have half a dozen I shall send them along.

Yesterday I went to Fontvieilles to visit Bock and MacKnight, only these gentlemen had gone on a little trip to Switzerland for a week.

I think the heat is still doing me good, in spite of the mosquitoes and flies.

The grasshoppers – not like ours at home, but like those you see in Japanese sketch books, and Spanish flies, gold and green in swarms on the olives. The grasshoppers (I think they are called cicidas) sing as loud as a frog . . .

Vincent had for some time been having a quarrel with the paint dealer Tanguy. Here he vents his spleen against Tanguy's wife.

. . . Xantippe, Mother Tanguy and some other good ladies, have by some queer freak of Nature heads of silex or flint. Certainly these ladies are a good deal more dangerous in the civilized world they go about in than the poor souls bitten by mad dogs who live in the Pasteur Institute. And old Tanguy would be right a hundred times over to kill his lady . . . but he won't do it, any more than Socrates.

And for this reason, old Tanguy has more in common – in resignation and long suffering anyhow – with the ancient Christians, martyrs and slaves, than with the present day rotters of Paris.

That does not mean that there is any reason to pay him 80 francs, but it is a reason for never losing your temper with him, even if he loses his . . .

I think it is well to work especially at drawing just now, and to arrange to have paints and canvas in reserve for when Gauguin comes . . .

. . . to look at the stars always makes me dream, as simply as I dream over the black dots of a map representing towns and villages. Why, I ask myself, should the shining dots of the sky not be as accessible as the black dots on the map of France? If we take the train to get to Tarascon or Rouen, we take death to reach a star. One thing undoubtedly true in this reasoning is this, that while we are *alive* we *cannot* get to a star, any more than when we are dead, we can take the train.

So it seems to me possible that cholera, gravel, phthisis and cancer are the celestial means of locomotion, just as steamboats, omnibuses and railways are the terrestrial means. To die quietly of old age would be to go there on foot . . .

To Theo   (507)
Arles, undated [1888]

. . . Your letter brings great news, that Gauguin agrees to our plan.
Certain the best thing would be for him to make tracks down here at
once. Instead of getting out of a mess he will quite likely get into one if
he comes first to Paris . . .

✳ ✳ ✳

To Theo   (509)
Arles, undated [Summer 1888]

. . . The fascination that these huge plains have for me is very strong,
so that I felt no *weariness*, in spite of the really wearisome circumstances,
mistral and mosquitoes. If a view makes you forget these little annoy-
ances, it must have something in it. You will see, however, that there is
no attempt at effect. At first sight it is like a map, a strategic plan as far
as the *execution* goes. I walked there besides *with a painter*, and he said –
'There is something that would be boring to paint.' Yet I went fully fifty
times to Mont Majour to look at this flat landscape, and was I wrong?
I went for a walk there as well with someone who was *not a painter*, and
when I said to him 'Look, to me that is as beautiful and as infinite as
the sea,' he said – and he knows the sea, 'For my part I like this *better*
than the sea, because it is not less infinite, and yet you feel that it is
inhabited.'
    What a picture I would make of it if there was not this blasted wind.
That is the maddening thing here, no matter where you set up your
easel . . .

✳ ✳ ✳

To Theo   (513)
Arles, undated [1888]

. . . I am getting older than you, and my ambition is to be less of a burden
to you. And, if no actual obelisk of a catastrophe comes along, and there
isn't a rain of frogs in the meantime, I hope to get there sometime . . .
    Why, a canvas I have covered is worth more than a blank canvas.

215

That – believe me my pretensions go no further – that is my right to paint, my reason for painting, and by the Lord, I have one!

All it has cost me is a carcass pretty well crashed and wits pretty well crazed for any life that I might and should live, from the philanthropic standpoint.

All it has cost you is, say, fifteen thousand francs, which you have advanced to me . . .

My dear brother, if I were not broke and crazy with this blasted painting what a dealer I should make just for the Impressionists. But there, I am broke . . .

If Gauguin cannot pay his debts nor his fare, if he can guarantee me cheaper living in Brittany – why should I not go to him, if we want to help him?

If he says 'I am at the height of my powers and my talent,' why should I not say the same myself?

But then, we are not at the height of our finances, so we must do what comes cheapest.

Lots to paint, little to spend, that is the line we must take. So once again I tell you that I lay aside all preference, either for the north or the south. Whatever plans one makes, there's a root of difficulty somewhere. It would all be plain sailing with Gauguin, but once shift him, is he going to be content? . . .

But in the old days I used to feel myself less a *painter*, now painting is becoming a distraction for me, like rabbit hunting for crazyheads: they do it to distract themselves . . .

That is why I dare almost swear to you that my painting will improve. Because I have nothing left but that . . .

✳ ✳ ✳

To Theo (514)
Arles, 29 July 1888

. . . Now you talk of the emptiness you feel everywhere, it is just that very thing that I feel myself.

Taking if you like the time in which we live as a great and true renaissance of art, the worm-eaten official tradition still alive but really impotent and inactive, the new painters alone, poor, treated like madmen and because of this treatment actually becoming so at least as far as their social life is concerned . . .

I have had a letter from [John] Russell. He says that he would have written to me before, if his removal to Belle Isle had not occupied him. He is there now, and says that he would be pleased if sooner or later I would go and spend some time there. He is at it again that he wants to repaint my portrait . . .

Bernard has sent me ten sketches like his brothel; three of them were à la Redon; the enthusiasm he has for that I do not altogether share. But there is a woman washing herself, very Rembrandt-esque, an effect like Goya, and a landscape with figures, very strange. He expressly forbids me to send them to you, but all the same you will get them by the same post.

I think that Russell will take something more from Bernard. Meantime I have seen the work of this Bock; it is strictly Impressionist, but not powerful, it is the stage when this new technique still so preoccupies him that he cannot be himself. He will gain in force and then his individuality will break free, I think. But MacKnight does watercolours of the quality of those of Destrée, you remember that Dutchman we used to know. However he has washed in some small still-lifes; a yellow pot on a violet foreground, a red pot on a green, an orange pot on blue, better, but very poor.

The village where they are staying is *real Millet*, poor peasants and nothing else, absolutely *rustic* and homely. This quality completely escapes them. I think that MacKnight has civilized and converted to civilized Christianity his brute of a landlord. Anyway the swine and his worthy spouse, when you go there, shake hands with you – it is in a café, of course – when you ask for drinks they have a way of refusing money – 'Oh! I could not take money from an artiss' – with two ss. Anyway it is their own fault that it is so abominable, and this Bock must be pretty well besotting himself along with MacKnight.

I think that MacKnight has some money but not much. So they taint the village, only for that I would go there often to work. What one ought to do there is not to talk to the civilized people; now they know the station master and a score of sticky people, and that is partly why they get nowhere. Naturally these simple and artless country folk laugh at and despise them. But if they did their work without taking up with these village loungers with their collars, then they could go into the peasants' homes, and let them earn a few pence. And then this blessed

Fontvielles would be a mine for them, but the natives are like Zola's poor peasants, innocent and gentle beings, as we know.

Probably MacKnight will soon be making little landscapes with sheep for chocolate boxes.

✳ ✳ ✳

To Theo   (515)
Arles, undated [1888]

. . . I think it would make a tremendous difference to me if Gauguin were here, for now the days pass without my speaking a word to anyone. Oh well. In any case his letter gave me tremendous pleasure.

If you are alone too long in the country you get stupid, and not yet – but this winter – I may become sterile because of this. Now if he came there would be no danger of this, because there would be no lack of ideas.

✳ ✳ ✳

To Theo   (516)
Arles, early August [1888]

So at last our uncle's [Vincent] sufferings are over. I received the news this morning from our sister. It appears that they were more or less expecting you to be at the funeral, so perhaps indeed you will be there.

How short life is and how like smoke. Which is no reason for despising the living, but the contrary.

So we are right to care more for the artists than for the pictures . . .

I am now at work with another model, a postman [Roulin] in a blue uniform, trimmed with gold, a big bearded face, very like Socrates. A violent Republican like Tanguy. A man more interesting than most . . .

I saw a magnificent and strange effect this evening. A very big boat loaded with coal on the Rhone, moored to the quay. Seen from above it was all shining and wet with a shower, the water was of a yellowish white, and clouded pearl grey, the sky lilac, and barred with orange to the west, the town violet. On the boat some poor labourers in dirty blue and white came and went carrying the cargo on shore. It was pure Hokusai. It was too late to do it, but one day when that coal boat comes back, I must go for it . . .

218

To Theo   (517)
Arles, undated [August 1888]

. . . I have had a letter from Gauguin, in which he talks about painting, and complains of not having enough money to come here, but nothing new or different . . .

✳ ✳ ✳

To Theo   (518)
Arles, undated [August 1888]

I think you were right to go to our uncle's funeral, since Mother seemed to be expecting you. The best way about a death is to swallow the illustrious dead whatever he was as being the best man in the best of all possible worlds, where everything is for the best. Which not being contested, and consequently incontestable, it is doubtless allowable for us afterwards to return to our own affairs. I am glad that our brother Cor has grown bigger and stronger than the rest of us. And he must be stupid if he does not get married, for he has nothing but that and his hands . . .

I have another unpleasant thing to tell you about the money, which is that I shall *not* manage this week, because this very day I am paying out 25 frs; I shall have money for five days, but *not* for seven. This is Monday; if I get your next letter on Saturday morning there will be no need to increase the enclosure. Last week I did not one only but two portraits of my postman, a half-length with the hands, and a head, life size. The good fellow, as he would not accept money, *cost more* eating and drinking with me, and I gave him besides the Lantern of Rochefort. But that is a trifling evil, considering that he posed very well, and that I expect to paint his baby very shortly, for his wife has just been brought to bed . . .

Today I am probably going to begin the interior of the café where I eat, by gas light, in the evening.

It is what they call here a *Café de Nuit* (they are fairly frequent here), staying open all night. Night prowlers can take refuge there when they have no money to pay for a lodging, or are too tight to be taken to one. All those things – family, native land – are perhaps more attractive in the imaginations of such people as us, who pretty well do without native land or family either, than they are in reality. I always feel I am a traveller, going somewhere and to some destination.

If I tell myself that the somewhere and the destination do not exist, that seems to me very reasonable and likely enough . . .

The brothel keeper, when he kicks anyone out, has similar logic, argues as well, and is always right I know. So at the end of the course I shall find my mistake. Be it so, I shall find then that not only the Arts, but everything else, were only dreams, that one's self was nothing at all. If we are *as flimsy as that*, so much the better for us, for then there is nothing against the unlimited possibility of future existence. Whence comes it that in the present instance of our uncle's death, the face of the dead was calm, peaceful and grave, while it is a fact that while living he was rarely thus, either in youth or age. I have often observed a like effect as I looked at the dead as though to question them. And that for me is *one* proof, though not the most serious, of a life beyond the grave.

And in the same way, a child in the cradle, if you watch it at leisure, has the infinite in its eyes . . .

✳ ✳ ✳

To Theo (520)
Arles, undated [August 1888]

. . . What a mistake Parisians make in not having a palate for crude things, for Monticellis, for clay. But there, one must not lose heart because Utopia is not coming true. It is only that what I learnt in Paris is leaving me, and that I am returning to the ideas I had in the country before I knew the Impressionists. And I should not be surprised if the Impressionists soon find fault with my way of working, for it has been fertilized by the ideas of Delacroix rather than by theirs. Because, instead of trying to reproduce exactly what I have before my eyes, I use colour more arbitrarily so as to express myself forcibly . . .

✳ ✳ ✳

To Theo (521)
Arles, undated [August 1888]

. . . I am thinking about Gauguin a lot, and I am sure that in one way or another, whether it is he who comes here, or I who go to him, he and I will like practically the same subjects, and I have no doubt that I could work at Pont-Aven, and on the other hand I am convinced that he would fall in love with the country down here. Well, at the year's end, supposing he gives you one canvas a month, which would make altogether a dozen per year, he will have made on it, not having incurred any debts and working steadily without interruption, certainly he won't have been the loser, while the money which he will have had from us would be largely made good by the economies that will be possible if we set up house in the studio instead of both of us living in cafés. Besides that, provided we keep on good terms and are determined not to quarrel, we shall be in a stronger position as far as reputation goes . . .

* * *

To Theo (522)
Arles, undated [August 1888]

. . . After such a coolness it is certainly not bad of uncle [Vincent] to have left you a legacy, but I cannot easily get it out of my head that C. M. and he did not actually condemn you to penal servitude for life, that time they refused to lend you the necessary capital to set you up in business on your own. It's still something pretty heavy against them. But I won't harp on that. All the more reason for trying to do the most that is possible in art, even if as far as money is concerned we shall always be comparatively straitened. Well, my boy, at that time you were *ready on your side* to set up in business and consequently you have perfect right to feel that you are doing *your duty on your side*. This business of the Impressionists, considered as a whole, you have taken up, with their help. Without their help the thing can't go on; or will go on in some different way . . .

With regard to Gauguin, with all our feeling for him, I think that we must behave like the mother of the family and work out the actual expenses. If one listened to him, one would go on hoping for something vague in the future, and meantime stay on at the inn, and go on living in a hell with no way out.

I would rather shut myself in a cloister like the monks, free as the monks are to go to the brothel or the wine-shop if the spirit moves us.

221

But for our work we need a home. Altogether Gauguin leaves me quite in the dark about Pont-Aven; he tacitly accepts my suggestion of coming to him if necessary, but he writes nothing about any means of finding a studio of our own, or about what it would cost to furnish it. And I can't help feeling there's something queer about it.

So I have decided not to go to Pont-Aven . . .

✳ ✳ ✳

To Theo (523)
Arles, undated [August 1888]

. . . it's very good of you to promise the two of us, Gauguin and me, that you'll put us in the way of carrying out our alliance. [Theo set aside part of his uncle's legacy to carry out Vincent's plan.]

I have just had a letter from Bernard, who went some days ago to join Gauguin, Laval and somebody else at Pont-Aven. It was a very decent letter, but not one syllable in it about Gauguin intending to join me, and not a syllable either about wanting me to come there. All the same it was a very friendly letter.

From Gauguin himself not a word for almost a month.

I think myself that Gauguin would rather mess about with his friends in the north, and if by good luck he sells one or more pictures, he may have other views for himself than coming to join me.

. . . Look here. As soon as you could, would you, not give, but lend me for a year 300 francs at one sweep? Then, if I say that you send me at present 250 francs a month, you will only send me 200 after this, until the 300, all laid out at once, would be paid off.

Then I should buy two decent beds all complete at 100 fr. each, and 100 fr. worth of other furniture.

That would mean that I could sleep at home, and could put up Gauguin or anybody else . . .

✳ ✳ ✳

To Theo (524)
Arles, undated [August 1888]

. . . I am working just now on a study of boats seen from the quay

222

above, the two boats are rose-colour tinged with violet, the water is bright green, no sky, a tricolour flag on the mast. A workman with a barrow is unloading sand . . .

I am afraid that I shall not get a beauty of a model, she promised, then – as it appears – earned some ha'pence by going gay, and has something better to do.

She was extraordinary, the expression like that one by Delacroix, the figure primitive and strange. I take these things with patience, failing any other way of bearing them, but this continual difficulty over models is maddening . . .

It is a gloomy enough prospect to have to say to myself that perhaps the painting I am doing will never be of any value whatever . . .

If you are a painter, they think you are either a fool or a rich man; a cup of milk costs you a franc, a slice of bread two, and meanwhile your pictures are not selling. That is what makes it necessary to combine as the old monks did, and the brothers of the common life of our Dutch heaths. I can see already that Gauguin is hoping for success, he cannot do without Paris, he does not realize the *eternity* of poverty . . .

I had begun to sign canvases, but I soon stopped, because it seemed too foolish . . .

✻ ✻ ✻

To Theo (526)
Arles, undated [August 1888]

I write in great haste, to tell you that I have had a note from Gauguin to say that he has not written much, but that he is quite ready to come south as soon as the opportunity offers.

They are enjoying themselves very much painting, arguing and fighting with the worthy English; he speaks well of Bernard's work, and B. speaks well of Gauguin's.

I am hard at it, painting with the enthusiasm of a Marseillais eating bouillabaisse, which won't surprise you when you know that what I'm at is the painting of some great sunflowers.

I have three canvases on hand – 1st, three huge flowers in a green vase, with a light background, a canvas of 15; 2nd, three flowers, one gone to seed, one in flower and the third a bud against a royal blue background, canvas of 25; 3rd, twelve flowers and buds in a yellow vase (canvas of 30). The last is therefore light on light, and I hope will be the best. I probably shall not stop at that. Now that I hope to live with Gauguin in a studio of our own, I want to make decorations for the studio. Nothing but big flowers. Next door to your shop, in the restaurant, you know there is a lovely decoration of flowers; I always remember the big sunflowers in the window there.

If I carry out this idea there will be a dozen panels. So the whole thing will be a symphony in blue and yellow. I am working at it every morning from sunrise, for the flowers fade so soon, and the thing is to do the whole at a flash . . .

✳ ✳ ✳

To Theo   (527)
Arles, undated [August 1888]

. . . If we painted like M. Gérôme and the other stereoscopic photographers, we should doubtless ask for very finely powdered colours. But on the contrary we do not object to the canvas having a rough look. If then instead of pounding the colour on the stone for God knows how many hours, it was crushed just long enough to make it manageable, without worrying too much about the fineness of the powder, you would get fresher colours which would perhaps darken less. If he likes to make a trial of it with the three chromes, the malachite, the vermilion, the orange lead, the cobalt and the ultramarine, I am almost certain that at much less cost I should get colours which would be both fresher and more lasting. Then what is the loss? I am sure that this could be done. Probably also with the reds and the emerald, which are transparent.

I enclose also an order which is urgent.

I am now at the fourth picture of sunflowers. This fourth is a bunch of fourteen flowers, against a yellow background, like a still-life of quinces and lemons that I did some time ago.

Only as it is much bigger, it gives a rather singular effect, and I think that this one is painted with more simplicity than the quinces and lemons.

Do you remember that one day we saw at the Hotel Drouot a very extraordinary Manet, some huge pink peonies with their green leaves against a light background? As much the open air and as much a flower as anything could be, and yet painted in perfectly solid *pâte* and not like Jeannin's.

That is what I should call simplicity of technique. And I must tell you that nowadays I am endeavouring to find a brushwork without stippling or anything else, nothing but the varied stroke. But some day you will see . . .

Gauguin and Bernard talk now of 'painting like children' – I would rather have that than 'painting like decadents'. How is it that people see something decadent in Impressionism? It is very much the reverse . . .

One of the decorations of sunflowers on royal blue ground has 'a halo', that is to say each object is surrounded by a glow of the complementary colour of the background against which it stands out . . .

✻ ✻ ✻

To Theo (528)
Arles, undated [August 1888]

. . . As for stippling and making haloes and other things, I think they are real discoveries, but we must see to it already that this technique does not become a universal dogma any more than any other. That is another reason why Seurat's Grande Jatte, the landscapes with broad stippling by Signac and Anquetin's boat, will become in time still more individual and still more original . . .

✻ ✻ ✻

To Theo (529)
Arles, undated [August 1888]

. . . I have two models this week; an Arlésienne, and the old peasant . . .

Unfortunately I am afraid that the little Arlésienne will not turn up for the rest of the picture. As a matter of fact she asked me for all the money I had promised her for posing, in advance, last time she came, and as I made no objection to that, she has made off and I have not seen her again . . .

✻ ✻ ✻

To Theo (530)
Arles, [1 September 1888]

. . . My life is disturbed and restless, but then if I make a change and move about much, I shall perhaps only make things worse.

It is a terrible loss to me that I don't speak the Provençal patois.

I keep seriously thinking of using coarser colours which will not be any less solid for being less pounded.

Often now I hold myself up from planning a picture because of what the colours would cost us. But all the same that is rather a pity, for the simple reason that perhaps we have power to work today, but we do not know if it will hold out till tomorrow . . .

✳ ✳ ✳

To Theo (531)
Arles, undated [September 1888]

I spent yesterday with the Belgian [Eugène Boch], who also has a sister [Anna Boch] among the 'vingtistes' [a group of avant-garde artists in Brussels]. It was not fine, but a very good day for talking; we went for a walk and anyway saw some very fine things at the bull fight and outside the town. We talked more seriously about the plan, that if I keep a place in the south, he ought to set up a sort of post among the collieries. Then Gauguin and I and he, if the importance of a picture made it worth the journey, could change places – and so be sometimes in the north, but in familiar country with a friend in it, and sometimes in the south.

You will soon see him, this young man with the look of Dante, because he is going to Paris, and if you put him up – if the room is free – you will be doing him a good turn; he is very distinguished in appearance, and will become so, I think, in his painting.

He likes Delacroix, and we talked a lot about Delacroix yesterday. He even knew the violent sketch of the *Barque of Christ*. Well, thanks to him, I have at last a first sketch of that picture which I have dreamt of for so long – the poet. He posed for me. His fine head with that keen gaze stands out in my portrait against a starry sky of deep ultramarine; for clothes, a short yellow coat, a collar of unbleached linen, and spotted tie. He gave me two sittings in one day . . .

And in a picture I want to say something comforting as music is comforting. I want to paint men and women with that something of the eternal which the halo used to symbolize, and which we seek to give by the actual radiance and vibration of our colourings . . .

The Belgian was saying that he paid 80 francs board and lodging with MacKnight, so what a difference there is in living together, since I have to pay 45 a month for nothing but lodging. I always come back to the same reckoning, that with Gauguin I should not spend more than I do alone, and be no worse off.

But we must consider that they were very badly housed, not for sleeping, but for the possibility of work at home. So I am always between two currents of thought, first the material difficulties, turning round and round to make a living, and second, the study of colour. I am always in hope of making a discovery there, to express the love of two lovers by a marriage of two complementary colours, their mingling and their opposition, the mysterious vibrations of kindred tones. To express the thought of a brow by the radiance of a light tone against a sombre background.

To express hope by some star, the eagerness of a soul by a sunset radiance. Certainly there is nothing in that of stereoscopic realism, but is it not something that actually exists? . . .

***

To Theo (532)
Arles, undated [1888]

. . . Neither Gauguin nor Bernard have written again. I think that Gauguin doesn't care a damn for it, seeing that it is not going to be done at once, and I for my part, seeing that for six months Gauguin has managed to muddle along by himself, am ceasing to believe in the urgent necessity of helping him . . .

Naturally we can still remain friends with Gauguin, but I see only too clearly that his mind is elsewhere. So I say, let us behave as if he was not there, then if he comes so much the better, if he does not so much the worse . . .

Counting the sunflowers, I have at the moment another fifteen new studies here . . .

***

Arles, 8 September [1888]

Thank you a thousand times for your kind letter and the 300 francs it contained; after some worrying weeks I have just had one of the very best. And just as worries do not come singly, neither do the joys. For just because I am always bowed down under this difficulty of paying my landlord, I made up my mind to take it gaily. I swore at the said landlord, who after all isn't a bad fellow, and told him that to revenge myself for paying him so much money for nothing, I would paint the whole of his rotten shanty so as to repay myself. Then to the great joy of the landlord, of the postman whom I had already painted, of the visiting night prowlers, and of myself, for three nights running I sat up to paint and went to bed during the day. I often think that the night is more alive and more richly coloured than the day. Now, as for getting back the money I have paid to the landlord by my painting, I do not dwell on that, for the picture [*The Night Café*] is one of the ugliest I have done. It is the equivalent, though different, of the *Potato Eaters*.

I have tried to express the terrible passions of humanity by means of red and green.

The room is blood red and dark yellow with a green billiard table in the middle; there are four lemon yellow lamps with a glow of orange and green. Everywhere there is a clash and contrast of the most alien reds and greens in the figures of little sleeping hooligans, in the empty dreary room, in violet and blue. The blood red and the yellow green of the billiard table for instance contrast with the soft tender Louis XV green of the counter on which there is a nosegay in rose colour. The white coat of the patron, on vigil in a corner of this furnace, turns lemon yellow, or pale luminous green . . .

I am greatly pleased that Pissarro thought something of the *Young Girl*. Has Pissarro said anything about the *Sower*? Afterwards, when I have gone further in these experiments, the *Sower* will still be the first attempt in that style. The *Night Café* carries on the *Sower*, and so also the head of the old peasant and of the poet, if I manage to do this latter picture.

It is colour not locally true from the point of view of the stereoscopic realist, but colour to suggest any emotion of an ardent temperament.

When Paul Mantz saw at the exhibition the violent and inspired sketch of Delacroix that we saw at the Champs Elysées – the *Barque of Christ* – he turned away from it, exclaiming:

'I did not know that one could be so terrible with a little blue and green.'

Hokusai wrings the same cry from you, but he does it by his *line*, his *drawing*, when you say in your letter – 'the waves are *claws* and the ship is caught in them, you feel it.' . . .

❋ ❋ ❋

To Theo   (534)
Arles, undated [September 1888]

I have just posted the sketch of the new picture, the *Night Café*, as well as another that I did some time ago. I shall end perhaps by making some prints.

Well now, yesterday I was busy furnishing the house. Just as the postman and his wife told me, the two beds, to be really substantial, will come at 350 fr. apiece. I found everything that they told me about prices was true. So I had to go on another tack, and this is what I have done. I have bought one walnut bed, and another in white wood which will be mine and which I'll paint later.

Then I got bedclothes for one of the beds, and two mattresses.

If Gauguin comes or someone else, there is his bed ready in a minute. I wanted to arrange the house from the start not for myself only, but so as to be able to put someone up. Naturally this has swallowed up the greater part of the money. With the rest I have bought twelve chairs, a mirror and some small necessary things. Altogether it means that next week I shall be able to go and live there already.

For a visitor there will be the prettier room upstairs, which I shall try to make as much as possible like the boudoir of a really artistic woman.

Then there will be my own bedroom, which I want extremely simple, but with large, solid furniture, the bed, chairs and table all in white wood.

Downstairs will be the studio, and another room, a studio too, but a kitchen as well.

You shall have a picture some day or other of the little house itself in bright sunshine, or else with the window lit up, and a starry sky.

Henceforth you can feel that you have your country house at Arles. For I am very keen to arrange it so that you will be pleased with it, and so that it will be a studio in an absolutely individual style, so if in a year, say you come here and to Marseilles for your holidays, it will be ready then, and the house, as I intend, will be full of pictures from top to bottom.

The room you will have then, or Gauguin, if Gauguin comes, will have white walls with a decoration of great yellow sunflowers.

In the morning when you open the window, you see the green of the gardens and the rising sun, and the road into the town.

But you will see these great pictures of the sunflowers, twelve or fourteen to the bunch, crammed into this tiny boudoir with its pretty bed and everything else dainty. It will not be hackneyed. And in the studio the red tiles of the floor, the walls and ceiling white, rustic chairs, white wood table, and I hope a decoration of portraits. It will have a feeling of Daumier about it, and I think I can promise you it will not be hackneyed . . .

In my picture of the *Night Café* I have tried to express the idea that the café is a place where one can ruin oneself, run mad, or commit a crime. So I have tried to express as it were the powers of darkness in a low drink shop, by soft Louis XV green and malachite, contrasting with yellow green and hard blue greens, and all this in an atmosphere like a devil's furnace, of pale sulphur.

And all under an appearance of Japanese gaiety, and the good nature of Tartarin.

But what would Monsieur Tersteeg say about this picture when he said before a Sisley – Sisley the most discreet and gentle of the Impressionists – 'I cannot help thinking that the artist who painted that was a bit tipsy.' If he saw my picture he would say that it was delirium tremens in full career . . .

✳ ✳ ✳

To Theo   (535)
Arles, undated [September 1888]

. . . If the plan of a more serious combination cannot be carried out, all right, but then each should resume his liberty of action. I have sent off my letter to Gauguin, I asked them for an exchange. If they are willing, I would very much like to have here the portrait of Bernard by Gauguin and that of Gauguin by Bernard.

I enclose an article which will interest you. You would be very wise to go and see this.

Ideas for my work come to me in swarms, so that although solitary I have no time to think or to feel, I go on like a steam engine at painting. I think there will hardly ever be a standstill again. And my view is that a living studio you will never find ready-made, but that it is created from day to day by patient work and going on and on in one place . . .

The idea of the *Sower* continues to haunt me all the time. Exaggerated studies like the *Sower*, and like this *Night Café*, seem to me usually atrociously ugly and bad, but when I am moved by something, as now by this little article on Dostoievsky, then these are the only ones which appear to have any deep meaning . . .

I am very glad to have finished my letter to Gauguin, without having said that his wavering between staying with Laval or me has left me rather at sea. It would not be fair not to leave him perfectly free to choose and to do the best he can . . .

Bernard says it grieves him to see how Gauguin is often prevented from doing what he otherwise could, for wholly material reasons, paints, canvas, etc. Well, in any case that can't go on. The worst that can happen to him is that he will be obliged to leave his pictures in pledge for what he owes his landlord, and to take refuge either with you or with me by making the single journey. But in this case if he does not want to lose his pictures, he must cope very definitely with his landlord . . .

❋ ❋ ❋

To Theo (536)
Arles, 11 September [1888]

Enclosed is a letter from Gauguin, which arrived at the same moment as a letter from Bernard. It is just a cry of distress. 'I am getting deeper into debt every day.' . . .

I am rather curious to know what he will say to you himself. I reply to him exactly as I feel, but I do not want to say depressing or dismal or malicious things to so great an artist. But from the point of view of money the business is taking on serious proportions – there is the journey, there is the debt, and there is also the furnishing which is not yet complete . . .

❋ ❋ ❋

231

To Theo (537)
Arles, 17 September [1888]

. . . The second [picture this week] represents the outside of a café, the terrace lit up by a big gas lamp in the blue night, and a corner of starry blue sky.

The third picture this week is a portrait of myself, *almost colourless*, in grey tones against a background of pale malachite.

I have bought of set purpose a mirror good enough for me to be able to work from myself in default of a model, because if I can manage to paint the colouring of my own head, which is not to be done without some difficulty, I shall likewise be able to paint the heads of other good souls, men and women.

The problem of painting night scenes and effects on the spot and actually by night, interests me enormously. This week I have done absolutely nothing but paint and sleep and take my meals. That means sittings of twelve hours, of six hours and so on, and then a sleep of twelve hours at a time . . .

✳ ✳ ✳

To Theo (538)
Arles, undated [September 1888]

. . . Now if I set up a studio and refuge right at the gates of the south, it's not such a daft scheme. And it means that we can work serenely on. And if other people say that it is too far from Paris, etc. let them, so much the worse for them. Why did the greatest colourist of all, Eugène Delacroix, think it essential to go south and right to Africa? Obviously, because not only in Africa but from Arles onwards, you are bound to find beautiful contrasts of red and green, of blue and orange, of sulphur and lilac.

And all true colourists must come to this, must admit that there is another kind of colour than that of the north. I am sure if Gauguin came he would love this country; if he does not it is because he has already had experience of more brightly coloured lands, and he will always be a friend, and one with us in principle . . .

✳ ✳ ✳

I wrote to you already, early this morning, then I went away to go on with a picture of a garden in sunshine. Then I brought it back and went out again with a blank canvas, and that also is finished. And now I want to write to you again.

Because I have never had such a chance, nature here is so *extraordinarily* beautiful. Everywhere and over all the vault of the sky is a marvellous blue, and the sun sheds a radiance of pale sulphur, and it is soft and as lovely as the combination of heavenly blues and yellows in a Van der Meer at Delft. I cannot paint it as lovely as that is, but it absorbs me so much that I let myself go, never thinking of a single rule.

That makes three pictures of the gardens opposite the house. Then the two cafés, and then the sunflowers. Then the portrait of Bock and of myself. Then the red sun over the factory, and the men unloading sand, and the old mill. Leaving out the other studies, you see that I have got some work behind me. But my paints, my canvas and my purse are all completely exhausted today. The last picture, done with the last tubes of paint on the last canvas, of a garden, green of course, is painted with real green, nothing but Prussian blue and chrome yellow.

I am beginning to feel that I am quite a different creature from what I was when I came here. I have no doubts, no hesitation in attacking things, and this may increase . . .

Today while I was working I thought a lot about Bernard. His letter is steeped in admiration for Gauguin's talent. He says that he thinks him so great an artist that he is almost afraid, and that he finds everything that he himself does poor in comparison with Gauguin. And you know that this winter Bernard was always picking quarrels with Gauguin . . .

I have such joy in the house and in my work, that I dare even to think that the joy will not always be solitary, but that you will have a share in it and the zest of it too.

Some time ago I read an article on Dante, Petrarch, Boccaccio, Giotto and Botticelli. Good Lord! it did make an impression on me reading the letters of those men.

And Petrarch was quite near here at Avignon, and I am seeing the same cypresses and oleanders . . .

I have tried to put something of that into one of the pictures painted in very thick *pâte*, lemon yellow and lemon green. Giotto moved me most – *always in pain*, and always full of kindness and enthusiasm, as though already he were living in a different world from this.

And besides Giotto is extraordinary. I understand him better than the poets, Dante, Petrarch and Boccaccio.

I always think that poetry is more *terrible* than painting, though painting is dirtier and much more of a mess. And then the painter never says anything, he holds his tongue, and I like that too . . .

What is Seurat doing? I should not dare to show him the studies already sent, but the ones of the sunflowers, and the cabarets, and the gardens, I would like him to see those. I often think over his method, though I do not follow it at all, but he is an original colourist, and Signac the same, though to a different degree, their stippling is a new discovery, and I like them very much still. But I myself – I tell you frankly – am returning rather to what I was looking for before I came to Paris. I do not know if anyone before me has talked about suggestive colour, but Delacroix and Monticelli, without talking about it, did it.

But I have got back to where I was at Nuenen, when I made a vain attempt to learn music, so much did I already feel the relation between our colour and the music of Wagner.

It is true that I see in Impressionism the resurrection of Eugène Delacroix, but the interpretations of it are so divergent and in a way so irreconcilable, that it will not be Impressionism that will give us the final doctrine.

That is why I myself remain among the Impressionists, because it gives away nothing, and binds you to nothing, and as one of the crowd I have not to declare my formula . . .

❋ ❋ ❋

To Theo (540)
Arles, undated [September 1888]

. . . For the second time I have scraped off a study of Christ with the angel in the garden of olives.

Because here I can see real olives, but I cannot or rather I will not paint any more without models, but I have the thing in my head with the colours, a starry night, the figure of Christ in blue, all the strongest

234

blues, and the angel blended lemon yellow. And every shade of violet from a blood-red purple to ashen, in the landscape . . .

Here my life will become more and more like a Japanese painter's, living close to nature like a petty tradesman . . .

✳ ✳ ✳

To Theo   (541)
Arles, undated [September 1888]

. . . Today again from 7 o'clock in the morning till 6 in the evening I worked without stirring except to eat a bite a step or two away. That is why the work is getting on fast.

But what will you say to it, and what shall I think of it myself, a little while from now?

I have a lover's clear sight or a lover's blindness for work just now.

Because these colours about me are all new to me, and give me extraordinary exaltation.

I have no thought of fatigue, I shall do another picture this very night, and I shall bring it off . . .

✳ ✳ ✳

To Theo   (542)
Arles, undated [September 1888]

. . . If we study Japanese art, you see a man who is undoubtedly wise, philosophic and intelligent, who spends his time how? In studying the distance between the earth and the moon? No. In studying the policy of Bismarck? No. He studies a single blade of grass.

And you cannot study Japanese art, it seems to me, without becoming much gayer and happier, and we must return to nature in spite of our education and our work in a world of convention . . .

I envy the Japanese the extreme clearness which everything has in their work. It never is wearisome, and never seems to be done too hurriedly. Their work is as simple as breathing, and they do a figure in a few sure strokes with the same ease as if it were as simple as buttoning your coat . . .

235

To Theo   (543)
Arles, [September 1888]

... Enclosed a little sketch of a canvas of 30 square, the starry sky painted
actually at night under a gas jet. The sky is greenish blue, the water royal
blue, the ground mauve. The town is blue and violet, the gas is yellow
and the reflections are russet gold down to greenish bronze. On the blue-
green field of the sky the Great Bear sparkles green and rose, its discreet
pallor contrasts with the brutal gold of the gas.

Two little figures of lovers in colour in the foreground . . .

I have a letter from Gauguin, who seems very unhappy and says that
as soon as he has sold something, he will certainly come, but he still
does not make it clear whether, if he had his fare paid, he would agree
to shake himself free and come.

He says that the people where he lodges are and have been wonderful
to him, and that to leave them like that would be an outrage. But that I
would be turning a knife in his heart if I were to think that he would not
come straight off if he could. And he says too that if you could sell his
pictures at a low price he would be quite content . . .

I wanted to do some more sunflowers . . . but they were already over.
Yes, during the autumn I very much want to be able to do a dozen
canvases of 30 square, and so far as I can see, I may very well manage
to do it. I have a terrible lucidity at moments, these days when nature
is so beautiful, I am not conscious of myself any more and the picture
comes to me as in a dream. I am rather afraid that this will mean a
reaction and depression when the bad weather comes . . .

❈ ❈ ❈

To Theo   (544)
Arles, undated [1888]

Enclosed a very very remarkable letter from Gauguin. Do put it on one
side as a thing of extraordinary importance.

I mean his description of himself, which moves me to the depths. I
got it with a letter from Bernard which Gauguin probably read and
perhaps approved, in which Bernard says once more that he wants to
come here, and proposes to me on behalf of Laval, Moret, another
novice, and himself, to make an exchange with the four of them.

He also says that Laval will come as well, and that the other two want to come. I should not ask anything better, but when it is a question of several painters living in community life, I stipulate before everything that there must be an abbot to keep order, and that would naturally be Gauguin. That is why I would like Gauguin to be here first (besides Bernard and Laval will only come in February, Bernard having to pass his Military Board in Paris). As for me I want two things, I want to win back the money which I have already spent, so as to give it to you, and I want Gauguin to have peace and quiet in which to produce, and be able to breathe freely as an artist . . .

Well yes, I am ashamed of it, but I am vain enough to want to make a certain impression on Gauguin by my work, so I cannot help wanting to do as much work as possible alone before he comes. His coming will alter my way of painting and I shall gain by it, I believe, but all the same I am rather keen on my decorations, which are almost like pottery. And these days are magnificent.

I have ten canvases of 30 in hand now . . .

We have to add over and above all this Gauguin's fare, but if Thomas isn't willing to be free-handed, *Gauguin's fare before everything*, to the detriment of your pocket and mine. *Before everything.* All the expenses I have mentioned are all with the idea of making a good impression on him at the moment of his arrival . . .

The essential thing is the fare, and even my paints can wait, though I venture to think that I shall some day earn with them more than they cost. I shouldn't make light of Gauguin's giving you the monopoly of his work, and straight off his prices will go up. Nothing below 500 frs. He has only to have confidence, and now he will have that . . .

If Gauguin gives his work to you, officially because you are with the Goupils, and privately as your friend and under an obligation to you, then in return Gauguin can consider himself head of the studio, and control the money as he thinks fit, and if it can be done, help Bernard, Laval and others by exchanging studies or pictures, whilst I shall abide by the same conditions, giving my studies for 100 francs and my share of canvas and paints. But the more Gauguin realizes that when he joins with us he will have the standing of headship of a studio, the sooner he will get better, and the more eager he will be to work . . .

❋ ❋ ❋

To Theo   (545)
Arles, undated [1888]

. . . I have just received the portrait of Gauguin by himself and the portrait of Bernard by Bernard, and in the background of the portrait of Gauguin there is Bernard's on the wall, and vice versa. The Gauguin is of course remarkable, but I very much like Bernard's. It is no more than the suggestion of a painter, a few abrupt tones, a few dark lines, but it has the distinction of a real true Manet. The Gauguin is more studied, carried farther.

That, along with what he says in his letter, gave me absolutely the impression of its representing a prisoner. Not a shadow of gaiety. Not the slightest relief of flesh, but one can confidently put that down to his determination to make a melancholy effect, the flesh in the shadows is gone a dismal blue.

So now at last I have a chance to compare my painting with what the crowd are doing. My portrait which I am sending to Gauguin in exchange holds its own with it, I am sure of that. I have written to Gauguin in reply to his letter that if I might be allowed to exaggerate my own personality in a portrait, I had done so in trying to convey in my portrait not only myself but an Impressionist in general, had conceived it as that of a Bonze, a simple worshipper of the eternal Buddha.

And when I put Gauguin's conception and my own side by side, mine is as grave, but less despairing. What Gauguin's portrait says to me above everything, is that he must not go on like this, he must become again the richer Gauguin of the *Negresses* . . .

✳ ✳ ✳

To Theo   (546)
Arles, undated [October 1888]

Thanks for your letter, but I have had a very thin time of it these days, as my money ran out on Thursday, so it was a damnably long time till Monday noon. I have lived principally for these four days on twenty-three cups of coffee, with bread which I still have to pay for. It is not your fault, it is mine if it is anyone's. Because I was wild to see my pictures in frames, and I had ordered too many for my budget, seeing that the month's rent and the charwoman had to be paid as well. And even now today is going to run me short, because I must also buy some canvas and prepare it myself, as Tasset's has not yet come. Would you as soon as possible ask him if he has sent it off, 10 metres or at least 5 of ordinary canvas at 2·50 fr. . . .

I venture to think that if you saw the studies you would say I was right to work at white heat as long as it was fine. It wasn't so the last few days, there is a pitiless mistral sweeping along the dead leaves in a rage. But between now and the winter there will be another spell of magnificent weather and magnificent effects, and then the thing will be to make another headlong spurt. I am so much taken up with the work, that I cannot pull myself up . . . Do you know what I have left today for the week, and that after four days of strict fasting? Just 6 francs. It is Monday, the very day I received your letter.

I ate at noon, but already this evening I must sup on a crust of bread . . .

✳ ✳ ✳

To Theo   (548)
Arles, undated [October 1888]

. . . I am working on a portrait of mother, because the black and white photograph annoys me so. Ah, what portraits could be made from nature with photography and painting! I always hope that we are still to have a great revolution in portraiture.

I am writing home for father's portrait also. I do not want to have black photographs, but I do want to have a portrait. That of mother, a canvas of 8, will be ashen grey, against a green background, the dress *carmine.*

I do not know if it will be like her, but anyhow I want to give the impression of fairness. You shall see it one day, and if you like I will make one for you as well. It will again be in very thick *pâte* . . .

✳ ✳ ✳

To Theo (549)
Arles, undated [October 1888]

A letter from Gauguin, paying me heaps of undeserved compliments, and adding that he will not be coming till the end of the month.

And that he has been ill, and dreads the journey. What can I do about it . . . but after all, when you come to think, is it such an annihilating journey when the worst lung cases undertake it? . . .

Reply to Gauguin's letter

My dear Gauguin,

Thanks for your letter – far too flattering to me. So you are not coming till the end of the month.

Very good – since you really think that you will get better more quickly in Brittany than here.

I don't insist on it, only if your recovery is not very speedy in Brittany, consider that *we* claim to be able to cure you more quickly here than there. Come, everything is always for the best in this best of worlds, in which we have – according to good old Pangloss anyhow – the ineffable happiness of living. In this case I have no doubt at all – everything will be for the best. But is it absolutely true that the journey to Arles is as exhausting as you say? Nonsense, since the worst lung cases make it. You well know that the P.L.M. exists for that.

Or are you more seriously ill than you say? I am afraid so, and if you can, either reassure me on this head, or else write definitely that you are ill and in a bad way. But you write about business, and talk of lithographs. This is what I think:

For you, me, Bernard and Laval to make lithographs at night is *all right* – I am sure of that, but about their periodical publication I am *not sure*, as long as I am no better off than this. I have more than enough with the painting. There is always something to spend money on in lithography *even if you do not buy* the stone. That would not cost so very much – I do not say that – but then for publishing, however humbly, the four of us would be let in for at least 50 francs *each. And more besides* . . .

Contradict me if you like, I don't press it, but still I say what I say. I have already had a small experience of one attempt, but the 'besides' that I add, means that it would not last, and above all, would never take at all with the public. And it will go on costing us money.

Even if it did cost us money, I am actually all for *making* the lithographs in question. But for *publication*, on the other hand, even *free of cost* – never.

If it is at our expense and for our own pleasure and use, then I tell you again, I am for it. If you are thinking of something else, I am not for it; do not tell me that one costs as little as the other, if it's a question of publishing.

Yours,
Vincent

And do come as soon as you possibly can!

P.S. to Gauguin. If you are not ill, do please come at once. If you are too ill, a wire and a letter, please.

P.S. to Theo. Perhaps you will think the P.S. to Gauguin too curt, but let him say whether or not he is ill, and anyhow he will recover better here. Have you got any canvases? . . .

✳ ✳ ✳

To Theo   (553)
Arles, undated [October 1888]

. . . I have been and still am nearly dead with the work of the past week. I cannot do any more, and besides there is a very violent mistral that raises clouds of dust which whiten the trees all up and down the arena. So I am forced to keep quiet. I have just slept 16 hours at a stretch, and it has restored me considerably.

And tomorrow I shall have recovered from this queer turn.

But I have done a good week, truly, with five canvases. If that rather takes its revenge on this one, well, it's natural. If I had worked more quietly, you can easily see that the mistral would have caught me again. If it is fine here, you must make use of it, if not you would never do anything . . .

I do wish we had the portrait of Seurat by himself. I said to Gauguin that when I pressed him to make an exchange of portraits it was because I thought that Bernard and he were sure to have made several studies of one another already. And since that was not so and he had

241

done the portrait expressly for me, I did not want it as an exchange, as I thought it was too considerable for that. He wrote to say that he was determined I should have it in exchange, his letter is again very complimentary, as I don't deserve it we will say no more . . .

✳ ✳ ✳

To Theo   (554)
Arles, undated [October 1888]

. . . Another canvas of 30. This time it's just simply my bedroom, only here colour is to do everything, and giving by its simplification a grander style to things, is to be suggestive here of *rest* or of sleep in general. In a word, to look at the picture ought to rest the brain or rather the imagination.

The walls are pale violet. The ground is of red tiles.

The wood of the bed and chairs is the yellow of fresh butter, the sheets and pillows very light greenish lemon.

The coverlet scarlet. The window green.

The toilet table orange, the basin blue.

The doors lilac.

And that is all – there is nothing in this room with closed shutters.

The broad lines of the furniture again must express inviolable rest. Portraits on the walls, and a mirror and a towel and some clothes.

The frame – as there is no white in the picture – will be white.

This by way of revenge for the enforced rest I was obliged to take.

I shall work at it again all day, but you see how simple the conception is. The shadows and the shadows thrown are suppressed, it is painted in free flat washes like the Japanese prints . . .

✳ ✳ ✳

To Theo   (555)
Arles, [October 1888]

. . . Gauguin writes that he has already sent off his promises to come about the 20th of this month, that is within a few days. I shall be very glad of it, because I do believe that it will be good for each of us.

. . . I believe that a new school of *colourists* will take root in the south,

242

as I see more and more that those in the north rely on ability with the brush, and the so-called 'picturesque', rather than on the desire to express something by colour itself. Your news gave me great pleasure, but it so astonishes me not to know what there was in that frame.

Here, under a stronger sun, I have found true what Pissarro said, and what Gauguin wrote to me as well, the simplicity, the lack of colour, the gravity of great sunlight effects.

Never in the north do you come near suspecting it . . .

✳ ✳ ✳

To Theo (556)
Arles, undated [October 1888]

. . . I am not ill, but I should get ill without the slightest doubt if I did not take plenty of food, and if I did not stop painting for days at a time. As a matter of fact I am pretty nearly reduced again to the madness of Hugo van der Goes in the picture by Emil Wauters. And if it were not that I have almost a double nature, as it were of a monk and a painter, I should have been reduced, and that long ago, completely and utterly, to the condition aforesaid.

Yet even then I do not think that my madness could take the form of persecution, since my feelings when in a state of excitement lead me rather to the consideration of eternity, and eternal life.

But in any case I must beware of my nerves, etc. . . .

✳ ✳ ✳

To Theo (557)
Arles, 20 October [1888]

Thanks for your letter and the 50 fr. note. As you learnt from my wire Gauguin has arrived in good health. He even seems to me better than I am.

He is naturally very pleased with the sale you have effected, and I no less, since in this way certain expenses absolutely necessary for the installation have no need to wait, and will not weigh wholly on your shoulders. Gauguin will certainly write to you today. He is very interesting as a man, and I have every confidence that with him we shall do heaps of things. He will produce a great deal here probably, and I hope perhaps I shall too.

And then I dare to hope that the burden will be a *little* less heavy for you, and I dare to hope *much* less heavy. I myself realize even to the pitch of being mentally crushed and physically drained by it, the necessity of producing, just because I have not after all any other means of ever getting back what we have spent.

I cannot help it that my pictures do not sell.

Nevertheless the time will come when people will see that they are worth more than the price of the paint and my own living, very meagre after all, that is put into them.

I have no other desire nor other interest as to money or finance, than first to have no debts.

But my dear lad, my debt is so great that when I have paid it, which I hope nevertheless to succeed in doing, the pains of producing pictures will have taken my whole life from me and it will seem to me then that I have not lived. The only thing is that perhaps the production of pictures will become a little harder for me, and as to numbers, there will not always be so many.

That there is no sale for them now, it gives me agony because you suffer for it, but as far as I am concerned – if only you were not too much pinched by my bringing nothing in – it would be pretty well all one to me . . .

We shall probably give Tasset [his usual paint supplier] the go by altogether, because in great measure we are going to use cheaper colours, Gauguin as well as I. And in the same way with the canvas, we are going to prepare it ourselves. I had for a while rather a feeling that I was going to be ill, but Gauguin's arrival has so much taken my mind off that I am sure it will pass off. I must not neglect my food for a time, and that is all, absolutely all there is to it.

And at the end of some time you shall have some work.

Gauguin has brought a magnificent canvas which he has exchanged with Bernard, Breton women in a green field, white, black, green, and a note of red, and the dull flesh tints. After all, we must all be of good cheer.

✳ ✳ ✳

To Theo (558)
Arles, 22 October [1888]

. . . Gauguin is astonishing as a man, he does not let himself get out of hand, and he will wait here very quietly, working hard, for the right moment to make a great step forward. Rest he needs as much as I do. With the money he has just earned he certainly could have treated himself to a rest in Brittany just as well, *but as things are now he is sure of being able to wait without once more getting fatally into debt.* We shall not spend *together* more than 250 fr. a month. And we shall spend *much less* on paint, since we are going to make it ourselves. So do not on your part have any anxiety for us, and have a breathing space as well, you need it badly . . . Gauguin has already nearly found his Arlésienne, and I could wish I had got that length, but for my part it is the landscape that comes to me, and I find it varied enough. So after all my little work goes on as usual.

I dare to think that you will like the new *Sower.*

✳ ✳ ✳

To Theo (559)
Arles, November [1888]

. . . Just now he [Gauguin] has in hand some women in a vineyard, altogether from memory, but if he does not spoil it or leave it unfinished it will be very fine and very unusual. Also a picture of the same night café that I painted too.

I have done two canvases of autumn, which Gauguin liked I think, and I'm working now on a vineyard all purple and yellow.

Then I have an Arlésienne at last, a figure (30 canvas) slashed on in an hour, background pale lemon, the face grey, the clothes black, black, black, with perfectly raw Prussian blue. She is leaning on a green table and seated in an armchair of orange wood.

Gauguin has bought a chest of drawers for the house, and various household utensils, and also 20 metres of very strong canvas, a lot of things that we needed, and that at any rate it was more convenient to have. Only we have kept an account of all he has paid out, which comes almost to 100 francs and either at the New Year or say in March we should pay him back, and then the chest of drawers etc. will naturally be ours.

I think this is right on the whole, since he intends to put money by when he sells, till the time (say in a year) when he has enough to risk a second voyage to Martinique.

We are working hard, and our life together goes very well . . .

Gauguin is still homesick for hot countries. And then it is unquestionable that if you went to Java, for instance, with the one idea of working for colour, you would see heaps of new things. Then in those brighter countries, with a stronger sun, direct shadow, as well as the thrown shadow of objects and figures, becomes quite different, and is so full of colour that one is tempted simply to suppress it. That happens even here . . .

Gauguin and I are going to have our dinner at home today, and we feel as sure and certain that it will turn out well as that it will seem to us better or cheaper.

✳ ✳ ✳

To Theo   (560)
Arles, November [1888]

. . . Our days pass in working, working all the time, in the evening we are dead beat and go off to the café, and after that, early to bed! That is life. Of course it's winter here with us too, though it still keeps on being very fine from time to time. But I do not dislike trying to work from imagination, since that allows me to stay in. It does not worry me to work in the heat of a stove, but cold does not suit me as you know . . .

Gauguin works a lot. I very much like a still-life, background and foreground yellow, he has in hand a portrait of me which I do not reckon among his fruitless undertakings, just now he is doing some landscapes, and lastly he has a good canvas of washerwomen, even very good I think.

You should be getting two drawings from Gauguin in return for the 50 fr. you sent him to Brittany. But mother Bernard has simply appropriated them. Speaking of tales without a name, that really is one. I think that she will end by giving them up. Mind you, in my opinion, Bernard's things are very fine, and will have a Parisian success that will be deserved . . .

You know that Gauguin is invited to exhibit at the 'Vingtistes'. His imagination already leads him to think of settling at Brussels and that certainly would be a means towards his being able to see his Danish wife again.

Since in the meantime he has plenty of luck with the Arlésiennes, I should not consider this entirely insignificant. He is married and has very little look of it. In short I fear that there is entire incompatibility of character between his wife and himself, but he naturally cares more for his children who are very pretty according to the portraits.

❋ ❋ ❋

To Theo   (561)
Arles, undated [1888]

I have received a letter from M. C. Dujardin on the subject of the exhibition of my pictures in his black hole. I am so disgusted at the idea of handing over a canvas in payment for the proposed exhibition that really there is only one possible answer to our gentleman's letter. That one you will find enclosed. Only I send it to you and not to him so that you may know what I think, and that you may simply say to him that I have changed my mind, and at the moment have no desire to exhibit. It isn't the least bit of good in the world getting angry with the scoundrel, it is better to be conventionally polite. So no exhibition at the *Revue Indépéndante*, I boldly venture to think that Gauguin also is of this opinion. In any case he makes no attempt to persuade me to do it.

I am going to set myself to work from memory often, and the canvases from memory are always less awkward, and have a more artistic look than studies from nature, especially when one works in mistral weather.

Gauguin has also almost finished his night café. He is very interesting as a friend, I must tell you that he knows how to cook *perfectly*, I think I shall learn it from him, it is very convenient. We find it very easy to make frames with plain strips of wood nailed on the stretcher and painted, and I have begun doing this. Do you know that Gauguin is really partly the inventor of the white frame? . . .

❋ ❋ ❋

To Theo (562)
Arles, undated [1888]

Many thanks for the 100 francs you sent and for your letter. I know you will be pleased to hear that I have had a letter from Jet Mauve to thank us for the picture . . .

Gauguin is working at a very original nude woman in the hay with some pigs. It promises to be very fine, and of great distinction. He has sent to Paris for a magnificent jar with two rats' heads.

He is a very great artist and a very excellent friend . . .

I have worked at two canvases. A memory of our garden at Etten, with cabbages, cypresses, dahlias and figures, then a Woman reading a novel in a library like the Lecture Française, a woman all in green. Gauguin gives me courage to imagine things, and certainly things from the imagination take on a more mysterious character . . .

✳ ✳ ✳

To Theo (563)
Arles, December [1888]

Gauguin's canvas, *Breton Children*, has arrived and he has improved it a very great deal.

But though I quite like this canvas, it is all to the good that it is sold, and the two he is just going to send you from here are thirty times better.

I am speaking of the *Women at the Vintage*, and the *Woman with the Pigs*.

The reason of this is that Gauguin is beginning to get over that disorder of the liver or the stomach, which has been tormenting him this last while. But I am now writing to answer what you said about having a little canvas of mine of a pink peach tree framed, I imagine to send to these gentlemen [Boussod Valadon & Co.]. I don't want to leave any doubt as to what I think of that.

First, if it is your wish to let them have something of mine, good or bad, upon my honour if it can in any way give you any pleasure now or later, you have absolute *carte blanche* . . .

Gauguin, in spite of himself and in spite of myself, has rather brought me to see that it is time I was varying my work. I am beginning to compose from memory, and for that sort of work all my studies will still be useful, by recalling to me things I have once seen. What then does it matter about selling if we are not absolutely pressed for money . . .

It does me tremendous good to have such intelligent company as Gauguin's, and to see him work.

You will see that some people will soon be reproaching Gauguin with being no longer an Impressionist.

His two last canvases, which you will soon be seeing, are very firm in the *pâte*, there is even some work with the knife. And they will overshadow his Breton canvases rather, not all, but some.

I have hardly any time to write. Only for that I should have written already to these Dutchmen. I have had another letter from Bock, you know, the Belgian who has a sister among the 'Vingtistes', he is enjoying his work up there.

I do hope we shall always remain friends with Gauguin and in business together, and if he could succeed in founding a studio in the tropics it would be magnificent.

But for that it needs more money according to my reckoning than it does according to his. Guillaumin has written to Gauguin. He seems to be very hard up, but he must have done some fine things. He has a child now but he was *terrified* by the confinement, and he says that he has the red vision of it always before his eyes. But to this Gauguin aptly replied that he himself had seen it six times . . .

Gauguin was telling me the other day that he had seen a picture by Claude Monet of sunflowers in a great Japanese vase, very fine, but – he likes mine better. I don't agree – only do not think that I am deteriorating . . .

Meanwhile I can at all events tell you that the last two studies are odd enough.

Canvases of 30, a wooden rush-bottomed chair all yellow on red tiles against a wall (daytime).

Then Gauguin's armchair, red and green night effect, walls and floor red and green again, on the seat two novels and a candle, on thin canvas with thick *pâte* . . .

✼ ✼ ✼

To Theo (564)
Arles, undated [December 1888]

Gauguin and I went yesterday to Montpellier to see the gallery there and especially the Brias room. There are a lot of portraits of Brias, by Delacroix, Ricard, Courbet, Cabanel, Couture, Verdier, Tassaert and others. Then there are pictures by Delacroix, Courbet, Giotto, Paul Potter, Botticelli, Th. Rousseau, very fine. Brias was a benefactor of artists, I need say no more to you than that. In the portrait by Delacroix he is a gentleman with red beard and hair, uncommonly like you or me, and made me think of that poem of de Musset – *'Partout ou j'ai touché la terre – un malheureux vêtu de noir, aupres de nous venait s'asseoir, qui nous regardait comme un frère.'* It would have the same effect on you I am sure. Please do go to that bookshop where they sell the lithographs of past and present artists, and see if you could get, not too dear, the lithograph from Delacroix *Tasso in the Madhouse*, since I think the figure there must have some affinity with this fine portrait of Brias ...

Gauguin and I talked a lot about Delacroix, Rembrandt, etc.

Our arguments are terribly *electric*, we come out of them sometimes with our heads as exhausted as an electric battery after it is discharged. We were in the midst of magic, for as Fromentin well says: Rembrandt is above all else a magician ...

Gauguin wrote to Theo that Vincent and he could not go on living together 'in conse-quence of incompatibility of temper'. The quarrel was made up, and Gauguin wrote another letter, speaking of the first as a bad dream.

✳ ✳ ✳

To Theo (565)
Arles, 23 December [1888]

... I think myself that Gauguin was a little out of sorts with the good town of Arles, the little yellow house where we work, and especially with me.

As a matter of fact there are bound to be for him as for me grave difficulties to overcome here too.

But these difficulties are rather within ourselves than outside.

Altogether I think that either he will definitely go, or else definitely stay.

Before doing anything I told him to think it over and reckon things up again.

Gauguin is very powerful, strongly creative, but just because of that he must have peace.

Will he find it anywhere if he does not find it here?

I am waiting for him to make a decision with absolute serenity.

On the following day, 24 December, a telegram arrived from Gauguin that called Theo to Arles. Vincent, in a state of terrible excitement and high fever, had cut off a piece of his own ear, and brought it as a gift to a woman in a brothel. There had been a violent scene; Roulin the postman managed to get him home, but the police intervened, found Vincent bleeding and unconscious in bed, and sent him to the hospital. Theo found him there, 'poor fighter and poor poor sufferer', and stayed over Christmas. Gauguin went back with Theo to Paris. By 31 December the news was better, and on 1 January, Vincent wrote this letter in pencil.

✳ ✳ ✳

To Theo   (566)
Arles, 1 January [1889]

I hope that Gauguin will completely reassure you, and a bit about the painting business too.

I expect soon to begin work again.

The charwoman and my friend Roulin had taken care of the house, and had put everything in order.

When I come out I shall be able to take the little old road here again, and soon the fine weather will be coming and I shall begin again on the orchards in bloom.

My dear lad, I am so terribly distressed at your journey. I could have wished you had been spared that, for after all no harm came to me, and there was no reason why you should be so upset . . .

However, keep a good heart, address letters direct to me at Place Lamartine 2. I will send Gauguin's pictures that are still at the house as soon as he wishes. We owe him the money that he spent on the furniture.

A handshake, I must go back to hospital, but shall soon be out for good.

Write a line too to mother for me, so that no one will be worried.

On the back of the page was written, also in pencil, the following letter.

My dear friend Gauguin,

I take the opportunity of my first leave from hospital to write you a few words of very deep and sincere friendship. I often thought of you in hospital and even in the height of fever and comparative weakness.

Look here – was my brother Theo's journey really necessary, old man?

Now at least do reassure him altogether, and do I entreat you be confident yourself that after all no evil exists in this best of worlds in which everything is for the best.

Then I should like you to give many messages from me to good old Schuffenecker, to refrain until after riper reflection on both sides, from speaking ill of our poor little yellow house, and to greet from me the painters whom I saw in Paris. I wish you prosperity in Paris, with a good handshake.

Yours,
Vincent

Roulin has been truly kind to me, it was he who had the presence of mind to make me come out of that place before the others were convinced.

Please answer this.

❊ ❊ ❊

To Theo   (567)
Arles, 2 January 1889

So as to reassure you altogether on my account I write you these few lines in the office of M. Rey, the house-surgeon whom you saw yourself. I shall stay here at the hospital some days more, then I think I can count on returning quite quietly to the house.

Now I do beg of you one thing only, not to worry, because that would cause me one worry *too much*.

Now let's talk about our friend Gauguin. Have I scared him? In short, why doesn't he give me a sign of life? He must have left along with you. Besides, he needed to go back to Paris, and in Paris he will perhaps feel himself more at home than here. Tell Gauguin to write to me, and that I am always thinking about him . . .

I add a few words to your brother's letter to reassure you for my part on his account.

I am happy to inform you that my predictions have been realized, and that the over-excitement has been only temporary. I am firmly convinced that he will be himself in a few days. I made a point of his writing to you himself, so as to give you a better idea of his condition. I have made him come down to my office for a little chat. It will entertain me and will be good for him.

With kind regards,
I am, yours very truly,
Rey

✳ ✳ ✳

To Theo   (568)
Arles, undated [January 1889]

Perhaps I shall not write you a very long letter today, but anyway a line to let you know that I got back home today. I do so regret that you had all the trouble for such a trifle. Forgive me, who am, after all, probably the first cause of it. I did not foresee that it would be important enough for you to be told of it. Enough . . . Monsieur Rey came to see the painting with two of his friends, doctors, and they were uncommonly quick at understanding at least what complementaries are.

I intend now to make a portrait of M. Rey and possibly other portraits as soon as I have got a bit used to painting again. Thanks for your last letter. Indeed I always feel your presence, but do realize on your side too that I am working at the same thing as yourself . . .

If you agree – now that Gauguin has gone – we will put the month back again at 150 fr. I think I shall yet see calmer days here than the year that is gone . . .

Only I think that we must still keep quiet with regard to my own painting. If you want any, certainly I can send you some already, but when my peace of mind comes back to me I hope to do something different. However, as to the *Independents* do as seems good to you, and what the others do.

But you have no idea how much I regret that your journey to Holland has not yet come off.

After all we cannot alter what has happened, but make up for it yourself by letter, or any way you can, as far as possible, and tell the Bongers [Theo had recently become engaged to Johanna Bonger] how I regret having involuntarily caused delay. I shall be writing to mother and Wil one of these days, and I must also write to Jet Mauve.

Write to me soon, and set your mind at rest about my health. It will completely cure me to know that things are going well with you. What is Gauguin doing? As his family are in the north, and he has been invited to exhibit in Belgium, and has now some success in Paris, I like to think that he has found his feet . . .

※ ※ ※

To Theo   (569)
Arles, undated [January 1889]

. . . I am going to set to work again tomorrow. I shall begin by doing one or two still-lifes so as to get back the habit of painting. Roulin has been splendid to me, and I dare to think that he will remain a lasting friend. I shall have need enough of that still, for he knows the country well.

We had our dinner together today.

If ever you want to make the house-surgeon Rey *very happy* this is what would please him hugely. He has heard of a picture by Rembrandt, the *Anatomy Lesson*. I told him that we would get him the engraving of it for his study.

As soon as I feel myself fairly up to it, I hope to do his portrait . . .

Last Sunday I met another doctor, who is at least theoretically up in things about Delacroix and Puvis de Chavannes, and who is very curious to know about Impressionism . . .

I assure you that some days at the hospital were very interesting, and perhaps it is from the sick that one learns how to live.

I hope I have just had simply an artist's freak, and then a lot of fever after *very* considerable loss of blood, as an artery was severed, but my appetite came back at once, my digestion is all right and my blood revives, from day to day, and so from day to day serenity returns to my brain. So please do quite deliberately forget your unhappy journey and my illness . . .

✳ ✳ ✳

To Theo   (570)
Arles, 9 January [1889]

Even before receiving (this very moment) your kind letter, I had had a letter this morning from your fiancée announcing the engagement. So I have already sent her in reply my sincere congratulations, and I repeat them to you in this.

My fear that my indisposition might hinder you from that very necessary journey which I had so much and so long hoped for, this fear having now disappeared I feel myself again quite normal.

This morning I was again at the hospital to get another dressing, and I walked for an hour and a half with the house-surgeon, and we talked a bit about everything, even about natural history.

What you tell me of Gauguin gives me tremendous pleasure, that is to say that he has not given up his project of returning to the tropics. That for him is the right road. I think I see light in his plan, and I approve it heartily. Naturally I regret it, but you understand that provided it goes well for him, that is all I want.

What is the '89 Exhibition going to be? . . .

The mistake in old Gauguin's calculations to my mind was that he is rather too much in the habit of blinding himself to the inevitable expenses of rent for the house, charwoman and a lot of terrestrial things of the kind. Now all those things weigh rather on *our* shoulders, but once we took them on, other artists could lodge with me without having those expenses.

They have just told me that during my absence the owner of my house here made a contract with a fellow who has a tobacco shop to turn me out, and to give this tobacconist the house.

This has rather upset me, for I am not much disposed to have myself turned out of this house practically in disgrace, when it was I who had it repainted inside and out, and had gas put in, etc. – in fact who had made habitable a house which had been shut up and uninhabited for a considerable time, and which I took in a very poor condition. This is to warn you that perhaps at Easter say, if the owner persists, I shall ask your advice about it, and that I only consider myself in all this as a representative to defend the interests of our artist friends. Besides, between now and then it is more than likely that a good deal of water will have run under the bridge . . . the great thing is not to worry about it . . .

Physically I am well, the wound is healing very well and the great loss of blood is getting made up for, because I eat and digest well. What is most *to be feared* would be insomnia, and the doctor has not spoken to me about it, nor have I spoken of it to him either. But I am fighting it myself.

I fight this insomnia by a very, very strong dose of camphor in my pillow and mattress, and if ever you do not sleep I recommend you this. I was very much afraid of sleeping alone in the house, and I have been fearing I should not be able to sleep. But that is quite over and I dare to think that it will not reappear. The suffering from this in the hospital was frightful, and yet through it all, when I was even a stage beyond fainting, I can tell you as a curiosity that I kept on thinking about Degas. Gauguin and I had been talking before about Degas and I had pointed out to Gauguin that Degas had said . . .

'I am saving myself up for the Arlésiennes.'

Now you know how subtle Degas is, so when you get back to Paris, just tell Degas that I admit that up to the present I have been powerless to paint them, the women of Arles, as anything but poisonous, and that he must not believe Gauguin if Gauguin speaks well of my work before its time, for it's only a sick man's so far.

Now if I recover I must *begin again,* and I shall not again attain the heights to which sickness partially led me . . .

✳ ✳ ✳

To Theo (571)
Arles, 17 January [1889]

. . . I cannot commend you enough for paying Gauguin in such a way that he can only congratulate himself on any dealings he has had with us. There again is by ill hap another expenditure perhaps greater than it should have been, but yet I catch a glimpse of hope in it. Must he not, or at least should he not begin to see that we were not exploiting him, but on the contrary were anxious to secure him a living, possibly of work and . . . and . . . decency?

If that is not up to the grandiose prospectus of the association of artists which he proposed, and how keen he is on it you know, if it is not up to his other castles in the air – why not then consider him as irresponsible for the trouble and waste which in his blindness he may have caused both you and me?

If this theory still seems to you too bold, I do not insist on it, but we shall see . . .

If Gauguin were in Paris for a while to examine himself thoroughly, or have himself examined by a specialist, I don't honestly know what the result might be.

I have seen him on various occasions do things which you and I would not let ourselves do, because we have consciences that feel differently about things. I have heard one or two things of this kind said of him, but having seen him at very very close quarters, I think that he is carried away by imagination, perhaps by pride, but . . . practically irresponsible.

This conclusion does not imply that I advise you to pay very much attention to what he says on any occasion. But in the matter of settling his bill I see that you have acted with higher ideals, and so I think that we need not fear that we will be involved in the errors of 'Paris banking' by him.

But as for him . . . Lord, let him do anything he wants, let him have his independence? ? (whatever he means by that) and his opinions, and let him go his own way directly he thinks he knows it better than we do.

I think it is rather strange that he claims a picture of sunflowers from me, offering me in exchange I suppose, or as a gift, some studies he left here. I will send him back his studies which will probably have a use for him that they would in no way have for me.

But for the moment I am keeping my canvases here and I am definitely keeping my sunflowers in question . . .

How can Gauguin pretend that he was afraid of upsetting me by his presence, when he can hardly deny that he knew I was asking for him continually, and that he was told over and over again that I insisted on seeing him at once.

Just to tell him that we would keep it between him and me, without upsetting you. He would not listen . . .

It will always be a pity, in spite of everything, that Gauguin and I gave up too soon perhaps the question of Rembrandt and light, which we had broached. Are de Haan and Isaäcson still on it? Do not let them get discouraged. After my illness my eyes have naturally been very sensitive. I have been looking at that *Croque-mort* of an undertaker of de Haan's, of which he was good enough to send me the photograph. Well, it seems to me that there is a real touch of Rembrandt in that figure, which seems to be lit up by the reflection of a light coming from the open tomb in front of which the *croque-mort* stands like a man walking in his sleep.

It is done with great subtlety. I myself do not try to get effects by means of charcoal, and de Haan has taken for his medium this very charcoal, again a colourless substance.

I should like de Haan to see a study of mine of a lighted candle and two novels (one yellow, the other pink) lying on an empty armchair (really Gauguin's chair), a canvas of 30, in red and green. I have just been working again today at its fellow, my own empty chair, a chair of white wood with a pipe and a tobacco pouch. In these two studies as in others, I have tried for an effect of light by means of clear colour, probably de Haan would understand exactly what I was trying to get, if you read him what I have written.

. . . Gauguin has a fine, free and absolutely complete imaginary conception of the south, and with that imagination he is going to work in the north! My word, we may get some fun out of it yet.

And now, dissecting the situation in all boldness, there is nothing to hinder us seeing him as the little Bonaparte tiger of Impressionism as far as . . . I don't quite know how to say it, his vanishing, say, from Arles would be comparable or parallel to the return from Egypt of the aforesaid little corporal, who also presented himself afterwards in Paris, and who always left the army in the soup.

Fortunately Gauguin and I and other painters are not yet armed with machine guns and other very destructive weapons of warfare. I for one am quite decided to go on being armed with nothing but my brush and my pen.

But with a good deal of clatter however, Gauguin has none the less demanded in his last letter 'his masks and fencing gloves' hidden in the little closet in my little yellow house.

I shall hasten to send him his toys by post.

Hoping that he will never use more serious weapons.

He is physically stronger than we are, so his passions must be much stronger than ours. Then he is a father, he has a wife and children in Denmark, and at the same time he wants to go to the other end of the earth, to Martinique. It is frightful, all the vice versa of incompatible desires and needs, which this must cause him.

✳ ✳ ✳

To Theo (573)
Arles, 23 January [1889]

. . . Roulin left yesterday (of course my wire yesterday was sent off before the arrival of your letter of this morning). It was touching to see him with his children this last day, especially with the quite tiny one when he made her laugh and jump on his knee, and sang for her.

His voice has a strangely pure and touching quality in which there was for my ear at once a sweet and mournful cradle-song, and a kind of far away echo of the trumpet of revolutionary France. He was not sad however. On the contrary he had put on his brand new uniform which he had received that very day, and every one was making much of him . . .

I feel remorse too when I think of the trouble that, however involuntarily, I on my side caused Gauguin. But up to the last days I saw one thing only, that he was working with his mind divided between the desire of going to Paris to carry out his plans, and the life at Arles.

What will come of all this for him? . . .

Meantime the great thing is that your marriage should not be delayed. By getting married you set mother's mind at rest and happy, and it is after all almost a necessity in view of your position in society and in commerce. Will it be appreciated by the society to which you belong, perhaps not, any more than the artists ever suspect that I have sometimes worked and suffered for the community . . . So from me, your brother, you will not want banal congratulations and assurances that you are about to be transported straight into paradise. And with your wife you will not be lonely any more, which I could wish for our sister as well.

That, after your own marriage, is what I should set my heart on more than anything.

When you are married, perhaps there will be others in the family, and in any case you will see your way clear and the house will not be empty any more.

Whatever I think on other points, our father and mother were exemplary as married people.

And I shall never forget mother at father's death, when she only said one word: it made me begin to love dear old mother more than before. In fact as married people our parents were exemplary, like Roulin and his wife, to quote another instance.

Well, go ahead the same way. During my illness I saw again every room of the house at Zundert, every path, every plant in the garden, the views in the fields round about, the neighbours, the graveyard, the church, our kitchen garden behind – down to a magpie's nest in a tall acacia in the graveyard.

It's because I still have earlier recollections of those first days than any of the rest of you. There is no one left who remembers all this but mother and me . . .

But if you like you can exhibit the two pictures of sunflowers.

Gauguin would be glad to have one, and I should very much like to give Gauguin a real pleasure. So if he wants one of the two canvases, all right, I will do one of them over again, whichever he likes.

You will see that these canvases catch the eye. But I would advise you to keep them for yourself, just for your own private pleasure, you and your wife.

It is a kind of painting that changes rather to the eye, and takes on a richness the longer you look at it . . .

✳ ✳ ✳

To Theo   (574)
Arles, 28 January [1889]

. . . Since it is winter still, look here, leave me to go quietly on with my work; if it is that of a madman, well, so much the worse. I can't help it.

However, the unbearable hallucinations have ceased, and now reduce themselves to a simple nightmare, by dint of my taking bromide of potassium, I think.

. . . If it is not absolutely necessary to shut me up in a cell, then I am still good for paying at least in stock what I am reckoned to owe. In conclusion I have still to tell you that the chief superintendent of police paid me a very friendly visit yesterday. He told me as he shook hands, that if ever I needed him I could consult him as *a friend*. I am far from refusing that, and I may soon be in just that position, if they raise difficulties about the house.

I am waiting till the time comes for me to pay the month's rent, to interview the agent or the proprietor face to face.

But if they try to kick me out they will find their own heels up this time anyhow.

What would you? We have gone all out for the Impressionists, and now as far as in me lies I am trying to finish canvases which will undoubtedly secure me the little corner among them that I have claimed. Ah, the future there ... but since old Pangloss assures us that everything is always for the best in the best of worlds – can we doubt it? ...

The work distracts my mind. And I *must* have some distraction. Yesterday I went to the Folies Arlésiennes, the budding theatre here. It was the first time that I slept without a bad nightmare. They were giving (it was a Provençal literary society) what they called a *Noël* or *Pastorale,* reminiscent of the Christian theatre of the Middle Ages. It was very carefully planned, and must have lost them a lot of money.

It represented of course the birth of Christ, mixed up with the burlesque story of a family of gaping Provençal peasants.

But the amazing thing about it, like a Rembrandt etching, was the old peasant woman, just such another as Mme Tanguy, with a head of silex or flint, dishonest, treacherous, silly, all that very evident from the preceding play.

Now that woman, led in the play before the mystic crib, began to sing in her quavering voice, and then the voice changed, changed from the voice of a witch to that of an angel, and from an angel's voice to a child's, and then the answer came in another voice, strong and warm and vibrant, the voice of a woman behind the scenes.

It was amazing ...

Old Gauguin and I at bottom understand each other, and if we are a bit mad, what of it. Aren't we also thoroughly artists enough to contradict suspicions on that head by what we say with the brush.

Perhaps someday everyone will have neurosis, St Vitus' dance or something else.

But does not the antidote exist? In Delacroix, in Berlioz and Wagner? And really as for the artist madness of all the rest of us, I do not say that I especially am not infected through and through, but I say and will maintain that our antidotes and consolations may, with a little good will, be considered as ample compensations . . .

✳ ✳ ✳

To Theo (576)
Arles, 3 February [1889]

. . . But I can tell you this, that in its words the language native to this place is extraordinarily musical in the mouth of an Arlésienne.

Perhaps in the *Woman Rocking* there's an attempt to get all the *music* of the colour here. It is badly painted and the chromos in the little shops are infinitely better painted technically, but all the same.

By the way – this here so-called *good* town of Arles is such an odd place, that old Gauguin calls it with good reason 'the dirtiest hole in the south' . . .

. . . I have no illusions about myself any more. It is going very well, and I shall do everything the doctor says, but . . .

When I came out of the hospital with kind old Roulin I thought that there had been nothing wrong with me, but *afterwards* I felt that I had been ill. Well, well, there are moments when I am wrung by enthusiasm or madness or prophecy like a Greek oracle on the tripod.

And then I have great readiness of speech and can speak like the Arlésiennes, but with all this I feel so weak.

It will be all right when my bodily strength comes back, but at the slightest grave symptom I have already told Rey that I would come back and put myself under the mental specialists at Aix, or under him.

Can anything come of it but trouble and suffering if we are not well, either you or I? So completely has our ambition foundered.

Then let us work on very quietly, let us take care of ourselves as much as we can and not exhaust ourselves in barren efforts of mutual generosity.

You will do your duty and I will do mine, and as far as that goes we have already both paid in other ways than words, and at the end of the march we may meet each other again with a quiet mind. And as for that delirium of mine in which everything I dearly loved was shaken, I do not accept it as reality and I am not going to be a false prophet . . .

As for the Independants I think that six pictures is too much by half. To my mind the *Harvest* and the *White Orchard* are enough, with the little *Provençal Girl* or the *Sower* if you like. But I don't mind about that. The one thing I have set my heart on is some day to give you a more heartening impression of this painting job of ours, by a collection of thirty or so more serious studies. That will prove again to our real friends like Gauguin, Guillaumin, Bernard, etc., that we are producing something. Well, about the little yellow house, when I paid my rent the landlord's agent was very nice, and behaved like an Arlesien by treating me as an equal. Then I told him that I had no need of a lease or a written promise of preference, and that in case of illness I should pay as a matter of friendly agreement.

People here are sound at heart, and the spoken word is more binding than the written word. So I am keeping the house provisionally, since for the sake of my mental recovery I need to feel that I am in my own home.

. . . I always say to the people here who ask after my health, that I shall start off by dying among them, and after that my malady will be dead.

This doesn't mean I shall not have long spells of respite, but once you are ill in earnest you know quite well that you cannot contract an illness twice, you are well, or you are ill, just as you are young or you are old. I will, like you, do what the doctor tells me as much as I can, and I consider that as a part of the work and the duty which I have to fulfil.

I must tell you this, that the neighbours, etc., are particularly kind to me, as everyone suffers here either from fever, or hallucination or madness, we understand each other like members of the same family. I went yesterday to see the girl I had gone to when I was astray in the wits. They told me there that in this country things like that are not out of the way. She had been upset by it and had fainted but had recovered her calm. And they spoke well of her too.

But as for considering myself as altogether sane, we must not do it . . .

In February Theo wrote to his wife that there was bad news from Arles, and that Vincent had again been taken to the hospital. He had imagined that people wanted to poison him, and did not say a word after coming into the hospital. Dr Salles, the Protestant clergyman in Arles whom Theo had interested in Vincent during his visit in December, wrote asking what was to be done now. Nothing further was heard from Arles for a few days, when Theo wired on 13 February to Dr Rey, and got the following reply: 'Vincent much better, hope getting better, keeping him here. Do not worry now.' Five days later a letter from Vincent himself arrived.

✳ ✳ ✳

To Theo (577)
Arles, February [1889]

I have been so altogether out of sorts mentally that it would have been useless to try to write an answer to your kind letter. Today I have just come home provisionally, I hope for good. I feel so often quite normal, and really I should think that if what I have is only a malady peculiar to this place, I must wait here quietly till it is over, even if it returns again (and let's say that it won't) . . .

But this is what I told M. Rey once for all. If sooner or later it is desirable that I should go to Aix, as has already been suggested, I consent beforehand and I will submit to it.

But in my character as a painter and a workman it is not permissible for anyone, not even you or a doctor, to take such a step without warning me and consulting *me* about it, also because since up till now I have always kept comparative presence of mind in my work, it would be my right then to say (or at least to have an opinion on) whether it would be better to keep my studio here or to move altogether to Aix . . .

It seems that people here have some superstition that makes them afraid of painting, and that they have talked about it in the town. Very good, I know it is the same thing in Arabia, but we have nevertheless heaps of painters in Africa, haven't we ? . . .

The unfortunate thing is that I am rather inclined to be affected by and to feel myself the beliefs of others, and cannot always laugh at the foundation of truth that there may be in absurdity . . .

On 27 February, Vincent was taken into hospital again.

✳ ✳ ✳

To Theo (579)
Arles, 19 March [1889]

I seemed to see so much brotherly anguish in your kind letter, that I think it my duty to break my silence. I write to you in full possession of my faculties and not a madman, but as the brother you know. This is the truth. A certain number of people here addressed to the Mayor (I think his name is M. Tardieu) a petition (there were more than eighty signatures) describing me as a man not fit to be at liberty, or something like that.

The inspector of police and the general inspector then gave the order to shut me up again . . .

Anyhow here I am shut up the livelong day under lock and key and with keepers in a cell, without my guilt being proved, or even capable of proof.

Needless to say in the secret tribunal of my soul I have much to reply to all that. Needless to say I cannot be angry, and to excuse myself I think is to accuse myself in such a case . . .

Only to let you know so as to set me free – yet I do not ask it, being persuaded that the whole accusation will be reduced nothing.

But I do say that as for getting me free, you would find it difficult. If I did not restrain my indignation I should at once be thought a dangerous lunatic. Let us hope and have patience. Besides, strong emotion can only aggravate my case. That is why I beg you for the present to let be without meddling in it.

Take it as a warning from me that it might only complicate and confuse things.

All the more because you will understand that while I am absolutely calm at the present moment, I may easily relapse in a state of over-excitement on account of fresh mental emotion.

So you understand what a staggering blow between the eyes it was, to find so many people here cowardly enough to join together against one man and that man ill . . .

Do not try to release me, that will settle itself, but warn Signac not to meddle in it, for he would be putting his hand into a wasp's nest – unless I write again. I take your hand in thought. Give my kind regards to your fiancée, and to our mother and sister.

. . . I am myself rather afraid that if I were at liberty outside, I should not always keep control of myself if I were provoked or insulted, and then they would be able to take advantage of that. The fact remains that a petition has been sent to the Mayor. I answered roundly that I was quite prepared for instance to chuck myself into the water if that would please these good folk once for all, but that in any case if I had in fact inflicted a wound on myself, I had done nothing of the sort to them, etc. . . .

Theo had heard from Signac that he was going to the South, and had asked him to visit Vincent.

✳ ✳ ✳

To Theo (580)
Arles, undated [March 1889]

. . . Certainly I should be pleased to see Signac, if he has after all to pass through here. They must then let me go out with him to show him my canvases.

. . . If sooner or later I become really mad, I think I should not want to stay on here at the hospital, but just now I want to go out and in freely.

The best thing for me would certainly be not to live alone, but I would rather live for ever in a cell, than sacrifice another life to mine. For this business of painting is a sorry poor job at the moment . . .

✳ ✳ ✳

To Theo (581)
Arles, 24 March [1889]

I am writing to tell you that I have seen Signac, and it has done me quite a lot of good. He was so good and downright and simple when the difficulty of opening the door by force or not presented itself, the police had closed it and destroyed the lock. They began by not wanting to let us do it, and after all in the end we got in. I gave him as a keepsake a still-life which had annoyed the good *gensd'armes* of the town of Arles, because it represented two smoked herrings, and they, the *gensd'armes*, are called that as you know. You remember that I did this same still-life in Paris two or three times, and exchanged it once for a carpet in the old days. That is enough to show you how these people meddle and what idiots they are.

I found Signac very quiet, though he is said to be so violent; he gave me the impression of someone who has balance and poise, that is all. Rarely or never have I had a conversation with an Impressionist so free on both sides from discords or conflict. So he has been to see Jules Dupré, and he admires him. Doubtless you had a hand in his coming to stiffen my morale a bit, and thank you for it: I took advantage of my outing to buy a book, *Ceux de la Glèbe*, by Camille Lemonnier. I have devoured two chapters of it – it has such gravity, such depth! Wait till I send it you. This is the first time for several months that I have had a book in my hand. That means a lot to me and does a good deal towards my cure.

Altogether there are several canvases to send you as Signac was able to affirm, he did not take fright at my painting as far as I saw. Signac thought, and it is perfectly true, that I looked healthy.

And with it I have the desire and the inclination for work. Still of course if I had daily to stand being messed up in my work and way of living by *gensd'armes* and poisonous slackers of municipal electors petitioning against me to the Mayor whom they have elected and who consequently clings to their votes, it would be no more than human of me to succumb all over again. I am inclined to think that Signac will tell you very much the same thing. We must in my opinion roundly oppose the loss of the furniture, etc. Then – my word – I must have liberty to carry on my trade.

M. Rey says that instead of eating enough and at regular times, I was keeping myself going by coffee and alcohol. I admit all that, but it is true all the same that to attain the high yellow note that I attained last summer, I really had to be pretty well strung up. And that finally the artist is a man with his work to do, and it is not for the first slacker who comes along to do him down for good.

Am I to suffer imprisonment or the madhouse? Why not? . . .

✳ ✳ ✳

To Theo (582)
Arles, 29 March [1889]

A few more lines before you leave; just now things are going well. The day before yesterday and yesterday I went out into the town to get things to work with. When I went home I was able to ascertain that the real neighbours, those whom I knew, were not among those who made that petition.

However it may be in other quarters, I saw that I had still friends among them.

M. Salles in case of need undertakes to find me in a few days a flat in another part of the town. I have sent for a few more books so as to have a few solid ideas in my head. I have read again *Uncle Tom's Cabin*, you know Beecher Stowe's book on slavery, Dickens' *Christmas Books* . . .

And now for the fifth time I am taking up my portrait of the *Woman rocking a Cradle*. And when you see it, you will agree with me that it is nothing but a chromolithograph from the cheap shops, and again that it has not even the merit of being photographically correct in its proportions or in anything whatever.

But after all I want to make such a picture as a sailor who could not paint would imagine to himself when away at sea he thinks of his wife ashore.

At the hospital these days they are very attentive to me, and this like many other things upsets me and makes me rather confused . . .

These last three months do seem so strange to me. Sometimes moods of indescribable mental anguish, sometimes moments when the veil of time and of inevitable circumstance seemed for the twinkling of an eye to be parted . . .

✳ ✳ ✳

To Theo   (583)
Arles, [beginning of April 1889]

By the way – only yesterday our friend Roulin came to see me. He told me to give you many messages from him and to congratulate you. His visit gave me a lot of pleasure, he has often to carry loads you would call very heavy, but it doesn't hinder him, as he has the strong constitution of the peasant, from always looking well and even jolly. But for me, who am perpetually learning from him, what a lesson for the future it is when one gathers from his talk that life does not grow any easier as one gets on in life.

I talked to him so as to have his opinion as to what I ought to do about the studio, which I ought to leave in any case at Easter, according to the advice of M. Salles and M. Rey.

I said to Roulin that having done a good many things to put the house in a better state than when I took it, especially considering the gas I had put in, I considered it as a definite piece of work.

They are forcing me to leave.

I am well just now, except for a certain undercurrent of vague sadness difficult to define – but anyway – I have rather gained than lost in physical strength, and I am working.

And now, my dear lad, I do believe I shall soon not be ill enough to have to stay shut up. Except for that I am beginning to get used to it and if I had to stay for good in an asylum, I should make up my mind to it and I think I could find subjects for painting there as well.

✳ ✳ ✳

To Theo   (585)
Arles, 21 April [1889]

You will probably be back in Paris at the moment when this letter arrives. I wish you and your wife a great deal of happiness. Thank you very much for your kind letter and for the 100 franc note it contained . . .

After the hospital, after I have settled up today, there is still almost enough for the rest of the month from the money I have still on deposit. At the end of the month I should like to go to the Hospital at St Rémy, or another institution of this kind, of which M. Salles has told me. Forgive me if I don't go into details to argue the pros and cons of such a step.

It would absolutely split my head to talk about it.

It will be enough, I hope, if I tell you that I feel quite unable to take a new studio and to stay there alone, here at Arles or elsewhere, it is all one for the moment; I have tried to bring myself to the thought of beginning again, but at the moment it's not possible.

I should be afraid of losing the power to work, which is coming back to me now, by forcing myself and having all the other responsibilities of a studio on my shoulders besides.

And temporarily I wish to remain shut up as much for my own peace of mind as for other people's.

What comforts me a little, is that I am beginning to consider madness as a disease like any other and accept the thing as such, whereas during the crises themselves, I thought that everything I imagined was real. Anyway, I just do not want to think or talk about it. You'll spare me any explanations, but I ask you, and Messrs Salles and Rey to arrange so that at the end of this month or the beginning of May I can go there as a resident boarder.

To begin again that painter's life from now on, isolated in the studio so often, and without any other means of distraction than going to a café or a restaurant with all the neighbours criticising, etc., *I can't face*

269

it: to go and live with another person, say another artist – difficult, very difficult – it's taking too much responsibility on oneself. I dare not even think of it.

So let's try three months to begin with, and we shall see afterwards . . .

Meantime you do understand that if alcohol has undoubtedly been one of the great causes of my madness, then it came very slowly and will go slowly too, supposing it does go, of course. Or if it comes from smoking, the same thing. But I should only hope that it – this recovery [word omitted] the frightful superstition of some people on the subject of alcohol, so that they prevail upon themselves never to drink or smoke . . .

✳ ✳ ✳

To Theo   (586)
Arles, undated [April 1889]

. . . I feel deeply that this has been working upon me for a very long time, and that other people, seeing symptoms of derangement, have naturally had apprehensions better founded than the certainty I thought I had that I was thinking normally, which was not the case. So that has much softened many of the judgments which I have too often passed with more or less presumption on people who nevertheless were wishing me well. Anyhow it is certainly a pity that with me these reflections reach the *stage of feeling* rather late. And that I can naturally alter nothing in the past.

But I want you to consider all that and to consider the step we are taking now, just as I spoke of it to M. Salles, this going into an asylum, as a pure formality, and in any case the repeated attacks seem to me to have been serious enough to leave no hesitation . . .

Besides, as to my future, it is not as if I were 20, since I have turned 36.

Really I think it would be torture for other people as well as for myself, if I were to leave the hospital, for I feel and am as it were paralysed when it comes to acting and shifting for myself. Later on – well, well, wait and see . . .

✳ ✳ ✳

To Theo (587)
Arles, 28 April [1889]

. . . Sometimes, just as the waves crash themselves against the sullen, hopeless cliffs, I feel a tempest of desire to embrace something, a woman of the domestic hen type, but after all, we must take this for what it is, the effect of hysterical over-excitement rather than the vision of actual reality.

Besides Rey and I have laughed about it sometimes, for he says that love is a microbe too, which does not surprise me much, and could not annoy anyone, it seems to me. Isn't Renan's Christ a thousand times more comforting than so many *papier mâché* Christs that they serve up to you in the Duval establishments called protestant, catholic or something or other churches? And why should it not be so with love? As soon as I can I am going to read Renan's *Antichrist*. I have not the least idea what it will be like, but I believe beforehand that I shall find in it one or two ineffable things.

Oh, my dear Theo, if you saw the olives just now . . . The leaves old silver and silver turning to green against the blue. And the orange coloured ploughed earth. It is something quite different from your idea of it in the North, the fineness, the distinction!

It is like the pollard willows of our Dutch meadows or the oak bushes of our dunes, that is to say the rustle of an olive grove has something very secret in it, and immensely old. It is too beautiful for us to dare to paint it or be able to imagine it. The oleander – ah! that speaks of love and is beautiful like the Lesbos of Puvis de Chavannes, with women on the sea shore. But the olive is different, if you want to compare it to something, it is a Delacroix . . .

❋ ❋ ❋

To Theo (588)
Arles, 30 April [1889]

. . . Today I am packing a case of pictures and studies. One of them is flaking off and I have stuck some newspapers on it; it is one of the best and I think that when you look at it you will see better what my now shipwrecked studio might have been.

This study, like some others, has got spoiled by the damp during my illness.

The water of a flood came up to within a few feet of the house, and on the top of that, the house itself having had no fires in it during my absence, when I came back the walls were oozing water and saltpetre.

That touched me to the quick, not only the studio wrecked, but even the studies which would have been a souvenir of it, ruined; it is so final and my enthusiasm to found something very simple but lasting was so strong. It was to fight against the inevitable or rather it was weakness of character on my part, for I am left with feelings of profound remorse, difficult to describe. I think that was the reason why I have cried out so much during the attacks, it was because I wanted to defend myself and could not manage to . . .

✳ ✳ ✳

To Theo   (589)
Arles, 2 May [1889]

. . . In the town . . . nobody says anything to me now, and I actually paint in the public garden without being much bothered by anything but the curiosity of passers-by . . .

Here are the ones [paintings] I think worth putting on stretchers out of the batch I'm sending:

> The Night Café
> The Green Vineyard
> The Red Vineyard
> The Bedroom
> The Furrows
> Ditto
>
> Portrait of Bock
> Portrait of Laval
> Portrait of Gauguin
> Portrait of Bernard
> Les Aliscamps (Path by the Tombs)
> Ditto

Garden with big bush of Conifers and Oleanders
    Ditto, Cedar and Geraniums
Sunflowers
Scabious Flowers, etc.
    Ditto, Asters and Marigolds, etc.

The case contains some of Gauguin's studies, which belong to him, and the two fencing masks and the fencing gloves. If there is room in the case I will put in some stretchers.

✳ ✳ ✳

To Theo   (590)
Arles, 3 May [1889]

. . . the main thing is to feel our closeness to one another and that is not yet shaken.

I have a sort of hope that with what on the whole I know of my art, the time will come when I shall produce again, even in the asylum. What use to me would be the more artificial life of an artist in Paris; I should never be more than half taken in by it, and so should lack the primary enthusiasm, indispensable to start me off.

Physically it is amazing how well I am, but it isn't enough to build any hope on it that it's the same with me mentally.

I would willingly, once I am a little known there, try to become a hospital orderly bit by bit, in short to work at something and have some occupation again – whatever offers.

. . . I must try to have less passion and more good humour.

The passionate factor is no great matter to me, so long as the power remains, as I dare to hope, of feeling attachment for the fellow creatures with whom one will live.

. . . it is only too true that heaps of painters go mad, it is a life that makes you, to say the least of it, very absent-minded. If I throw myself into full work again, very good, but I shall always be cracked . . .

Vincent moved to the mental asylum at St Rémy in May 1889, and would stay there for a whole year.

✳ ✳ ✳

. . . I wanted to tell you that I think I have done well to come here, first of all that by seeing the actual truth about the life of the various madmen and lunatics in this menagerie I am losing the vague dread, the fear of the thing. And bit by bit I can come to consider madness as being a disease like any other. Then the change of surroundings, I think, does me good.

As far as I can make out the doctor here is inclined to consider what I have had as some sort of epileptic attack. But I did not ask any more . . .

(Enclosed was a letter to his new sister-in-law Johanna, who was now living with Theo in Paris.)

✳ ✳ ✳

My dear sister
St Rémy, [9 May 1889]

Many thanks for your letter in which I especially looked for news of my brother. And I find it excellent. I see you have already noticed that he likes Paris and this surprises you more or less, since you do not like it at all, or rather like mostly the flowers there, the wisteria, I suppose, which is probably coming into bloom.

Might it not be the case that when you are fond of something you see it better and more truly than when you are not fond of it? For him and me Paris is certainly already in some sort a graveyard where many artists have perished whom directly or indirectly we once knew.

Certainly Millet, whom you are learning to like very much, and many others with him, tried to get out of Paris. But for Eugène Delacroix for instance, it is difficult to imagine him, as a man, otherwise than a Parisian.

All this is to urge you – with all caution it is true – to believe in the *possibility* that there are *homes* in Paris and not only flats.

Anyway – fortunately *you* are yourself his home.

It is rather queer perhaps that the result of this terrible attack is that there is hardly any very definite desire or hope left in my mind, and I wonder if this is the way one thinks, when with the passions dying out, one descends the hill instead of climbing it. And anyhow, my sister, if you can believe, or almost believe, that everything is always for the best in the best of worlds, then you will be able perhaps also to believe that Paris is the best of towns in it.

Have you yet noticed that the old cab horses there have large beautiful eyes, as heartbroken as Christians sometimes? . . .

Anyway if you do not like Paris, above all do not like painting nor those who are directly or indirectly concerned in it, for it is only too doubtful whether it has any beauty or use . . .

And though here you continually hear terrible cries and howls like beasts in a menagerie, in spite of that people get to know each other very well and help each other when their attacks come on. When I am working in the garden, they all come to look, and I assure you they have more discretion and manners to leave me alone than the good people of the town of Arles for instance.

It may well be that I shall stay here long enough – I have never been so peaceful as here and at the hospital at Arles – to be able in the end to paint a little. Quite near here there are some little mountains, grey and blue, and at their feet some very very green cornfields and pines . . .

✳ ✳ ✳

To Theo (592)
St Rémy, 25 May [1889]

. . . I *assure* you I am quite all right and that temporarily I see no reason at all for coming to board in Paris or near it. I have a little room with greenish grey paper with two curtains of sea-green with a design of very pale roses, brightened by slight touches of blood-red.

These curtains, probably the relics of some rich and ruined defunct, are very pretty in design. From the same source probably comes a very worn armchair, recovered with an upholstery splashed like a Diaz or a Monticelli, with brown, red, rose, white, cream, black, forget-me-not blue and bottle green. Through the iron-barred window I see a square of corn in an enclosure, a perspective like Van Goyen, above which I see in the morning the sun rising in his glory. As well as this – as there are more than thirty rooms empty – I have another as well to work in . . .

The room where we stay on wet days is like a third-class waiting room in some dead-alive village, the more so as there are some distinguished lunatics who always wear a hat, spectacles and cane, and travelling cloak, like at a bathing resort almost, and they represent the passengers.

I am forced to ask you again for some paints and especially for canvas. When I send you the four canvases of the garden I have in hand, you will see that considering life is spent mostly in the garden, it is not so unhappy. Yesterday I drew a very big, rather rare night moth, called the death's head, its colouring of amazing distinction, black, grey, cloudy white tinged with carmine or shading indistinctly to olive green; it is very big. To paint it I had to kill it and it was a pity, the beastie was so beautiful. I will send you the drawing with some other drawings of plants.

I am again – speaking of my condition – so grateful for another thing. I gather from others that they also have heard in their attacks strange sounds and voices as I did, and that to their eyes too things seemed to be changing. And that lessens the horror that I retained at first of the attack I have had, and which when it comes on you unawares cannot but frighten you beyond measure. Once you know that it is part of the disease, you take it like anything else. If it had not been that I have seen other lunatics close to, I should not have been able to free myself from constantly dwelling upon it. For the anguish and suffering are no joke once you are caught by an attack. Most epileptics bite their tongue and wound themselves. Rey told me that he had seen a case where someone had wounded himself like me in the ear, and I think I heard a doctor here say, when he came to see me with the superintendent, that he also had seen it before. I really think that once you know what it is, once you are conscious of your condition and of being subject to attacks, that then you can do something yourself not to be so taken aback by the suffering or the terror. Now for five months it has been going on lessening, I have good hope of getting over it, or at least of not having attacks of such violence. There is someone here who has been shouting and talking like me *all the time* for a fortnight, he thinks he hears voices and words in the echoes of the corridors, probably because the nerves of the ear are diseased and too sensitive, and in my case it was sight and hearing at once, which according to what Rey told me one day is usual in the beginning of epilepsy. Then the shock was such that it sickened me even to make a movement, and

276

nothing would have pleased me better than never to have wakened again. At present this *horror of life* is less strong already and the melancholy less acute. But of *will* I have none, of desires hardly any or none, and of everything belonging to ordinary life, the desire for instance to see my friends, although I keep thinking about them, almost none. That is why I am not yet at the point when I ought to think of leaving here, I should have this depression anywhere.

And it is only during these very last days that my repulsion for life is in any way radically modified. From that to will and action there is still some way to go . . .

✳ ✳ ✳

To Theo   (594)
St Rémy, 9 June [1889]

. . . Now as to the Impressionists – once again, if an interior is not complete without a work of art, a picture is not complete either if it is not at one with surroundings originating and resulting from the period in which it was produced. And I do not know if the Impressionists are better than their time or instead are not yet so good. In a word, are there minds and interiors of homes more important than anything that has been expressed by painting? I am inclined to think so.

I have seen the announcement of a coming exhibition of Impressionists, described as Gauguin, Bernard, Anquetin and other names. So I am inclined to think that a new sect has again been formed, not less infallible than those already existing.

Was it of that exhibition that you spoke? What storms in teacups . . .

It is queer that every time I try to reason with myself to get a clear idea of things, why I came here and that after all it is only an accident like any other, a terrible dismay and horror seizes me and prevents my thinking . . . it seems to me to prove that there is quite definitely something or other deranged in my brain, it is astounding to be afraid like this of nothing and not to be able to recollect yourself. Only you may be sure I shall do all I can to become active again and perhaps useful, in this sense at least that I want to do better pictures than before . . .

✳ ✳ ✳

To Theo (595)
St Rémy, 19 June [1889]

. . . I think that you were right not to show any pictures of mine at the exhibition that Gauguin and the others had. It is reason enough for me keeping out of it without giving them offence, seeing that I am not yet recovered . . .

What I should very much like to have to read here now and then, would be a Shakespeare. There is one at a shilling, *Dick's Shilling Shakespeare,* which is complete. There are plenty of editions and I think the cheap ones are less altered than the dearer ones. In any case I do not want one that costs more than three francs . . .

✳ ✳ ✳

To Theo (596)
St Rémy, 25 June [1889]

. . . Speaking of Gauguin and Bernard, and that they may well give us painting of greater consolation, I must however add what I have also said many a time to Gauguin himself, that we must not then forget that others have done it already. But however it may be, out of Paris you quickly forget Paris, by throwing yourself into the heart of the country your ideas change, but I for one cannot forget all those lovely canvases of Barbizon, and that anyone will do better than that seems to me hardly probable and besides not necessary . . .

The cypresses are always occupying my thoughts, I would like to make something of them like the canvases of the sunflowers, because it astonishes me that they have not yet been done as I see them.

It is as beautiful in line and proportion as an Egyptian obelisk. And the green has a quality of such distinction.

It is a splash of black in a sunny landscape, but it is one of the most interesting of the black notes, and the most difficult to strike exactly, that I can imagine.

But then you must see them against the blue, *in* the blue rather. To paint nature here, as everywhere, you must be in it a long time . . .

✳ ✳ ✳

To Theo (597)
St Rémy, undated [1889]

. . . Thank you also very heartily for the *Shakespeare*. It will help me not
to forget the little English I know, but above all it is so fine. I have
begun to read the series of which I knew least, the series of the Kings:
I have already read *Richard II*, *Henry IV* and half of *Henry V*. I read
without wondering if the ideas of the people of those times were
different from our own, or what would become of them if you set them
over against republican and socialist beliefs and so on. But what
touches me, as in some novelists of our day, is that the voices of these
people, which in Shakespeare's case reach us from a distance of several
centuries, do not seem unfamiliar to us. It is so much alive that you
think you know them and see the thing.

And so what Rembrandt has alone or almost alone among painters,
that tenderness in the gaze which we see whether it's in *Pilgrims of
Emmaus*, or in the *Jewish Bride*, or in some such strange angelic figure as
the picture you have had the luck to see – that heartbroken tenderness,
that glimpse of a superhuman infinite that there seems so natural, in
many places you come upon it in Shakespeare. And then portraits
grave or gay, like the *Six* and like the *Traveller*, and like the *Saskia*, he is
full of them, above all . . .

✳ ✳ ✳

To his mother (598)
St Rémy, undated [1889]

When you say you are a mother nearly seventy years old, it must be
true, but one would not notice it from your handwriting, for it struck
me as being very firm. Also Theo and Wil wrote to me that you seem
to be getting young again, and I think this is very good, and is necessary in life sometimes. The news about Cor – no wonder that you are
occupied by it, and it will be hard for both sides to have to separate.
[His brother Cor was taking up a position in the Transvaal.] He is
right though, I think, not to hesitate to accept this position, as it seems
that one can get on better and happier in the world by being at a
distance from these big cities, not only Paris, but Amsterdam,
Rotterdam and so many others in Europe. There is more that is

natural and good in the world than one would suppose here in our continent.

I have often heard talk, not exactly about the Transvaal, but for instance about Australia, by people who came from there and were always longing to go back. Also about Haiti for instance and Martinique, where Gauguin who was with me at Arles, has been. And I suppose that the Transvaal will have several things in common with Australia. One has the chance to develop oneself better there and to use one's energy better than in this European circumlocution.

As far as the sorrow, dear mother, is concerned, which we have and keep in separation and loss, it seems to me it is instinctive, that we, without that, could not resign ourselves to separations, and probably it will help us to recognise and find each other again later. It seems impossible for things to remain in their place . . .

. . . the blue sky never tires me. One never sees here buckwheat or rape, and perhaps there is in general less variety than with us. And I should like so much to paint a buckwheat-field in flower, or the rape in bloom, or flax, but maybe I will have an occasion for this later in Normandy or in Brittany. Also one never sees here those moss-covered roofs on the barns or huts as with us, nor the oak-bushes for cutting, nor spurry, nor beech hedges with their white crossed old stems. Nor the real heather, and heather birches which were so beautiful in Nuenen. But what is beautiful in the South, are the vineyards, but they are in the flat country or against the hills. I have seen some and even sent a picture of them to Theo, where a vineyard was quite purple, fire-red, and yellow and green and violet, like the Virginian creeper in Holland. I like as much to see a vineyard as a cornfield. Also too the hills full of thyme and other smelling plants are here very nice, and through the clearness of the air one sees here so much further than with us from the heights . . .

✳ ✳ ✳

To Theo and Johanna   (599)
St Rémy, [5 July 1889]

Jo's letter told me a very great piece of news this morning, I congratulate you on it and I am very glad to hear it. I was much touched by your thought when you said that neither of you being in such good health as seems desirable on such an occasion, you felt a sort of doubt, and in any case that a feeling of pity for the child who is to come passed through your heart.

I talked a little this morning with the doctor here – he told me exactly what I thought already – that I must wait a year before thinking myself cured, since anything at all might bring on another attack . . .

I live soberly, because I have a chance to do it, I drank in the past because I did not quite know how to do otherwise. Anyway, I don't care in the least!!! Very deliberate sobriety – it's true – leads nevertheless to a state of being, in which thought, if you have any, moves more readily. In short it is a difference like painting in grey or in colours. I am going in fact to paint more in grey . . .

I enjoyed myself very much yesterday reading *Measure for Measure*. Then I read *Henry VIII*, where there are such fine passages, such as that of Buckingham, and Wolsey's words after his fall.

I think that I am lucky to be able to read or re-read this at leisure and then I very much hope to read Homer at last.

Outside the cicadas are singing fit to burst, a harsh cry, ten times stronger than that of the crickets, and the burnt-up grass takes on lovely tones of old gold. And the beautiful towns of the south are in the state of our dead towns along the Zuyderzee that once were astir. Yet in the decline and decadence of things, the cicadas dear to the good Socrates abide. And here certainly they still sing in ancient Greek . . .

✳ ✳ ✳

To Theo (600)
St Rémy, undated [1889]

Tomorrow I shall send by goods a small roll of canvases. There are four, namely the following:

1. View from Arles – Orchards in bloom
2. Ivy
3. Lilacs
4. Red Chestnuts in the *Jardin des Plantes* at Arles

which will go along with the ones you have already, such as the red and green vineyard, the garden, the harvest, the starry sky . . .

Now the next parcel which will follow in a little will be made up mostly of the cornfields and olive gardens.

As you see I have been to Arles to get these canvases, the warder here accompanied me . . .

✳ ✳ ✳

To Theo   (601)
St Rémy, undated [1889]

. . . Dr Peyron is very kind to me and very patient. You can imagine that I am terribly distressed that the attacks have come back, when I was already beginning to hope that it would not return.

It would perhaps be well for you to write a line to Dr Peyron to tell him that the work on my pictures is almost necessary for me in order to recover, for these days without anything to do, and without being able to go to the room they had allotted to me to do my painting in, are almost intolerable.

My friend Roulin has written to me as well.

I have received a catalogue of the Gauguin, Bernard, Schuffenecker, etc., exhibition, which I find interesting. Gauguin has also written a kind letter, though a little vague and obscure, but after all I must say that I think they are right to have an exhibition among themselves. For many days I have been *absolutely wandering* as at Arles, quite as much if not worse, and it is to be presumed that the attacks will come back again in the future; it is *abominable* . . .

This new attack, my boy, came on me in the fields and when I was in the midst of painting, on a windy day. I will send you the canvas. I finished it in spite of it.

And truly it was a more sober attempt, matt in colour without showing it, in blended greens, reds and rusty ochre yellows, just as I told you that sometimes I felt a great desire to begin again with the same palette as in the north . . .

✳ ✳ ✳

To Theo   (602)
St Rémy, undated [1889]

. . . Yesterday I began to work again a little – on a thing that I see from my window – a field of yellow stubble that they are ploughing, the contrast of the violet tinted ploughed earth with the strips of yellow stubble, background of hills.

Work distracts me infinitely better than anything else and if I could once really throw myself into it with all my energy, it would possibly be the best remedy.

The impossibility of getting models, however, and a lot of other things prevents me managing it.

Altogether I really must try to take things passively a little and have patience . . .

If I get better or in the intervals I could sooner or later come back to Paris or into Brittany for a time.

But first of all it is *very expensive* here, and then just now I am afraid of the other patients. Altogether heaps of reasons make me feel that I haven't had any luck here either.

Perhaps I exaggerate in my wretchedness at having been again bowled over by my illness – but I am sort of afraid . . .

My dear brother, I wanted to write better than this but things aren't going very well. I get great pleasure from going into the mountains to paint the whole day. I hope they will let me some of these days . . .

To Theo   (603)
St Rémy, undated [1889]

The reason I am writing to you a second time today is that enclosed I have written a few lines to our friend Gauguin; as I felt my calm returning these last days, it seemed to me sufficiently so for my letter not to be absolutely ridiculous, besides when you over-refine scruples of respect or sentiment, it is not certain that you gain in consideration or common sense. That being so, it does one good to talk to the other fellows again even at a distance . . .

. . . I am working with a will in my room, it does me good and drives away, I think, these abnormal ideas.

So I have gone over the canvas of my bedroom. That study is certainly one of the best . . .

I am working on two portraits of myself at this moment – for lack of another model – because it is more than time I did a little figure work. One I began the day I got up, I was thin, and pale as a ghost. It is dark violet-blue and the head whitish with yellow hair, so it has a colour effect . . .

But since then I have begun another one, three-quarter length on a light background. Then I am touching up the studies of that summer – altogether I am working from morning till night . . .

My dear brother – it is always in between my work that I write to you – I am working like one actually possessed, more than ever I am in a dumb fury of work. And I think that this will help to cure me. Perhaps something will happen to me like what Eug. Delacroix spoke of, 'I discovered painting when I had no longer teeth or breath', in the sense that my unhappy illness makes me work with a dumb fury – very slowly – but from morning till night without slackening – and – the secret is probably here – work long and slowly. How can I tell, but I think I have one or two canvases in hand that are not so bad, first the reaper in the yellow corn and the portrait against a light background, that will do for the Vingtistes if indeed they remember me at the given moment, but then it is all absolutely one to me, if not preferable, that they should forget me . . .

And here we are in September already, we shall soon be right in the autumn and then the winter.

I will go on working very hard and then if about Christmas the attack returns we shall see, and that over, then I can see nothing to stop me sending the management here to blazes, and returning to the north for a longer or shorter time. To leave now, when I judge a new attack probable in the winter, that is to say in three months, would perhaps be too risky. It is six weeks since I put my foot outside, even in the garden, next week however when I have finished the canvases in hand, I am going to try . . .

. . . I am continuing this letter again in between times. Yesterday I began the portrait of the head warder and perhaps I shall do his wife too, for he is married and lives in a little house a few steps away from the establishment.

A very interesting face, there is a fine etching of Legros, representing an old Spanish noble, if you remember it, that will give you an idea of the type. He was at the hospital at Marseilles through two periods of cholera, altogether he is a man who has seen an enormous lot of suffering and death, and in his face there is a sort of contemplative calm, so that the face of Guizot – for there is something of that in this head but different – comes involuntarily to my memory. But he is of the people and simpler. Anyway you will see if I succeed with it and if I make a duplicate.

I am struggling with all my energy to master my work, thinking that if I win, that will be the best lightning-conductor for my illness. I take a lot of care of myself, shutting myself up carefully, it is egotistical if you like, not rather to accustom myself to my companions in misfortune and to go and see them, but I find myself none the worse for it, for my work is progressing and we have need of that, for it is more than necessary that I should do better than before, for that was not enough . . .

There! The *Reaper* is finished, I think it will be one of those you keep at home – it is an image of death as the great book of nature speaks of it – but what I have tried for is the 'almost smiling'. It is all yellow, except a line of violet hills, a pale fair yellow. I find it queer that I saw it like this between the iron bars of a cell . . .

What I dream of in my best moments, is not so much of striking colour effects, as once more the half-tones. And certainly the visit to the Montpellier gallery contributed to give this turn to my ideas. For what touched me there more than the *magnificent* Courbets, which are marvels – the *Village Girls*, the *Sleeping Spinner* – were the portraits of Brias by Delacroix and by Ricard, then the *Daniel* and *Odalisques* by Delacroix, all in half-tones. For these *Odalisques* are quite a different thing from those in the Louvre, mostly in shaded violet.

But in these half-tones, what choice and what quality! . . .

✳ ✳ ✳

To Theo (605)
St Rémy, 10 September [1889]

. . . I am now trying to recover like a man who meant to commit suicide and finding the water too cold, tries to regain the bank.

My dear brother, you know that I came to the South and threw myself into my work for a thousand reasons. Wishing to see a different light, thinking that to look at nature under a bright sky might give us a better idea of the Japanese way of feeling and drawing. Wishing also to see this stronger sun, because one feels that without knowing it one could not understand the pictures of Delacroix from the point of view of execution and technique, and because one feels that the colours of the prism are veiled in the mist of the North.

All this is still pretty true. Then when to this is added the natural incli- nation towards this South which Daudet described in *Tartarin*, and that here and there I have found besides friends and things here which I love.

Can you understand then that while finding this malady horrible, I feel that all the same I have fashioned myself links with the place perhaps too strong – links that may bring me later on to hanker to work here again – and yet in spite of everything, it may be that in a com- paratively short time I shall return to the North.

Yes, for I will not hide from you that in the same way that I take my food now with avidity, I have a terrible desire that comes over me to see my friends again and to see again the northern countryside . . .

When I realize that here the attacks tend to take an absurd religious turn, I should almost venture to think that this even *necessitates* a return to the North. Do not talk too much about this to the doctor when you see him – but I do not know if this does not come from living so many months both in the Arles hospital and here in these old cloisters. In fact, I really must not live in such an atmosphere, one would be better in the street. I am not indifferent, and even in the suffering sometimes religious thoughts bring me great consolation . . .

So old Pissarro is cruelly smitten by these two misfortunes at once. [Pissarro had lost his mother and had trouble with his eyes.]

As soon as I read that, I thought of asking him if there would be any way of going to stay with him.

If you will pay the same as here, he will find it worth his while, for I do not need much – except to work.

Ask him bluntly, and if he does not wish it, I could quite well go to Vignon's. I am a little afraid of Pont-Aven, there are so many people, but what you say about Gauguin interests me very much. And I still think that Gauguin and I will perhaps work together again.

I know that Gauguin is capable of better things than he has done, but to make that man comfortable!

I am still hoping to do his portrait . . .

Have you seen that portrait that he did of me, painting some sunflowers? After all my face got much brighter since, but it was really me very tired and charged with electricity as I was then . . .

Yes, we must finish with this place, I cannot do the two things at once, work and take no end of pains to live with these queer patients here – it is upsetting.

In vain I tried to force myself to go downstairs. And yet it is nearly two months since I have been in the open air.

In the long run I shall lose the faculty for work, and that is where I begin to cry a halt and I shall send them then – if you agree – about their business . . .

You understand that I have tried to compare the second attack with the first and I only tell you this, it seemed to me rather to be some influence or other from outside, than a cause coming from within myself. I may be mistaken, but however it may be, I think you will feel it quite right that I have rather a horror of all religious exaggeration . . .

✳ ✳ ✳

To Theo   (607)
St Rémy, undated [1889]

Many thanks for your letter. First of all, I am very pleased that you too had already thought of old Pissarro. You will see that there are still some chances, if not there, then elsewhere. Meantime, business is business, and you ask me to answer categorically – and you are right – about going into a home in Paris in case of an immediate removal for this winter. I answer yes to that, with the same calm and for the same reasons that I came into this place – even if this home in Paris should be a last shift, which might easily be the case, for the opportunities of working are not bad here and work is my one distraction.

But having said that, I ask you to note that in my letter I gave a very serious reason as a motive for wishing to move.

And I insist on repeating it. I am astonished that with the modern ideas that I have, and being so ardent an admirer of Zola and de Goncourt and caring for things of art as I do, that I have attacks such as a superstitious man might have and that I get embroiled and frightful ideas about religion such as never came into my head in the north . . .

I am sending you today my own portrait, you must look at it for some time; you will see I hope that my face is much calmer, though my look is vaguer than formerly, it seems to me. I have another which is an attempt made when I was ill, but this I think will please you better and I have tried to make it simple. Show it to old Pissarro if you see him. You will be surprised at the effect the *Work in the Fields* takes on in colour, it is a very profound series of his . . .

Thank you very much for the parcel of canvas and paints. Over against it I am sending you with the portrait some canvases, the following:

> Moonrise (ricks)
> Study of Fields
> Study of Olives
> Study of Night
> The Mountain
> Field of Green Corn
> Olives
> Orchard in Flower
> Entrance to a Quarry

. . . I rather like the *Entrance to a Quarry*, I was doing it when I felt this attack beginning, because the sombre greens go well to my mind with the ochre tones; there is something sad in it which is healthy, and that is why it does not bore me . . .

❋ ❋ ❋

To Theo   (608)
St Rémy, [undated 1889]

. . . I feel now quite normal and do not remember the bad days at all.

With the work and very regular food, this will probably last a pretty long time up and down, and anyhow I shall go on working like this unless the thing appears. For at the end of the month you will receive another dozen studies.

. . . the olive trees are very characteristic and I am struggling to catch them.

They are old silver, sometimes more blue, sometimes greenish, bronzed, whitening over a soil which is yellow, rose, violet-tinted or orange, to dull red ochre.

But very difficult, very difficult. But that suits me and draws me on to work right into gold or silver. And perhaps one day I shall do a personal impression of them like what the sunflowers were for the yellows. If I had had some of them last autumn! But this half-liberty often prevents me doing what I nevertheless feel I could. Patience, however, you will tell me, and I really must . . .

Pissarro had talked to Theo about Dr Gachet at Auvers, who was himself a great art-lover and art-collector, and who might be willing to have Vincent living with him.

❊ ❊ ❊

To Theo (609)
St Rémy, undated [1889]

. . . Now I must begin by some rather irritating news, as I see it. It is that there have been some expenses during my stay here, which I thought M. Peyron had notified you of as they occurred, which they told me the other day he had not done, so that it has mounted up to about 25 francs, deducting from it the 10 that you sent by postal order. It is for paints, canvas, frames and stretchers, my journey to Arles the other day, a linen suit and various repairs . . .

It surprises me very much that M. Isaäcson wants to write an article on my studies. I should be glad to persuade him to wait, his article will lose absolutely nothing by it, and with yet another year of work, I could – I hope – put before him some more individual things, with more definite drawing, and more knowledge of motive with regard to the Provençal south.

M. Peyron was very kind in speaking of my affairs in those terms – I have not dared to ask leave to go to Arles lately, which I very much want to do, thinking that he would disapprove. Not however that I suspected that he believed in any connection between my previous journey and the attack that followed it closely. The thing is, that there are some people there that I felt and again feel the need of seeing.

While not having like the good Prévot a mistress in the Midi who holds me captive, involuntarily I get attached to people and things.

And now that I am staying on here provisionally and as far as we can see shall stay the winter – till spring – shan't I stay here too till the summer? That will depend mostly on my health.

What you say of Auvers is nevertheless a very pleasant prospect and either sooner or later – without looking further – we must fix on that. If I come north, even supposing that there were no room at this doctor's house, it is probable that after your recommendation and old Pissarro's he would find me either board with a family or quite simply at an inn. The chief thing is to know the doctor, so that in case of an attack you do not fall into the hands of the police, and get carried off by force to an asylum.

And I assure you that the north will interest me like a new country . . .

. . . Altogether it is difficult to leave a country before you have done something to prove that you have felt and loved it.

If I return to the north, I propose to make heaps of Greek studies, you know studies painted with white and blue and a little orange only, as if in the open air . . .

❋ ❋ ❋

To Theo (610)
St Rémy, undated [1889]

I have just brought back a canvas on which I have been working for some time representing the same field again as in the *Reaper*. Now it is clods of earth and the background of parched land, then the cliffs of the Alps. A bit of green-blue sky with a little white and violet cloud. In the foreground a thistle and some dry grass. A peasant dragging a truss of straw in the middle. It is again a harsh study and instead of being almost entirely yellow, it makes a canvas almost entirely violet. Blended violet and neutral tints. But I am writing to you because I think this will complete the *Reaper* and will make clearer what that is. For the *Reaper* looks as though it were done at random and this will give it balance . . .

Then too I have done this week the *Entrance to a Quarry* which is like something Japanese; you remember there are Japanese drawings of rocks with grass growing on them here and there and little trees. There are moments in between whiles when Nature is superb, autumn effects glorious in colour, green skies contrasting with foliage in yellows, oranges, greens, earth in all the violets, burnt up grass amongst which however the rains have given a last energy to certain plants, which start again to put forth little flowers of violet, rose, blue yellow. Things that one is quite sad not to be able to reproduce.

And skies – like our skies in the north, but the colours of the sunsets and sunrises more varied and clean. Like in a Jules Dupré or a Ziem.

I have also two views of the park and the asylum, where this place looked very pleasing. I tried to reconstruct the thing as it might have been, simplifying and accentuating the haughty unchanging character of the pines and cedar clumps against the blue.

Anyway – if it should be that they remember me, which I don't build on – there will be something in colour to send to the Vingtistes. But I am indifferent to that . . .

I often think that if Gauguin had stayed here he would have lost nothing by it, for I can see clearly in the letter he has written me that he is not altogether at the top of his form either. And I know quite well what that is due to – they are too hard up to get models, and living as cheaply as they thought at first cannot have lasted. However if he has patience next year may perhaps be dazzling, but then he will not have Bernard with him, if he does his service . . .

That is the terrible thing about the Impressionists, that the development of the thing hangs fire, and they remain for years held up by obstacles over which the previous generation triumphed, the difficulty of money and models . . .

Does Jo's health continue good? I think that altogether this year has been happier for you than previous ones. As for me I am well just now. I think M. Peyron is right when he says that I am not strictly speaking mad, for my mind is absolutely normal in between and even more so than formerly. But in the attacks it is terrible – and then I lose consciousness of everything. But that spurs me on to work and in earnest as a miner who is always in danger makes haste in what he does . . .

✳ ✳ ✳

To Theo (611)
St Rémy, undated [1889]

. . . very often terrible fits of depression come over me, and besides the more my health come back to normal, the more my brain can reason in cold blood, the more foolish it seems to me, and a thing against all reason, to be doing this painting which costs us so much and brings in nothing, not even the net cost. Then I feel very unhappy and the trouble is that at my age it is damnably difficult to begin anything else.

In some Dutch newspapers which you put in with the Millets – I notice some Paris letters that I attribute to Isaäcson.

They are very subtle and one guesses the author to be a sorrowful, creature, restless, with a rare tenderness – tenderness that makes me instinctively think of the *Reisebilder* of H. Heine.

No need to tell you that I think what he says of me in a note extremely exaggerated, and it's another reason why I should prefer him to say nothing about me. And in all these articles I find, side by side with very fine things, something, I don't quite know what, that seems to me unhealthy . . .

I have worked on a study of the mad ward at the Arles Hospital and then having had no more canvas these last days, I have taken long walks in all directions across the country. I am beginning to feel more the effect as a whole of the scenery in which I am living . . .

Ah, now certainly you are yourself deep in nature, since you say that Jo already feels her child quicken – it is much more interesting even than landscape, and I am very glad that things should so have changed for you.

How beautiful that Millet is, *The First Steps of a Child*! . . .

✳ ✳ ✳

To his mother (612)
St Rémy, undated [1889]

. . . Well, I am ploughing on my canvases as they on their fields.

It goes badly enough in our profession – in fact that has always been so but at the moment it is very bad.

And yet never have such high prices been paid for pictures as these days.

What makes us still work is friendship between one another, and love for Nature, and finally if one has taken all the pains to master the brush, *one cannot keep from painting*. I belong, compared with others, still to the lucky ones, but think what it must be if one has begun the profession and has to leave it before one has done anything, and there are many so. Take ten years as necessary to learn the profession and somebody who has gone through six years and paid for them and then has to stop it, if you think how miserable that is, and how many there are like that!

292

And those high prices one hears about, paid for work of painters who are dead and who in their life were not paid like that, it is a kind of tulip-trade, from which the living painters suffer rather than have any benefit. And it will disappear also like the tulip-trade.

But one may reason that, though the tulip-trade has gone and is forgotten long since, yet the flower-growers remained, and will abide. And thus I consider painting too, that what abides is as a kind of flower-growing. And as far as that concerns, myself, I reckon myself happy to be in it . . .

✳ ✳ ✳

To Theo   (613)
St Rémy, undated [Autumn 1889]

. . . I am very well – except for a great depression sometimes, but I feel well, much better than last winter and even better than when I came here, and still better than in Paris.

Also in my work my ideas are becoming – it seems to me – more stable. But then I do not quite know if you will like what I am doing now. For in spite of what you said in your last letter, that the search for style often harms other qualities, the fact is that I feel much inclined to seek for style, if you like, but I mean by that a more masculine and deliberate drawing. If that makes me more like Bernard or Gauguin I can't help it . . .

For, yes, you must feel the whole of a country – isn't it that which distinguishes a Cézanne from anything else? . . .

✳ ✳ ✳

To Theo   (614)
St Rémy, November [1889]

Thank you for your letter and I am very glad that you tell me that Jo continues well. That is the one great thing now. I think very often about you. As for you, when you write that you are seeing so many pictures you would like for a time to see none, it proves that you have had too much worry in business. And then – yes, there is something else in life than pictures, and this something else one neglects, and nature seems then to revenge itself and fate itself is set on thwarting us. I think that in these circumstances one must stand by pictures as far as duty demands, but not more. As for the Vingtistes here is what I would like to exhibit:

1 and 2. The two companion pictures of Sunflowers.
3. The ivy, perpendicular.
4. Orchard in bloom (the one Tanguy is exhibiting just now), with some poplars lined across the canvas.
5 The Red Vineyard.
6. Cornfield at Sunrise, on which I am working at the moment.

Gauguin has written me a very nice letter and talks with animation about de Haan and their rough life at the seaside.

Bernard also has written to me, complaining of heaps of things, while resigning himself like the good lad he is, but not at all happy with all his talent, all his work, all his sobriety; it seems that his home is often hell for him.

And I am not an admirer of Gauguin's *Christ in the Garden of Olives*, for example, of which he sends me the sketch. And then as for Bernard's, he promises me a photograph of it. I don't know, but I fear that his biblical compositions will make me want something different. Lately I have seen the women picking and gathering the olives, but as I had no way of getting a model, I have done nothing at it. However it is not the moment now to ask me to admire our friend Gauguin's composition, and our friend Bernard has probably never seen an olive tree. Now he avoids getting the least idea of the possible, or of the reality of things, and that is not the way to synthetize – no, I have never taken any stock in their biblical interpretations.

I said that Rembrandt, and Delacroix, had done this admirably, that I liked it even better than the primitives, but stop! I do not want to begin again on that head. If I stay here, I shall not try to paint *Christ in the Garden of Olives*, but the glowing of the olives as you still see it, giving nevertheless the just proportion of the human figure in it, that would make people think perhaps . . .

If health remains stable, then if while I work I start again trying to sell, to exhibit, to make exchanges, perhaps I shall make some progress in being less a burden to you on the one hand and on the other might recover a little more zest. For I will not conceal from you that my stay here is very wearisome because of its monotony, and because the company of all these unfortunates, who do absolutely nothing, is enervating . . .

✳ ✳ ✳

To Theo (615)
St Rémy, undated [1889]

I have to thank you very much for a parcel of paints, which was accompanied also by an excellent woollen waistcoat.

How kind you are to me, and how I wish I could do something good, so as to prove to you that I would like to be less ungrateful. The paints reached me at the right moment, because what I had brought back from Arles were almost exhausted. The thing is that I have worked this month in the olive groves, because they have maddened me with their Christs in the Garden, with nothing really observed. Of course with me there is no question of doing anything from the Bible – and I have written to Bernard and Gauguin too, that I considered that to think, not to dream, was our duty, so that I was astonished looking at their work that they let themselves go like that. For Bernard has sent me photos from his canvases. The thing about them is that they are a sort of dream or nightmare – that they are erudite enough – you can see that it is some one who is mad on the primitives – but frankly the English Pre-Raphaelites did it much better, and then Puvis and Delacroix, much more healthy than the Pre-Raphaelites . . .

I am quite at the end of my canvas and when you can I beg you to send me 10 metres. Then I am going to attack the cypresses and the mountains. I think that that will be the core of the work that I have done here and there in Provence, and then we can conclude my stay here when it is convenient. It is not urgent, for Paris after all only distracts. I don't know however – not being a pessimist always – I still think that I have it yet in my heart to paint some day a book shop with the frontage yellow and rose, at evening, and the black passers by – it is such an essentially modern subject. Because it seems to the imagination such a focus of light – I say, there would be a subject that would go well between an olive grove and a cornfield, the seed time of books and prints. I have a great longing to do it like a light in the midst of darkness. Yes, there is a way of seeing Paris beautiful. But after all book shops do not run away like hares and there is no hurry, and I am quite willing to work here for another year, which will probably be wisest . . .

✳ ✳ ✳

To his mother   (619)
St Rémy, undated [December 1889]

. . . It is a year since I fell ill, and it is difficult for me to say how far I am recovered or not. Often I have much self-reproach about things in the past, my illness coming more or less through my own fault, in any case I doubt if I can make up for faults in any way.

But reasoning and thinking about these things is sometimes so difficult, and more than before my feelings overwhelm me sometimes. And then I think so much of you and of the past.

You and Father have been still more, if possible, to me than to the others, so much, so very much, and I seem not to have had a happy character. I discovered that in Paris, how much more than I Theo has done his best to help Father practically, so that his own interests were often neglected. Therefore I am so thankful now that Theo has got a wife and expects his baby. Well, Theo had more self-sacrifice than I, and that is deeply rooted in his character. And after Father was no more and I came to Theo in Paris, then he got so attached to me that I understood how much he had loved Father. And now I am saying this to you, and not to him, it is good that I did not stay in Paris, for we, he and I, would have interested ourselves too much in each other.

And life does not exist for this, I cannot but tell you how much better I think it is for him in this way, than before, he had too many tiresome affairs to think about, and his health suffered thereby. In the beginning when I became ill, I could not resign myself to the idea of having to go into a hospital.

And now at present I agree that I should have been treated even earlier, but it is human to err.

A French writer says that all painters are more or less crazy, and though quite a lot can be said against this, it is certain that one gets too lonely in it. Whatever may be the truth of it, I imagine that here, where I don't have to care for anything, etc., I am progressing in the quality of my work.

And thus, I go on with relative calmness, and do my best on my work, and don't consider myself amongst the unhappy ones.

For the moment I am working at a picture of a path between the mountains and a little brook, thrusting on between the stones. The rocks are of a plain violet-grey or pink, with here and there palm bushes and a kind of broom, which through the autumn has all kinds of colours, green, yellow, red, brown. And the brook in the foreground, white and foaming like soap-suds and further on reflecting the blue of the sky . . .

❋ ❋ ❋

To Theo   (620)
St Rémy, undated

. . . What a misfortune for Gauguin, that child falling from the window and his not being able to be there. I often think of him, what misfortunes that man has, in spite of his energy and so many unusual qualities. I think it is splendid that our sister is coming to help you when Jo has her confinement.

May that go well – I think a great deal about you two, I assure you . . .

I do not know what M. Peyron is going to advise, but while taking into account what he tells me, I think that he will dare less than ever to commit himself as to the possibility of my living as I used. It is to be feared that the attacks will return. But that is no reason at all for not trying a little to distract oneself.

For the crowding up of all these lunatics in this old cloister becomes I think a dangerous thing in which you risk losing any good sense that you may still have kept. Not that I am set on this or that by preference. I am used to the life here, but one must not forget to make a little trial of the opposite . . .

Oh, while I was ill there was a fall of damp and melting snow. I got up at night to look at the country. Never, never had nature seemed to me so touching and so full of feeling.

The rather superstitious ideas they have here about painting sometimes depress me more than I can tell you, because it is really at bottom fairly true that a painter as man is too much absorbed by what his eyes see, and is not sufficiently master of the rest of his life . . .

To Theo   (622)
St Rémy, January [1890]

... I have never worked with more calm than in my last canvases – you
will receive some at the same time as this letter I hope. For the moment
I am overcome by a great discouragement.

But since this attack was over in a week, what is the use of thinking
that it may in fact come back again? First of all you do not know, nor
can foresee, how or under what form.

Let us go on working then as much as possible as if nothing had
happened. I shall soon have an opportunity of going out when the
weather is not too cold, and then I should rather set my heart on trying
to finish the work I have begun here ...

In January 1890, an article by Albert Aurier, entitled 'Les Isolés', appears in
Mercure de France. *In it the author singles out van Gogh from among other
contemporary artists as 'sublime', a 'hyperaesthete' who perceives with 'abnormal
intensity the scarcely visible secret characteristics of lines and forms, and especially
the colours, lights, nuances invisible to healthy people' and the 'magic iridescences of
shadows'. He will, he said, never be truly understood except by true artists, and ordinary people who have escaped the conventional teachings of the day. Van Gogh is
possessed of a 'terrible and maddened genius'.*

✳ ✳ ✳

To Theo   (625)
St Rémy, 1 February [1890]

Today I have just received your good news that you are at last a father,
that the most critical time is over for Jo, and that finally the little boy is
well. That has done me more good and given me more pleasure than I
can put into words. Bravo – and how pleased mother is going to be. The
day before yesterday I received a fairly long and very contented letter
from her too. Anyhow, here it is, the thing I have for long so much
desired. No need to tell you that I have often thought of you these days
and it touched me very much that Jo had the kindness to write to me the
very night before. She is so brave and calm in her danger, it touched me
very much. Well, it contributes much to making me forget the last days
when I was ill, I don't know then where I am and my mind wanders.

I was extremely surprised at the article on my pictures which you sent me. I needn't tell you that I hope to go on thinking that not paint like that, but I do see in it how I ought to paint. For the article is very right in this way, that it indicates the gap to be filled, and I think that really the writer wrote it rather to guide not only me, but the other Impressionists as well, and even partly to make the breach at a good place. So he proposed an ideal collective self to the others quite as much as to me; he simply tells me that here and there there is something good, if you like, in my work which is at the same time so imperfect, and that is the consoling side, which I appreciate and for which I hope to be grateful. Only it must be understood, that my back is not broad enough to accomplish such an undertaking, and in concentrating the article on me, there's no need to tell you how set up with flattery I feel, and in my opinion it is as exaggerated as what a certain article by Isaäcson said about you, that at present the artists had given up squabbling and that an important movement was silently taking place in the little shop on the Boulevard Montmartre. I admit that it is difficult to say what one wants, to express oneself differently – in the same way as you cannot paint things as you see them – and so I do not mean to criticize the daring of Isaäcson or that of the other critic, but as far as we are concerned, really, we are *posing* a bit for *the model* and indeed that is a duty and a bit of one's job like any other. So if some sort of reputation comes to you and to me, the thing is to try to keep some sort of calm and if possible presence of mind . . .

Why not say what he said of my sunflowers, *with far more grounds*, of those magnificent and perfect hollyhocks of Quost's, and his yellow irises, and those splendid peonies of Jeannin's? And you will see as I do that praise like this *must* have its contrary, the reverse of the medal. But I am glad and grateful for the article, or rather '*le cœur à l'aise*' as the song in the *Revue* has it, since one may need it, as one may really need a medal . . .

Gauguin proposed, very vaguely it is true, to found a studio in his name, he, de Haan and I, but he said that he is insisting on going through with his Tonkin project, and seems to have cooled off greatly, I do not exactly know why, about continuing to paint. And he is just the sort to be off to Tonkin in earnest, he has a sort of need of expansion and he finds – and there's some truth in it – the artistic life mean. With his experience of travel, what can I say to him? . . .

✳ ✳ ✳

To Theo (626)
St Rémy, undated [1890]

I was in the midst of writing to you to send you the reply for M. Aurier when your letter arrived. I'm very glad that Jo and the little one are well and that she expects to be able to get up in a few days from now. Then what you tell me about our sister also interests me very much. I think she was lucky to see Degas at his home.

And so Gauguin has returned to Paris. I am going to copy my reply to M. Aurier to send to him and you must make him read this article in the *Mercure*, for really I think they ought to say things like that of Gauguin, and of me only very secondarily. Gauguin wrote me that he had exhibited in Denmark and that this exhibition had been a great success. It seems to me a pity that he did not stay on here a bit longer. Together we should have worked better than myself all alone this year. And now we should have a little house of our own to live and work in, and could even put up others . . .

About the Impressionists' exhibition in March, I hope to send you a few more canvases, which at the moment are drying; if they do not arrive in time, you could make a selection from the ones that are at old Tanguy's . . .

Aurier's article would encourage me, if I dared to let myself go, and risk still further leaving reality and making with colour a kind of music of tones, as some Monticellis are. But it is so dear to me, this truth, *to try to make it true*, after all I think, I think, that I still would rather be a shoemaker than a musician in colours.

In any case to try to remain true is perhaps a remedy in fighting the malady which still continues to disquiet me.

✳ ✳ ✳

To his mother (627)
St Rémy, 15 February [1890]

. . . These last days we had rather bad weather here, but today it was a real day of spring, and the fields of young corn, with the violet hills in the distance are so beautiful, and the almond-trees are beginning to bloom everywhere. I was rather taken aback at the article which they wrote about me. Isaäcson wanted to do it some time ago and I asked him not to

300

do it, I was sorry when I read it because it is so much exaggerated; the question is different – what keeps me up in working is just the feeling that there are several others who are doing the same as I, and why then an article on me and not on those six or seven others, etc.?

But I must admit that afterwards, when my surprise had passed a little, I felt at times very much cheered up by it; yesterday Theo wrote me moreover that they had sold one of my pictures at Brussels for 400 francs. [*The Red Vineyard* bought by Miss Anna Bock.] Compared with other prices, also the Dutch ones, this is little, but I try therefore to be productive to be able to go on working at a reasonable cost . . .

On 24 February, Dr Peyron wrote to Theo that Vincent had again had an attack, after spending two days in Arles. He had been brought back in a carriage to St Rémy, and it was not known where he had spent the night. The picture representing an Arlésienne which he had taken along with him to Arles was never found. On 1 April Dr Peyron wrote again that the attack was lasting longer this time, and that it finally proved that these trips were bad for him.

✳ ✳ ✳

To Theo (628)
St Rémy, April [1890]

Today I wanted to read the letters which had come for me, but I was not clear-headed enough yet to be able to understand them.

I take up this letter again to try to write, it will come bit by bit, the thing is that my head is so bad, without pain it is true, but altogether stupefied. I must tell you that there are, as far as I can judge, others who have the same thing wrong with them that I have, and who after having worked during part of their life, are reduced to helplessness now. Between four walls it isn't easy to learn much good, that is natural, but all the same it is true that there are people who can be no longer left at liberty as though they had nothing wrong with them. And that means I am pretty well or altogether in despair about myself . . .

My work was going well, the last canvas of branches in blossom – you will see, it was perhaps the best, the most patiently worked thing I had done, painted with calm and with a greater certainty of touch. And the next day, down like a brute. Difficult to understand things like that, but alas! it is like that. I have a great desire however to begin my work again, but Gauguin also writes that he, and he is robust, also despairs of being able to go on. And isn't it true that we often hear the same story of artists? My poor boy, just take things as they come, do not be grieved for me, it will encourage and sustain me more than you think, to know that you are managing your household well. Then after a time of trial, perhaps for me too peaceful days will come again. But meantime I will send you some canvases in a little while . . .

Give many messages to the Pissarros, I am going very shortly to read the letters more calmly, and tomorrow or the next day I hope to write again.

❋ ❋ ❋

To Theo (629)
St Rémy, 29 April [1890]

Until now I have not been able to write to you, but being a bit better just now, I did not wish to delay in wishing you a happy year, since it is your birthday, for you and your wife and child . . .

Here is the list of the colours I want:

Large tubes	12 zinc white	3 cobalt	5 malachite green
	1 crimson lake		2 chrome 2
	2 emerald green		4 chrome 1
	1 orange lead		2 ultramarine

Then (but at Tasset's) two geranium lake, medium sized tubes. You would do me a kindness if you sent me at least half at once, at once, because I have wasted too much time.

Then I shall need six brushes – six pole-cat brushes and seven metres of canvas or even ten . . .

What am I to say about these two last months, things didn't go well at all. I am sadder and drearier than I can express and I do not know at all where I have got to.

The order for paints is rather heavy, so let me wait for the half, if it is more convenient for you.

While I was ill I did all the same some little canvases from memory which you will see later, memories of the north, and now I have just finished a corner of a sunny meadow, which I think is fairly vigorous. You will see it soon . . .

Letters from home have come too, which I have not yet had courage to read, I feel so melancholy. Please do ask M. Aurier not to write any more articles on my painting, insist upon this, that to begin with he is mistaken about me, since I am too overwhelmed with trouble to be able to face publicity. To make pictures distracts me, but if I hear them spoken of, it gives me more pain than he knows. How is Bernard? . . .

I felt ill at the time that I was doing the almond blossom. If I had been able to go on working, you can judge from that that I would have done others of trees in bloom. Now the trees in bloom are almost over, really I have no luck . . .

✳ ✳ ✳

To Theo   (631)
St Rémy, May [1890]

. . . I do not feel competent to judge the way of treating the patients here, I do not want to go into details – but please do remember that I warned you almost six months ago, that if I had another attack of the same nature, I should wish to change my asylum. And I have already delayed too long having let an attack go by meanwhile, I was then in the midst of work and I wanted to finish some canvases in hand. But for that I should not be here now. Well then, I am going to tell you that I think that a fortnight at the most (a week would please me better, however) should be enough to take the necessary steps to move. I will have myself accompanied as far as Tarascon – even one or two stations further if you insist; once arrived in Paris (I will send off a wire at my departure from here) you would come and fetch me at the Gare de Lyon.

Now I should think it would be best to go and see this doctor [Dr Gachet of Auvers] in the country as soon as possible and we would leave the luggage at the station. So I should not stay with you more than say two or three days, then I would leave for this village where I would begin by staying at the inn . . .

My surroundings here begin to weigh on me more than I can express – my word, I have had patience for more than a year – I need air, I feel overwhelmed with boredom and depression . . .

303

I assure you it is something simply to resign yourself to living under surveillance, even supposing it were sympathetic, and to sacrifice your liberty, keep yourself out of society, and have nothing but your work with no distraction . . .

As for me I am at the end, at the end of my patience, my dear brother, I can't stand any more – I must move, even for a last shift . . .

✳ ✳ ✳

To Theo   (633)
St Rémy, undated [1890]

. . . At present things continue for the better, the whole horrible attack has disappeared like a storm and I am working to give a last stroke of the brush here with a calm and continuous enthusiasm. I have a canvas of roses on hand with a light green background and two canvases representing big bunches of violet iris flowers, one lot against a pink background in which the effect is soft and harmonious because of the combination of greens, pinks, violets. On the other hand the other violet bunch (ranging between carmine and pure Prussian blue) stands out against a startling lemon yellow background, with other yellow tones in the vase and the stand on which it rests, so it is an effect of tremendously unlike complementaries, which heighten each other by their opposition.

These canvases will take quite a month to dry, but the attendant here will undertake to send them off after my departure.

I intend to leave this week as soon as possible and I am beginning today to do my packing . . .

But another strange thing, just as that day we were so struck by Seurat's canvases, these last days here are like a fresh revelation of colour to me. As for my work, my dear brother, I feel more confidence than when I left, and it would be ungrateful on my part to miscall the Midi, and I confess to you that it is with great grief I come away from it.

Vincent left St Rémy on 16 May, visiting Theo, Johanna and their baby Vincent in Paris on the way to Auvers to see Dr Gachet, a homeopathic doctor who had written a treatise on neuroses in artists. At first Vincent stayed in an inn.

✳ ✳ ✳

After having made Jo's acquaintance, it will be difficult for me henceforth to write to Theo only, but Jo will allow me – I hope – to write in
French; because after two years in the south, I really think that so
doing I shall say better what I have to say. Auvers is very beautiful,
among other things a lot of old thatch, which is getting rare.

So I should hope that by settling down to do some canvases of this
there would be a chance of recovering the expenses of my stay – for
really it is profoundly beautiful, it is the real country, characteristic and
picturesque.

I have seen Dr Gachet, who gives me the impression of being rather
eccentric, but his experience as a doctor must keep him balanced
enough to combat the nervous trouble from which he certainly seems
to me to suffer at least as seriously as I do.

He piloted me to an inn where they ask 6 francs a day. I found for
myself one where I shall pay 3.50 fr. a day . . .

Probably you will see Doctor Gachet this week – he has a *very* fine
Pissarro, winter with a red house in the snow, and two fine flower
bunches by Cézanne.

Also another Cézanne, of the village. And I in my turn will gladly,
very gladly, do a bit of brush-work here.

. . . His house is full of black antiques, black, black, except for the
Impressionist pictures mentioned. The impression I got of him was not
unfavourable. When he spoke of Belgium and the days of the old painters,
his grief-hardened face grew smiling again, and I really think that I shall
keep on being friends with him and that I shall do his portrait.

Then he said that I must work boldly on, and not think at all of what
went wrong with me.

❋ ❋ ❋

. . . M. Gachet says that a father and mother must naturally feed up,
he talks of taking 2 litres of beer a day, etc., in those circumstances. But
you will certainly enjoy making his further acquaintance and he

already counts on you all coming, and talks about it every time I see him. He seems to me certainly as ill and distraught as you or me, and he is older and lost his wife several years ago, but he is very much the doctor and his profession and faith still hold him. We are great friends already and as it happens he already knew Brias of Montpellier and has the same idea of him that I have, that there you have someone significant in the history of modern art.

I am working at his portrait, the head with a white cap, very fair, very light, the hands also light flesh tint, a blue frock coat and a cobalt blue background, leaning on a red table, on which are a yellow book and a foxglove plant with purple flowers. It has the same feeling as the portrait of myself, which I took when I left for this place.

M. Gachet is absolutely *fanatical* about this portrait and wants me to do one for him, if I can, exactly like it. I should like to, myself. He has now got the length of understanding the last portrait of the Arlésienne, of which you have one in rose; he always comes back to these two portraits when he comes to see the studies and he accepts them utterly, yes utterly, just as they are.

. . . anyway I am living a day at a time, the weather is so beautiful. And I am well. I go to bed at 9 o'clock, but get up at 5 most of the time. I hope that it will not be unpleasant to come to oneself again after a long absence. And I also hope that this feeling I have of being much surer of my brush than before I went to Arles, will last. And M. Gachet says that he thinks it most improbable that it will return, and that things are going on quite well.

. . . Now nothing, absolutely nothing, keeps us here but Gachet – but he will remain a friend I should think. I feel that at his house I can do a not too bad a picture every time I go and he will continue to ask me to dinner every Sunday or Monday.

But till now, though it is pleasant to do a picture there, it is rather a tax on me to dine and lunch there, for the good soul takes the trouble to have dinners of four or five courses, which is as dreadful for him as for me – for he certainly has not a strong digestion. The thing that has rather prevented me from protesting about it, is that this recalls to him the old times when there were those family dinners, which we ourselves know so well.

But the modern idea of eating one – or at most two – courses is certainly an advance, and a remote return to real antiquity. Altogether old Gachet is very, yes very like you and me.

306

Theo and his wife and small baby were able to spend Sunday with Vincent at Dr Gachet's.

✳ ✳ ✳

To Theo and Johanna (640)
Auvers, 10 June [1890]

Sunday has left me a very pleasant memory; in this way we feel that we are not so far from one another, and I hope that we will often see each other again. Since Sunday I have done two studies of the house in the trees; by the side of the house where I am a whole colony of Americans have just established themselves, they are painting, but I have not seen yet what they are doing.

. . . It is odd all the same that the nightmares have ceased here to such an extent, I always told M. Peyron that returning to the north would free me from it, but it is odd also that under his direction, though he is very capable and certainly wished me well, it was rather aggravated . . .

✳ ✳ ✳

To Paul Gauguin (643)
Auvers, undated [1890]
[An unfinished letter found among Vincent's papers]

Thank you for having written to me again, old fellow, and be sure that since my return I have thought of you every day. I only stayed in Paris three days and the noise, etc., of Paris had such a bad effect on me that I thought it wise for the sake of my head to be off to the country, but for that I should soon have run round to see you. And it gives me enormous pleasure when you say the Arlésienne's portrait which was founded strictly on your drawing is to your liking.

I tried to be religiously faithful to your drawing while nevertheless taking the liberty of interpreting by the medium of colour the sober character and the style of the drawing in question. It is a synthesis of the Arlésiennes if you like; as syntheses of the Arlésiennes are rare, take this as a work belonging to you and me as a summary of our months of work together. For the doing of it I have paid for my part with another month of illness, but I also know that it is a canvas which will be under-stood by you, and very few others, as we would wish it to be understood. My friend Dr Gachet here has taken to it altogether after two or three hesitations, and says 'How difficult it is to be simple'. Very well – I want to underline the thing again by engraving it as an etching, then let it be. Anyone who likes can have it. Have you also seen the olives? Meantime I have a portrait of Dr Gachet with the heart-broken expression of our time. *If you like*, something like what you said of your *Christ in the Garden of Olives*, not meant to be understood, but there, anyhow I follow you and my brother caught that suggestion absolutely.

I have still from down there a cypress with a star, a last attempt – a night sky with a moon without radiance, the slender crescent barely emerging from the opaque shadow cast by the earth – a star with exaggerated brilliance, if you like, a soft brilliance of rose and green in the ultramarine sky across which are hurrying some clouds. Below a road bordered with tall yellow canes, behind these the blue *Basses Alpes*, an old inn with yellow lighted windows, and a very tall cypress, very upright, very sombre.

On the road a yellow cart with a white horse in harness, and two late wayfarers. Very romantic, if you like, but Provence also I think.

I shall probably engrave this as an etching and other landscapes and subjects, memories of Provence, then I shall look forward to giving you one, a whole summary, rather deliberate and studied. My brother says that Lauzet, who does the lithographs after Monticelli, liked the head of the Arlésienne in question.

But you will understand that arriving in Paris a bit confused I have not yet seen your canvases. But I hope soon to return for a few days. I'm very glad to learn from your letter that you are going back to Brittany with de Haan. It is very likely that – if you will allow me – I shall come there for a month to join you, to do a seascape or two, but especially to see you again and make de Haan's acquaintance. Then we will try to do something decisive and serious, as our work would have probably become if we had been able to carry on down there.

I say, here's an idea may suit you, I am trying to do some studies of corn like this, but I cannot draw it – nothing but ears of corn with green-blue stalks, long leaves like ribbons of green shot with rose, ears that are just turning yellow, edged with pale rose by the dusty efflores-cence – a rose coloured bindweed at the bottom twisted round a stem.

Above this, against a very vivid but yet tranquil background, I would like to paint some portraits. The thing is greens of a different quality, of the same value, so as to form a whole of green, which by its vibration, will make you think of the gentle rustle of the ears swaying in the breeze: it is not at all easy as to colour.

In a letter in which Theo had written that the child was ill, he also talked about a plan of giving up his position and setting up on his own account. So much was needed, and as they were, Vincent as well as Theo's family had to economize: Theo also wished in this letter that Vincent too might find a wife some day to share his life with him.

✳ ✳ ✳

To Theo and Johanna   (646)
Auvers, 30 June [1890]

I have just received the letter in which you say that the child is ill; I would much like to come and see you and what holds me back, is the thought that I should be even more powerless than you in the present state of anxiety. But I feel how dreadful it must be and I wish I could help you.

By coming point-blank, I am afraid of increasing the confusion. But I share your anxiety with all my heart. It is a great pity that M. Gachet's house is so encumbered with all sorts of things. But for that I think that it would be a good plan to come and stay here – with him – with the little one, for a full month at least. I think that country air has enormous effect. In this very street there are youngsters born in Paris and really sickly – who however are doing well. It would be possible also to come to the inn, it's true. So that you should not be too much alone, I could come myself to you for a week or a fortnight. That would not increase expenses . . .

As for the little one, really, I am beginning to fear that it will be necessary to give him fresh air and still more the little stir of other children that there is in a village. I think for Jo also who shares our anxieties and risks, she ought to have the variety of the country from time to time.

Rather a gloomy letter from Gauguin, he talks vaguely of having quite decided on Madagascar, but so vaguely that you can see that he is only thinking of this because he really does not know what else to think of.

And to carry out the plan seems to me almost absurd . . .

The people at the inn here used to live in Paris, there they were constantly unwell, parents and children, here they never have anything wrong at all and especially the smallest, who came when he was 2 months old and then the mother had difficulty in giving him the breast, whereas here everything came all right almost at once. On the other hand you are working all day and at present you probably hardly sleep. I should be quite willing to believe that Jo would have twice as much milk here and that when she comes here, you will be able to do without cows, asses and other quadrupeds. And as for Jo, so that in the daytime she should have some company, well, she could stay right opposite old Gachet's house, perhaps you remember that there is an inn just opposite at the bottom of the hill?

What can I say as to the future perhaps, without the Boussods? [Theo's employers] . . .

I am trying myself also to do as well as I can, but I will not conceal from you that I hardly dare to count on always having the necessary sanity. And if my malady returns, you would forgive me. I still love art and life very much, but as for ever having a wife of my own, I have no great faith in that. I rather fear that towards say forty – or rather say nothing – I declare I know nothing, absolutely nothing as to what turn this may still take. But I am writing to you at once that about the little one, I think you must not worry out of reason, if the thing is that he is getting his teeth, well, to make the job easier for him perhaps it would be possible to distract him more here where there are children and animals, and flowers, and fresh air . . .

Vincent did go to Paris to see Theo and his family, and spend an afternoon with Albert Aurier and Toulouse-Lautrec, but things did not turn out well.

✳ ✳ ✳

To Theo and Johanna   (649)
Auvers, undated [July 1890]

Jo's letter was really like a gospel to me, a deliverance from the agony which had been caused by the hours I had shared with you which were a bit too difficult and trying for us all. It was no slight thing when all together we felt our daily bread in danger, no slight thing when for other reasons than that we felt that our life was fragile.

Back here, I felt still very sad and continued to feel the storm which threatens you, weighing on me also. What was to be done – you see, I try generally to be fairly cheerful, but my life too is threatened at the very root, and my steps too are wavering.

I feared – not altogether but yet a little – that being a burden on you, you felt me rather a thing to be dreaded, but Jo's letter proves to me clearly that you understand that for my part I am in toil and trouble as you are.

There – once back here I set to work again – though the brush almost slipped from my fingers, and knowing exactly what I wanted, I have since painted three more big canvases.

They are vast stretches of corn under troubled skies, and I did not need to go out of my way to try to express sadness and the extreme of loneliness. I hope you will see them soon – or I hope to bring them to you in Paris as soon as possible, since I almost think that these canvases will tell you, what I cannot say in words, the health and strengthening that I see in the country. Now the third canvas is Daubigny's garden, a picture I have been meditating since I came here . . .

❊ ❊ ❊

To his mother and sister   (650)
Auvers, undated [July 1890]

In his mother's handwriting was written on top of this letter: 'Very last letter from Auvers'.

. . . Often I am thinking of you both, and should like very much to see you once again . . .

I myself am quite absorbed by the immeasurable plain with corn-fields against the hills, immense as a sea, delicate yellow, delicate soft green, delicate violet of a ploughed and weeded piece of soil, regularly chequered by the green of flowering potato-plants, everything under a sky with delicate blue, white, pink, violet tones.

I am in a mood of nearly too great calmness, in the mood to paint this.

I heartily hope that you will spend very happy days with Theo and Jo, and you will see, as I did, how well they take care of the little child, who looks well . . .

To Theo   (651)
Auvers, 23 July [1890]

Thanks for your letter of today and the 50 fr. note it contained.

I should rather like to write to you about a lot of things, but to begin with the desire to do it has left me so completely, and then I feel it is useless.

I hope that you will have found these worthies well disposed towards you.

As for what concerns me, I apply myself to my canvases with all my mind, I am trying to do as well as certain painters, whom I have much loved and admired.

What I think now I am back is that the painters themselves have more and more their backs to the wall.

Very well . . . but is not the moment for trying to make them understand the usefulness of a union, rather gone by already? On the other hand a union, if it should take shape, would founder if the rest must founder. Then perhaps you would say that some dealers would unite for the Impressionists, that would be very transient. Altogether I think that personal initiative is still powerless and having had experience of it would we begin it again?

I noticed with pleasure that the Gauguin of Brittany which I saw, was very fine and I think that the others he has done there must be so too.

Perhaps you will look at this sketch of Daubigny's garden. It is one of my most deliberate canvases . . .

Goodbye for the present and good luck in business, etc., remember me to Jo and handshakes in thought.

Yours,
Vincent.

✳ ✳ ✳

To Theo   (652)
Auvers, [letter found on Vincent on 29 July 1890]

Thanks for your kind letter and for the 50 fr. note it contained. Since the thing that matters most is going well, why should I say more about things of less importance, my word, before we have a chance of talking business more collectedly, there is likely to be a long way to go.

The other painters, whatever they think, instinctively keep themselves at a distance from discussions about the actual trade.

Well, the truth is, we can only make our pictures speak. But yet my dear brother, there is this that I have always told you and I repeat it once more with all the earnestness that can be given by an effort of a mind diligently fixed on trying to do as well as one can – I tell you again that I shall always consider that you are something other than a simple dealer in Corot, that through my mediation you have your part in the actual production of some canvases, which even in the deluge will retain their peace.

For this is what we have got to and this is all or at least the chief thing that I can have to tell you at a moment of comparative crisis. At a moment when things are very strained between dealers in pictures of dead artists, and living artists.

Well, my own work, I am risking my life for it and my reason has half-foundered in it – that's all right – but you are not among the dealers in men so far as I know, and you can still choose your side, I think, acting with humanity, but what's the use?

On 27 July 1890, Vincent went into the cornfields close by the château, and shot himself with a revolver. Severely wounded he struggled back to the inn. At first it looked as though he might rally, although he was in dreadful pain. Theo was summoned from Paris. No attempt was made to remove the bullet. Vincent lay suffering for two days and finally fell into a coma and died in his brother's arms on 29 July. He was thirty-seven years old.

Not long afterwards, Theo, in poor health and 'broken by grief', began to have hallucinations and violent headaches. He resigned from his job and had a complete breakdown. He died only six months after Vincent on 25 January 1891.

Index